AF556203

UNDERSTANDING HISTOLOGY

UNDERSTANDING HISTOLOGY

By

Dr. Veena

Dept. of Zoology

M.M.H. College

Ghaziabad (U.P.)

(India)

DISCOVERY PUBLISHING HOUSE PVT. LTD.

NEW DELHI-110 002

First Published - 2010

Reprinted - 2018

ISBN: 978-81-8356-525-7

Understanding Histology

Published by:

DISCOVERY PUBLISHING HOUSE PVT. LTD.

4383/4B, Ansari Road, Darya Ganj

New Delhi-110 002 (India)

Phone: +91-11-23279245, 43596064-65

Fax: +91-11-23253475

E-mail: discoverypublishinghouse@gmail.com

sales@discoverypublishinggroup.com

web: www.discoverypublishinggroup.com

Printed at:

Infinity Imaging Systems

Delhi

Preface

The present title "Understanding Histology" has been written for those students interested in careers in diverse fields of biological sciences. It provides a structured approach to learning by covering all the important topics in a uniform, systematic format. The book has been comprehensively designed incorporating recent advances in this fast moving field. It also provides accessible information on histelogy in compact form for undergraduate students in biology and related life sciences. It is intelligible to the educated layman, though it deals with some complex ideas. It is an adequate text for all the requirements of students in this area. In addition, busy lecturers who require a quick reference compendium will find it useful, particularly for tutional planning. Simple, yet hopefully clear figures and tables are provided throughout the book.

The over-riding goal of this book, and indeed of the whole *Understanding series*, is to present the essential information concering histology in a compact, readily accessible form which leads itself to student learning and revision. The convergence of various approaches has generated a rich panorama of detail, the significance of which we are still attempting to unraval. The present text has been written as an introduction to this rapidly growing field.

To make the work more comprehensive and informative, the author has consulted many authoritative books, research journals, abstracts, monographs etc., so there can be no claim to originality except in the manner of treatment.

The author expresses her thanks to her friends and colleagues whose continue inspirations have initiated her to bring out this book.

The author expresses her gratitude to Mr. Wasan and staff of M/s Discovery Publishing House Pvt. Ltd. for their whole hearted co-operation in the publication of this book.

In the mean time, the author will remain sincerely responsible for any shortcomings of the book and be grateful to the readers for their suggestions and constructive criticism for the continuous betterment of the book. She takes this opportunity to appeal to the readers to send their suggestions straightaway to his Publisher.

Author

Contents

1

EPITHELIAL TISSUES

An epithelium has the following characters:

1. The cells are generally arranged as an expansion covering a free surface, but may be disposed to form solid masses, as in the liver.
2. They lie close together, the cement-substance between the cells being small in amount.
3. The cells, or, if in more than one layer, those of the lowermost stratum, rest on a layer of homogeneous substance. This is the *basement membrane,* which intervenes between the epithelium and the underlying connective tissue of which it forms the superficial stratum.

The structure of epithelium-cells, and the changes which they undergo in division, are well seen in the epidermis of the newt or of the salamandertadpole; the cells and nuclei being much larger in these animals than in mammals. An epithelium-cell consists, like other cells, of *cytoplasm* and *nucleus*. The cytoplasm either may look granular, or may have a reticulated appearance, or may exhibit fibrils.

The nucleus is spherical or ovoid. Usually there is only one, but there may be two. The cell-substance is often modified in its chemical nature; its external layer may become hardened to form a sort of membrane, or the whole cell may become horny (keratinised); or there may be a special material in the form of well-marked granules or globules within the cell-material which is ultimately discharged and used by the organism, as occurs in secreting glands.

Absence of vitamin A in the diet prevents the normal specialisation

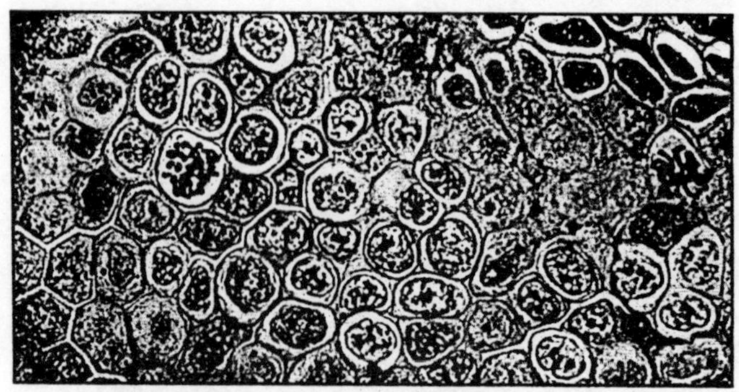

Figure 1.1: Epidermis-cells of a larval salamander.

of epithelia. In many parts of the body various columnar, glandular and other epithelia tend to be replaced by stratified squamous partially-cornified epithelia. On giving vitamin A again in the diet, the abnormal epithelia slough off as the normal specialised epithelia are once more formed from the basal undifferentiated cells.

The following table shows the types of epithelia and the more important sites where they are found in man and the monkey.

SIMPLE

Pavement

Peritoneum and pleura; alveoli of lungs in the embryo; covering of glomerulus of kidney and the lining of its capsule.

Cubical

Small ducts of digestive glands (e.g., salivary glands and liver). Also the smallest respiratory ducts.

Columnar

Alimentary canal (stomach to rectum, inclusive).

Pseudo-stratified columnar

Largest ducts of digestive glands.

Ciliated columnar

Respiratory ducts-except the smallest and the largest; many parts of the male and female genital tracts.

Pseudo-stratified ciliated columnar

Trachea.

Glandular

Many glands, including liver, mammary, sweat and sebaceous glands; also endocrines-thyroid, pituitary, etc..

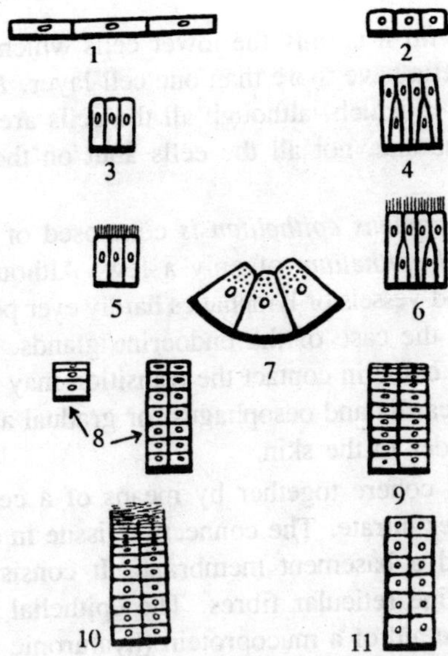

Figure 1.2: Diagram of the different types of Epithelia.

COMPOUND

Transitional

Urinary tract.

Stratified squamous (non-eornifled)

Buccal cavity, oesophagus, anus, cornea.

Stratified squamous (cornified)

Skin.

Stratified columnar

Membranous segment of male urethra.

Note—The terms in the above table are, in many cases, self-explanatory (e.q., ciliated, glandular, etc.). But in some cases explanation is necessary.

Pavement epithelium is composed of flattened cells, larger and broader than they are high; in *columnar epithelium* the opposite obtains; the height of the cells exceeds their other dimensions.

The term *cubical epithelium is* self-explanatory.

In nearly all (if not in all) epithelia the cells lie upon a homogeneous sheet known as the *basement membrane. Simple epithelia* are those in which all the cells lie in contact with the basement membrane, whereas in *compound epithelia* it is only the lower cells which do so; in other words, these epithelia have more than one cell-layer. *Pseudo-stratified epithelia* are those in which, although all the cells are in contact with the basement membrane, not all the cells abut on the surface of the epithelium.

A *stratified squamous epithelium is* composed of many layers of cells, a *transitional epithelium* of only a few. Although all epithelia receive nerves, blood-vessels or lymphatics hardly ever penetrate between the cells except in the case of the endocrine glands. When different types of epithelium come in contact the transition may be abrupt, as at the junction of the cardia and oesophagus, or gradual as in the passage of the urinary bladder to the skin.

Epithelial cells cohere together by means of a cement substance stainable. with silver nitrate. The connective tissue in contact with an epithelium is called a basement membrane. It consists usually of a dense network of fine reticular fibres. The epithelial cells cohere to these fibres with the aid of a mucoprotein (hyaluronic acid) substance (Robb Smith).

A physiological classification according to the function of the epithelium may also be used. We should then include under the term *protective epithelia,* the pavement, stratified and transitional varieties; under the term *secreting epithelia,* the cubical, columnar and glandular epithelia (some of the pavement epithelia would come also under this head); while *ciliated epithelium* would form a separate division, as in the classification usually adopted.

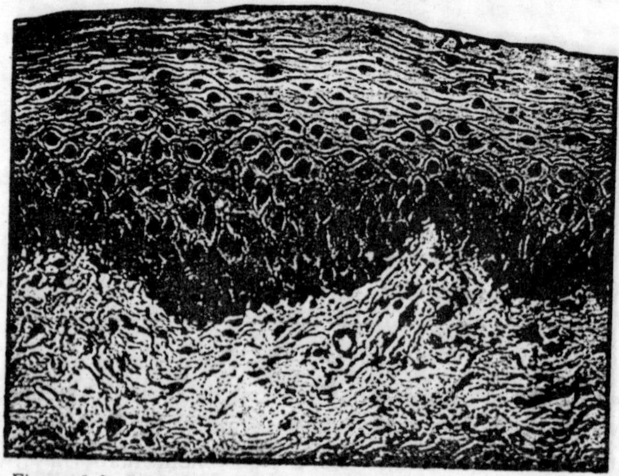

Figure 1.3: Section of stratified epithelium from fauces of rabbit.

PROTECTIVE EPITHELIA

Stratified epithelium covers the anterior surface of the cornea, lines the mouth, pharynx (lower part), oesophagus, anal canal and part of the urethra, and forms the epidermis which covers the skin. The vocal cords are covered by stratified epithelium. In the female it lines the vagina and covers the os uteri.

The cells nearest the surface are always flattened and scale-like, whereas the deeper cells are polyhedral, and those of the deepest layer are somewhat columnar in shape. Moreover, the deep cells are soft and protoplasmic, and are separated from one another by a system of inter-cellular channels, which are bridged across by numerous fibrils passing from cell to cell, giving the cells, when separated, the appearance of being beset with short spines *(prickle cells)*.

Figure 1.4: Section of epidermis of cat's foot, shjowing inter-cellular channels, with bridging fibrils.

The fibrils are traceable through the cell-substance and from cell to cell so that the cells are held firmly together and there is difficulty in isolating them. According to Shapiro some fibrils are confined to each cell and have a concentric arrangement. The fibrils are enlarg-ed as they cross the intercellular spaces.

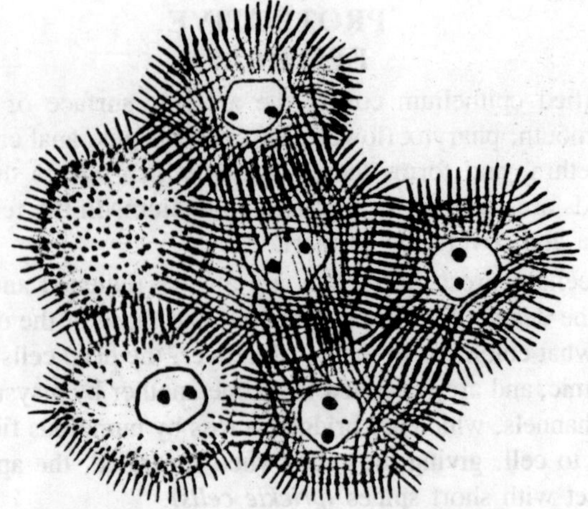

Figure 1.5: Fibres in deeper layer of epidermis.

Bridging fibrils have also been described in the pavement epithelium of Descemet's membrane at the back of the cornea.

The deeper cells multiply by mitosis. The newly formed cells tend as they enlarge to push those superficial to them nearer to the surface, from which they are eventually thrown off.

In certain .situations (e.g., the integument) the cells approach the surface, become keratinised, and in the case of the epidermis lose their nuclei and the appearance of distinct cells this can, however, be in a measure restored by the action of alkalies.

Such keratinised epithelia tend to be dry. The cast-off superficial cells of the stratified epithelium of the mouth, which are seen in abundance in the saliva, are less altered than those of the epidermis, and the remains of a nucleus are still visible in them. The stratified epithelium of the human epidermis shows many peculiarities; these will be considered when the skin is dealt with. The name *transitional*

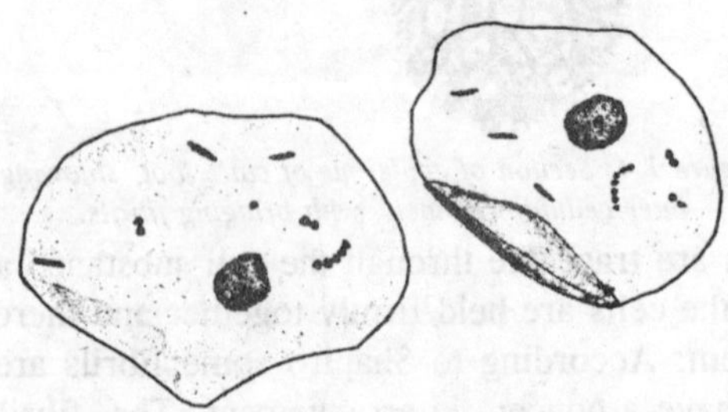

Figure 1.6: Dissociated epitherlium cells from the inside the mouth.

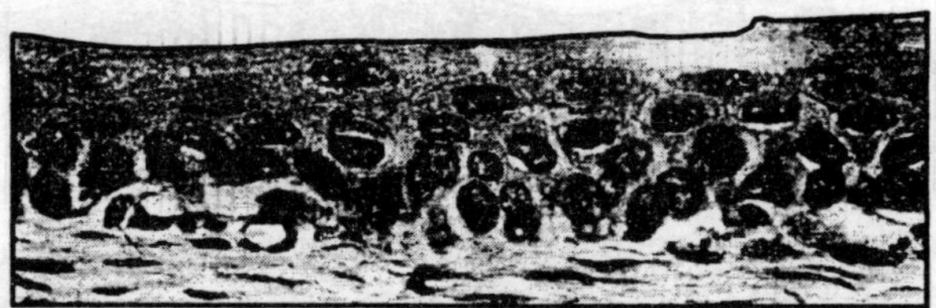

Figure 1.7: Transitional epithelium of urinary bladdeer of cat.

epithelium is given to a stratified epithelium consisting of only three or four layers of cells.

It occurs in the upper part of the urethra, in the urinary bladder, the ureter, and the pelvis of the kidney. The superficial cells are large and somewhat flattened; they often have two nuclei. Their free surface is covered with a cuticular stratum, and on their under surface they exhibit indentations, into which fit the rounded ends of pyriform or columnar cells, which form the next layer.

Next to this come one or two layers of smaller polyhedral cells. The epithelium is renewed by mitotic division of the deeper cells. It is possible that the superficial cells also multiply; if so, the division of their nuclei is amitotic.

If the organ is distended, the superficial cells may be nearly as flat as those of a stratified epithelium; but then the number of cell layers is much smaller. If the organ is collapsed, then the surface cells of the

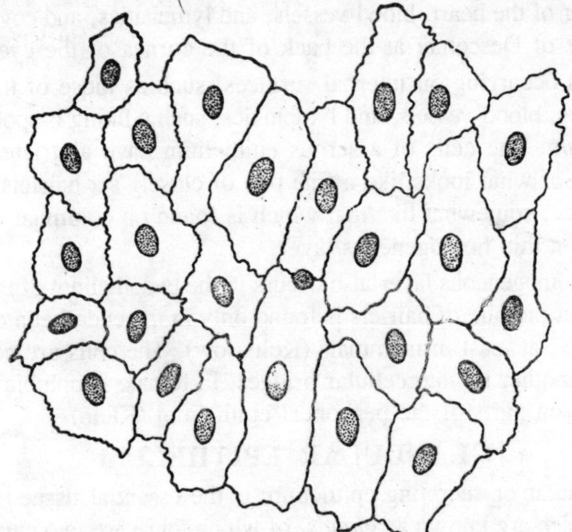

Figure 1.8: Pavement epithelium (endothelium of a serous membrane.

Figure 1.9: Endothelium-cells of serous membrane profile view, showing protoplasmic bridges stretching across the inter-cellular spaces.

transitional epithelium are much less flattened than those of a stratified epithelium; but the number of cell layers may now be as large. The cells can apparently glide over each other and are also capable of considerable deformation without loss of function.

Transitional epithelia, unlike the stratified epithelia, are not usually exposed to mechanical trauma. But they must be highly resistant to passage of water in order to prevent the osmotic pressure of the urine from withdrawing water from the blood.

It is possibly in connexion with this property that transitional epithelium contains alkaline phosphatase.

In some animals, such as the cat, the superficial cells are very large, with numerous indented facets into which the cells of the second layer fit; in others, as in man, they are much less extensive and have only one or two facets.

Endothelium and pavement epithelium are found in the alveoli of the lungs of the embryo, in the ducts of the mammary glands, in the kidney (in the tubes of Henle, also lining the capsules of the Malpighian body, and covering the glomeruli), lining the cavities of serous membranes, the interior of the heart, blood-vessels, and lymphatics, and covering the membrane of Descemet at the back of the cornea of the eye.

When occurring on internal surfaces, such as those of the serous membranes, blood-vessels, and lymphatics, such a lining is spoken of as *endothelium*. The cells of a serous epithelium have a striated border consisting of what looks like a fine pile of closely set hairlets on their free surface, somewhat like that which is found on columnar cells and resting on a thin homogeneous layer.

The homogeneous layer also occurs in the endothelium of the blood-vessels, but the pile of hairlets is found only in the endothelia of serous membranes, at least in mammals (Kolossow). The cells are connected with one another by intercellular bridges. In female Amphibia cilia are developed on parts of the peritoneal epithelium (Klein).

GLANDULAR EPITHELUM

Glandular or secreting epithelium is the essential tissue of all the organs which are known as *glands*, of which there are two chief kinds, known respectively as *externally* and *internally secreting glands*.

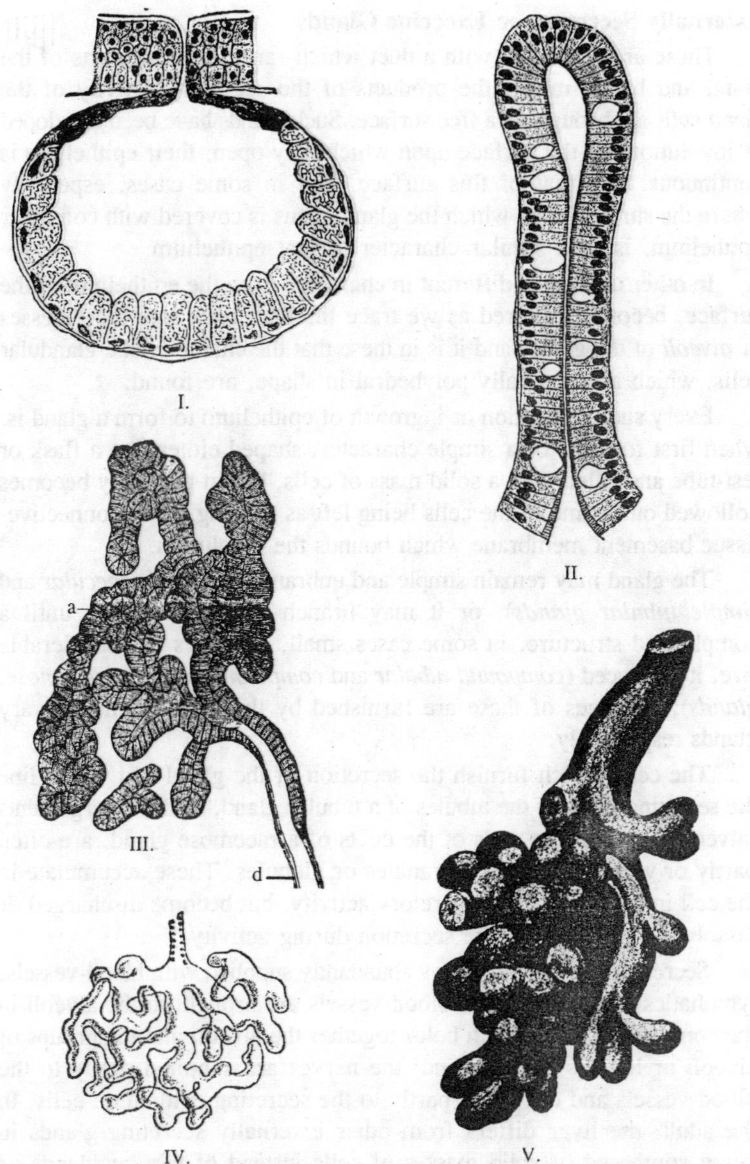

Figure 1.10: Various hinds of glands. I. Simple saccular gland from amphibian skin (Flemming). II. Simple tubular gland from intestine (Flemming). III. A small raoemose gland with a simple duct, d, into which a number of irregularly tubular acini, a, open (Klein). IV. Part of a tubulo-ràcemose gland with the acini unravelled (Flemming). V. Wax model of a small tubulo-racemose gland from the epiglottis (Maziarski).

Externally Secreting or Exocrine Glands

These are furnished with a duct which ramifies in all parts of the gland and by its means the products of the secretory activity of the gland-cells are brought to a free surface. Such glands have been developed as involutions of the surface upon which they open; their epithelium is continuous with that of this surface, and in some cases, especially where the surface upon which the gland opens is covered with columnar epithelium, is of a similar character to that epithelium.

In other cases it is different in character from the epithelium of the surface, becoming altered as we trace the duct back into the recesses or *alveoli* of the gland, and it is in these that the characteristic glandular cells, which are generally polyhedral in shape, are found.

Every such involution or ingrowth of epithelium to form a gland is, when first formed, of a simple character, shaped either like a flask or test-tube and filled with a solid mass of cells, but. it presently becomes hollowed out, some of the cells being left as a lining to the connective-tissue basement membrane which bounds the involution.

The gland may remain simple and unbranched *(simple saccular* and *simple tubular glands*), or it may branch again and again until a complicated structure, in some cases small, in others of considerable size, it produced (*compound tubular* and *compound saccular* (*racemose*) *glands*); instances of these are furnished by the kidneys and salivary glands respectively.

The cells which furnish the secretion of the gland and which line the secreting parts of the tubules of a tubular gland, or the enlargements (alveoli, acini) at the ends of the ducts of a racemose gland, are often partly or wholly filled with granules or globules. These accumulate in the cell in the intervals of secretory activity, but become discharged or dissolved and pass into the secretion during activity.

Secreting glands are always abundantly supplied with blood-vessels, lymphatics and nerves. The blood-vessels are brought to the alveoli in the connective tissue which holds together the alveoli and the groups of alveoli or lobules of the gland; the nerves are supplied partly to the blood-vessels and ducts and partly to the secreting epithelium-cells. In the adult, the liver differs from other externally secreting glands in being composed of solid masses of cells instead of tubular glands or saccular alveoli lined by epithelium.

It exhibits also other important differences in the nature of its blood supply, and the relation between the blood and the livercells. In many ways its structure resembles that of a gland of internal secretion which is not surprising because liver cells function both as internally and externally secreting cells.

Internally Secreting or Endocrine Glands

These are not furnished with ducts and were formerly classed with the spleen and lymphoid structures as *ductless glands*. But the true endocrine glands are, like the externally secreting organs, composed of epithelial cells, sometimes grouped in solid masses (as in the adrenal), in other cases disposed around hollow vesicles (thyroid) which become filled with the material of the secretion.

Since there is no duct in these glands the secretion is carried into the blood either directly by the blood-vessels of the gland or indirectly through the lymphatics.

MECHANISM OF SECRETION

This consists essentially of three phases.

1. ***Entry of substances into the cell***—The cell membrane is more permeable than when the cell is at rest but little else is known about the mechanisms involved. Probably most of the substances are water-soluble and enter the cell by diffusion. They continue to enter because they are immediately transformed into other substances; thus a constant diffusion gradient is maintained.

2. ***Elaboration of the secretion product***—This seems to occur in the neighbourhood of mitochondria and microsomes. It is possible that the anabolic process is related to the ribo-nucleoprotein content of these structures.

The process starts at the base of the cell and in a matter of hours the secretion products are migrating to the apical pole, but secretion may be modified by the Golgi apparatus. If the secretion product is not needed, it accumulates in granules or vacuoles which are stored at first in the apical pole and then gradually come to fill more and more of the cytoplasm.

Little is known of the factors affecting this elaboration. But it is known that in prolonged disuse, the secretion products diminish again. Thus in starvation the granules in the pepsin-secreting cells of the stomach diminish in number.

In some types of secreting cells, such as those of the islets of Langerhans of the pancreas, stimulation leads to an increased cell content of the secretion product (insulin) as well as to an increased rate of discharge. In many other types stimulation does not appear to affect directly the rate of elaboration but only that of discharge.

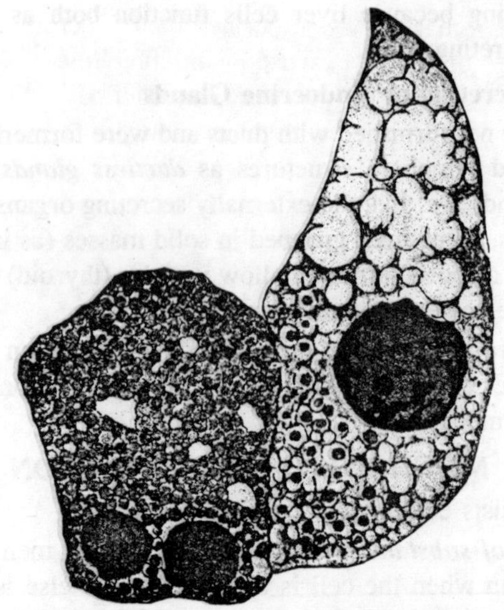

Figure 1.11: Two cells from a cutaneous gland of salamander-larva, showing secretion globules or granules.

3. *Discharge of the secretion product*—This phase is the one which is usuallly considered as being the true process of secretion, the previous two phases being merely preparatory phases.

For many years, it has been acknowledged that this phase occurs in a different manner in various cell types. In the *hjolocrine* type of cell, such as that of the sebaceous gland, the whole cell, with its inculded secretion product, disintegrates. This loss of cells is made good by division of relatively undifferentiated cells, which after elaboration of the secretion product also disintegrate.

In the *apocrine* type of cell, such as that of the mammary gland, the apical portion of the cell, containing the secretion product, is nipped off and disintegrates. The remainder, containing the nucleus then proceeds to elaborate more of the secretion product and to enlarge again in size.

In the *merocrine* type of cell no gross changes occur during the loss of the secretion product. Recent observations on the living cells of the pancreas of the white mouse have confirmed that, in this organ at least, merocrine secretion involves a more complicated process than mere diffusion. Small pseudopodia are projected from the apical pole and are nipped off. They contain either vacuoles of the secretion product or granules of it surrounded by a vacuole.

Often it seems that in the merocrine type of secretion the process is accompanied by or possibly caused by an imbibition of water into the cell; the consequent swelling may cause the eruptions from the surface. In the case of the mucus-secreting goblet-cells of the intestine such an explanation appears most likely. It is possible that the entry of water occurs when the cell membrane is depolarised by the arrival of a nerve impulse to the cell or the action of a stimulating chemical substance. The act of discharge is accompanied by an increased oxygen uptake.

Atypical Secretion

In the usual type of secretion such as that of the salivary glands, the substances present in solution in the fluid secreted differ from those of the blood and tissue fluid. But in other types, such as that of the sweat glands, the substances present in the secretion are the same as those in the blood and tissue fluid, but their relative concentrations are different.

Physical work must be done to effect this but the process both of formation and discharge of the secretion product may be quite different from that involved in the more usual type of secretion. Cerebro-spinal fluid of the brain and possibly the aqueous humour of the eye are other examples of this type of secretion.

The detailed study of glandular epithelium and of other epithelial structures may be reserved until the organs in which they occur are described, but columnar and ciliated epithelia will be dealt with in the next chapter. The *hairs* and *nails* and the *enamel* of the teeth are modified epithelial tissues. They will be described with the skin and mouth respectively.

COLUMNAR AND CUBICAL EPITHELIUM

Columnar epithelium occurs extensively in the body, lining the ducts of glands and covering the inner surface of mucous membranes. These are membranes moistened by *mucus* and they line passages in communication with the exterior, such as the alimentary canal, the respiratory and generative passages.

The cells of a columnar epithelium generally form a single layer, varying in thickness according to the length of the constituent cells. When the cells are short, the epithelium is spoken of as *cubical*. The cells are prismatic columns, which are set closely side by side, so that when seen in surface view a mosaic appearance is produced, the intercellular or cement substance forming a network around their ends

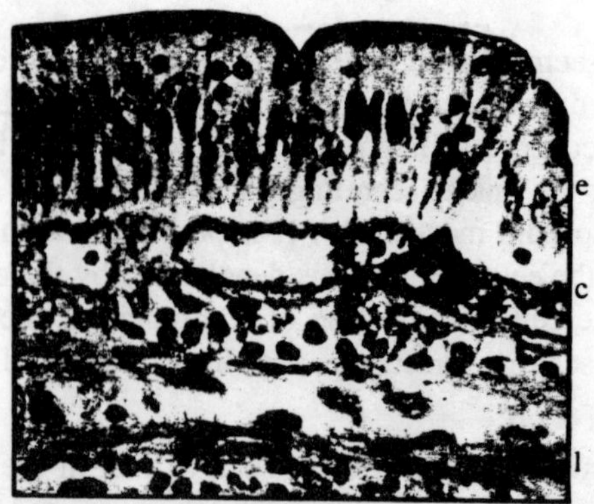

Figure 1.12: Secion of part of an intestinal villus (cat), showing columnar EPI thelium-cells covering the free surface.

(' Kittleisten ' of German authors). They often taper somewhat towards their attached end, which is generally truncated, and set upon a basement membrane. In the cells lining the intestine, the free surface is covered by a thick striated border which may sometimes become detached in teased preparations, and has the appearance of a dense mass of cilia.

The protoplasm of the cell exhibits fibres, vacuoles or granules according to the method which has been used for fixation. It contains numerous mitochondria, usually filamentous. Between the striated border and the protoplasm is a highly refractile disk, in the middle of which is a double centriole (diplosome) looking like a minute dumb-bell set vertically.

A Golgi apparatus lies between the nucleus and the free end of the cell. The nucleus is ovoid and usually has two nucleoli. The lateral borders of the cells are often irregular or jagged, due to the presence of lymphocytes, which are generally found between the columnar cells.

Columnar Epithelium

Cells are found lining the whole of the interior of the stomach and intestines: they are also present in the ducts of most glands, and sometimes also in their secreting tubes and saccules. The epithelium which covers the ovary is also of a modified columnar shape, but cells possessing the striated border and other structural peculiarities above described occur only in the alimentary canal and in certain of its diverticula.

Pseudo-stratified columnar epithelium is usually found in the larger ducts of the digestive glands such as the salivary glands. In this type of epithelium, all the cells are in contact with the basement membrane but not all reach to the free surface. The nuclei are arranged in two

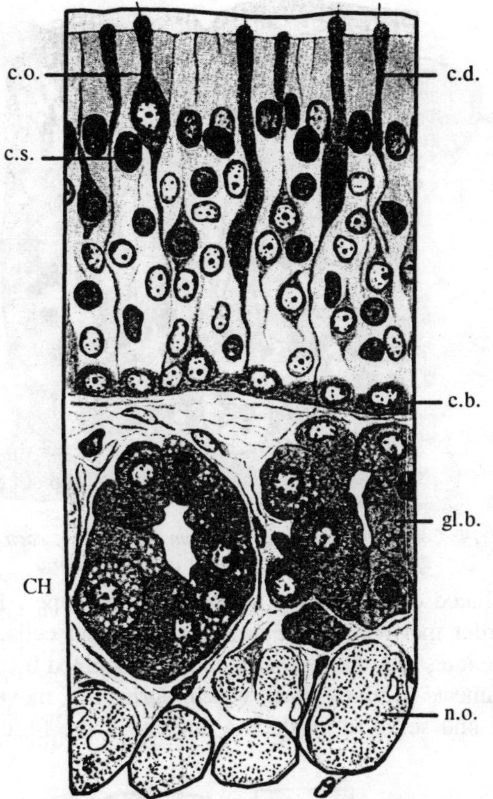

Figure 1.13: Stratified columnar epithelium of lafactor mucosa.

or more layers; the nuclei of the shortest cells are found nearest the basement membrane.

CILIATED EPITHELIUM

Ciliated epithelium is found in man throughout the whole extent of the air-passages and their prolongations, but not in the uppermost part of the nostrils, supplied by the olfactory tory nerves, nor in the lower part of the pharynx, nor in the terminal bronchioles.

Ciliated epithelium also occurs in the Fallopian tubes or oviducts and the greater part of the uterus; in the efferent tubes of the testicle; in the ventricles of the brain, and the central canal of the spinal cord. The cells may be only one layer deep, but in the trachea there is a basal layer from which the ciliated cells may be regenerated (pseudo-stratified columnar ciliated epithelium).

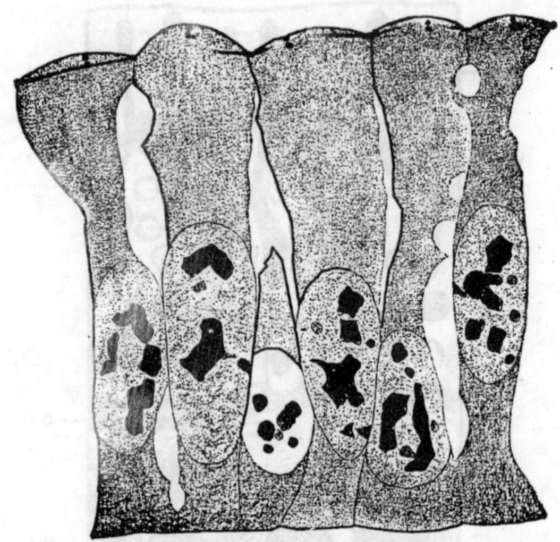

Figure 1.14: Columnar epithelium-cells from duck embro, each containing a diplosome (double centriole) at the free border.

The ciliated cells are usually columnar in shape . In place of the striated border met with in the ordinary columnar cells, such as those found in the intestine, the free surface is surmounted by a bunch of fine tapering filaments *(vibratile cilia),* which, during life, move spontaneously to and fro, and serve to produce a current in the fluid which covers them.

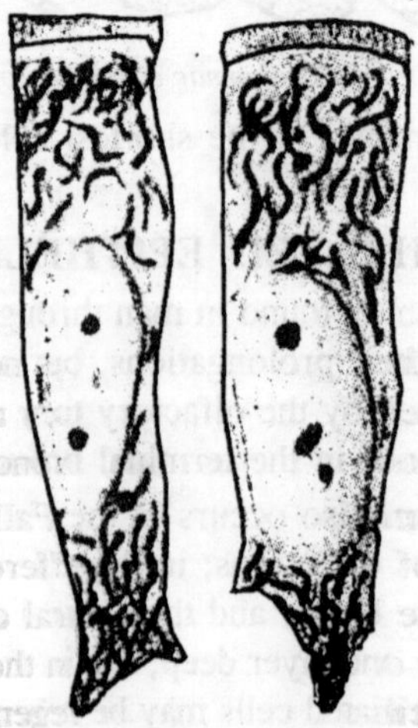

Figure 1.15: Two columnar epithelium-cells of intesting, stained to show the mitochondria.

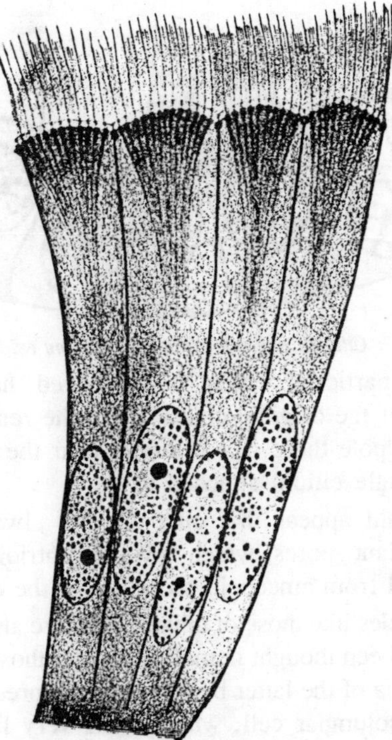

Figure 1.16: Four ciliated cells.

The border upon which the cilia are set has a bright appearance in the living condition: after fixation it appears formed of little juxtaposed *basal particles* to each of which a cilium is attached. In the large ciliated cells which line the alimentary canal of some molluscs, and with less distinctness in the ciliated cells of vertebrates, the cilia seem to be prolonged through the basal particles into the protoplasm of the cell as fine varicose filaments termed *rootlets*.

The nature of these has not been determined, but they resemble the fibrillar appearance seen in many cells and possibly are mere indications of lines of stress in the colloidal substance of the cytoplasm. The axial fibril in the tail of the spermatozoon (which is undoubtedly to be regarded as a cilium) is developed in connexion with the centriole, and it seems probable that the cilia of an ordinary ciliated cell may also be outgrowths from the multiplied centriole.

Corroboration of this is found in the epididymis of the rabbit, where there are both ciliated and non-ciliated cells; the latter have a double centriole (diplosome), whilst the ciliated cells have no centriole, but a

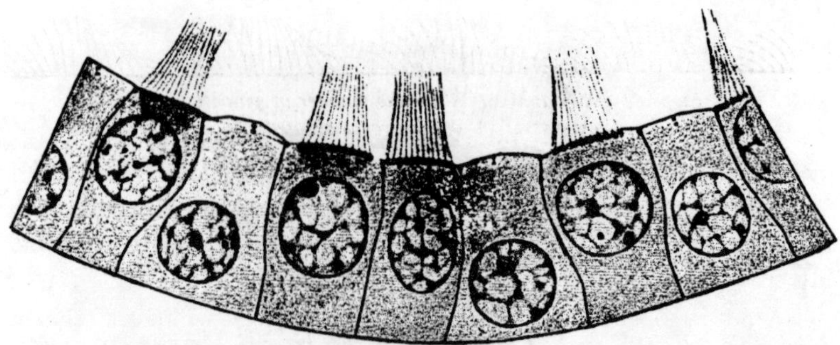

Figure 1.17: Ciliated and non-ciliated cells from epididymis of rabbit.

series of basal particles, which, it is believed, have been formed by multiplication of the original centriole. In the renal epithelium of the salamander -tadpole there is a centriole near the free border of each cell, with a single cilium attached to it.

But it would appear that cilia are not always developed from centrioles. In plant spores, which have no centrioles, the cilia are said to be developed from amceboid processes of the cytoplasm.

Basal particles like those of ciliated cells are also found in columnar cells they have been thought homologous with those of the ciliated cell, the bunch of cilia of the latter being perhaps represented by the striated border of the columnar cell, which looks very like a bunch of cilia although showing no ciliary movement. But the columnar cell contains an ordinary centriole, whereas the ciliated cell does not.

Cilia are remarkable in that they appear to beat permanently during life. Their movement has also been observed many hours after death.

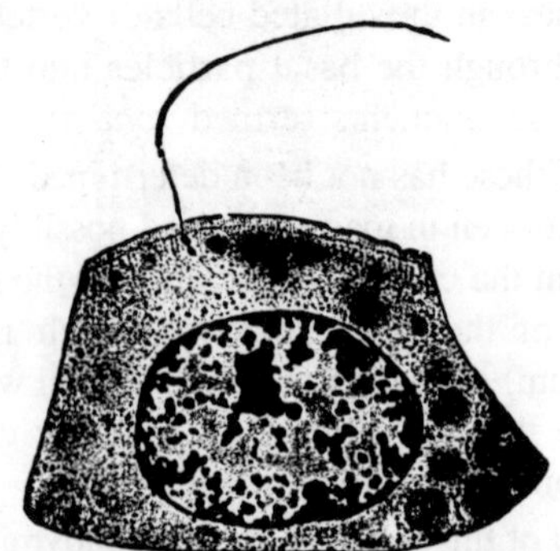

Figure 1.18: A ranal epithelium-cell of salamander-Tadpole, with centriole and cilium.

Figure 1.19: Diagram to show the manner in which ciliary movement passes in waves over a ciliated surface.

The Action of Cilia

When in motion a cilium is bent quickly over in one direction with a lashing whip-like movement, immediately recovering itself. In the effective direction it is stiff, in moving backward it is limp.

When vigorous the action is so rapid, and the rhythm so frequent (ten or more times in a second), that it is impossible to follow the motion with the eye. All the cilia upon a ciliated surface are not in the same phase of action at the same instant, but the movement travels in waves over the surface.

If a cell is detached from the general surface, its cilia continue to act for a while, but their movement at once ceases if they are completely detached from the cell, and if a ciliated cell (of the frog) is merely pierced by a fine glass point, so that the protoplasm undergoes coagulation, the cilia cease to act.

The rhythm is slowed by cold and quickened by warmth; but heat a few degrees above body temperature kills the cells and stops the action. The presence of calcium is essential for ciliary movement. It will continue for about an hour in water deprived of oxygen.

CO_2, ether vapour and chloroform vapour arrest the movement; but

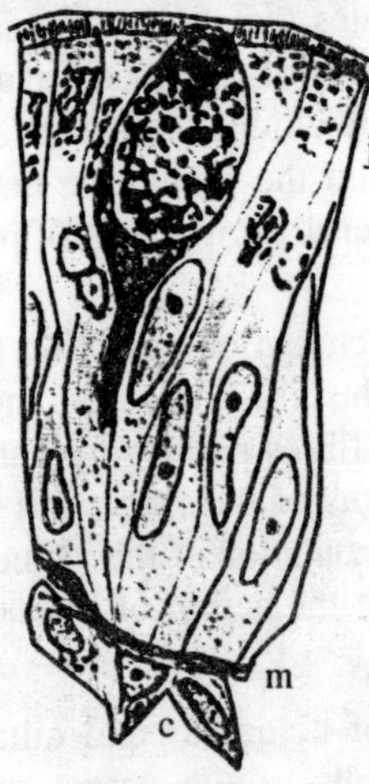

Figure 1.20: Five columnar cells and one globlet-cell from the small intesting of the cat.

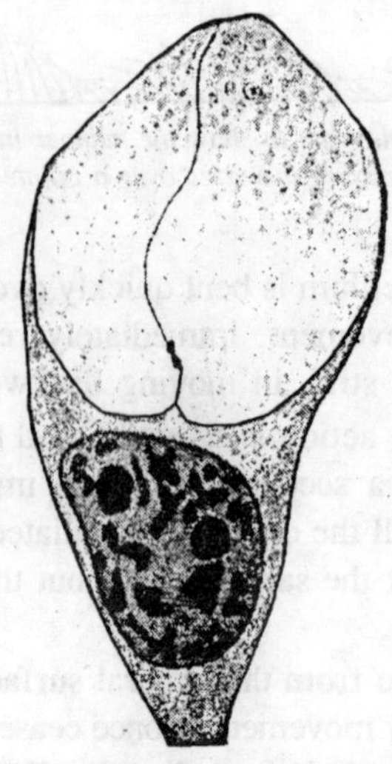

Figure 1.21: Globlet-cell of salamander-larva, with a diplosome in the mucin-containing portion of the cell.

it recommences on restoring air, if the action of those agents, especially of chloroform, is not too prolonged.

Very dilute alkaline solutions quic-ken the activity of cilia, or may even restore the movement shortly after it has ceased. It is probable (Gray) that ciliary movement is not due to displacement of hydrostatic pressure from the cell to its cilia, as has been previously supposed.

The evidence indicates that movement is generated in the cilium itself-probably as the result of localised changes in the distribution of water. In other words, the cilium can absorb with amazing speed more water on one side than on the other, the net effect, in Gray's view, being comparable to the curling of a strip of paper after moistening one side.

Most cilia are independent of activation by nerve stimulation, but inn the freshwater snail the cilia around the mouth can be set in activity by stimulating the nerve-fibres passing to that part. It is stated that the cilia lining the Oesophagus of the frog can be accelerated or retarded in their movements by stimulation of the vague and sympathetic nerves, either directly or through the action of hormones and drugs.

Goblet or Chalice Cells

Some of the cells of columnar and ciliated epithelia, which lie between the ordinary cells of the tissue, and occasionally cells in glandular and transitional epithelia, secrete mucin, which is laid down

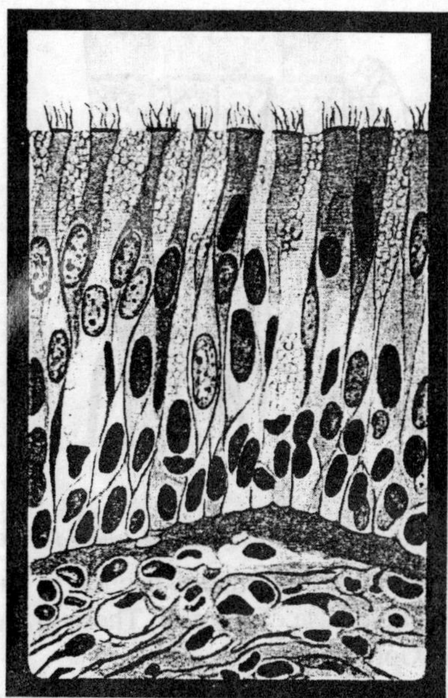

Figure 1.22: Human nasal mucosa.

within the cell in the form of granules or globules of mucin. The granules eventually swell up to form globular masses which clump together and greatly distend the part of the cell nearest the free border. When the mucin is extruded as mucus the free part of the cell becomes emptied and the cell then takes the form of a goblet or chalice, hence the above name.

The nucleus always lies near the attached end of the cell, in the stem of the goblet. The centriole or diplosome lies between the nucleus and the free border. The Golgi apparatus lies towards the base of the goblet in cells distended with mucus.

It has been shown that granules of mucin are formed in the region of the Golgi apparatus. The material of the latter is not apparently used up in the production of mucin, being dislocated towards the base of the cell by the accumulated secretion products.

Inflammation causes passage of water through the cells; the mucus is thereby dissolved and discharged through the open mouths of the goblet-cells. The latter are developed from the ordinary columnar elements at the bases of the crypts. It has also been shown that stimulation of the nervi errigentes of the cat's colon causes a discharge of mucus.

There is also evidence that the first appearance of the granules

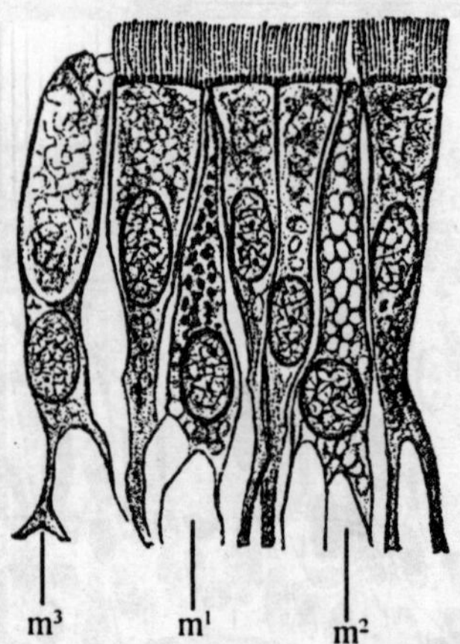

Figure 1.23: Ciliated epithelium from the trachea of the rabbit.

precursory to the formation of mucin occurs in the region of the mitochondrial group at the base of the cell. These granules then migrate into the area of the Golgi apparatus.

The *goblet-cells*, or, as they may be appropriately termed, *mucus-secreting cells*, are not mere temporary modifications of the ordinary columnar and ciliated cells amongst which they are found, but permanently differentiated cells, and they may therefore be regarded as unicellular glands.

After having got rid of their mucin by extrusion, they again form a fresh supply in the same way as before. In the gastric mucous membrane all the surface epithelium is composed of mucus-secreting cells, and here they extend also a certain distance into the tubular glands. In the small intestine they occur here and there between the ordinary columnar cells covering the general surface and the villi, and also. between those lining the crypts of Lieberkiihn.

In the large intestine most of the cells both of the surface and in the glands are goblet-cells. Goblet-cells also occur abundantly amongst the cells of some ciliated epithelia, such as that of the trachea. In ordinary preparations, the mucin is partially dissolved and the remainder is left as a reticulum stainable both by acidic and basic dyes.

Only in fresh preparations made in hypertonic solutions and in sections prepared with the greatest care can the mucin be seen in its natural granular form. It seems that mucoproteins are apt to resist fixation and hence remain watersoluble. Especially after de-fatting of tissues the mucoprotein dissolves in water as when the section is flattened out on water or when stained in an aqueous solution of dye.

2

Connective Tissues

The term *Connective Tissue* includes areolar, elastic, reticular, adipose and fibrous tissues and also cartilage and bone. Connective tissues are derived from mesoderm and resemble one another in their general manner of composition. They differ in the relative proportions of the contained elements and some show specialisation of one or more of the essential components.

Indeed all tissues of mesodermal origin conform to this pattern of structure, although it may be less obvious where the specialisation of the cells dominates the tissue, as in the case of muscular tissue or the suprarenal cortex.

The components to be considered are:

Cells

Some of these, the fibroblasts, are concerned with the production and maintenance of the fibres. Others, the histiocytes, are phagocytic. The remainder have specialised functions such as the production of pigment, the storage of fat and many other diverse actions in the metabolism of the body.

Fibres

These are of three kinds, elastic, collagen and reticular. The proportion of these varies and one or more may be lacking in some tissues.

Matrix

In some tissues, such as bone and cartilage, this component is obvious as well as dominant. But in the others even its demonstration is so difficult that its presence must still remain in some doubt.

Tissue fluid

This permeates all the spaces between the cells and fibres and the interstices of the matrix.

The following table gives the principal types of connective tissue and a brief summary of their contained components. Two other mesodermal tissues are included for comparison.

Tissue	*Principal cell type*	*Matrix.*	*Collagen fibres*	*Elastic fibres*	*Reticular fibres*
Areolar	Various	Doubtful	Present	Present	Present
Elastic	Fibroblasts	„	„	Predominate	Absent
Fibrous	„	„	Predominate	Absent	„
Reticular	Reticulo-endothelial	„	Present	„	Predominate
Hyaline cartilage	Chondro-blasts	Cartilaginous	Few	„	Present
Elastic	„	Present	Predominate	„	cartilage
White fibro cartilage	„	„	Predominate	Absent	„
Bone	Bone-cells (osteocytes)	Ostein and Calcium salts	Present near surface	„	Absent
Muscle	Muscle cells or syncytia	Doubtful	Present	Present	Present
Suprarenal cortex	Endocrine cells	„	„	Absent	Predominate

Connective tissues differ from epithelial tissues 'in the following ways :

(1) The cells tend to link their processes and form networks or to remain completely isolated. Epithelial cells tend to adhere to one another and form sheets.
This is true both in the body and in tissue-culture.

(2) Fibres, which give strength or elasticity are present in the intercellular spaces.
No such fibres are present between epithelial cells.

(3) The amount of the intercellular substance is very much greater in proportion.

(4) Transitions between the different types are common in places where they come into contact.

CELL TYPES

Fibroblasts

These cells lie among and upon the bundles of fibres The cell-body

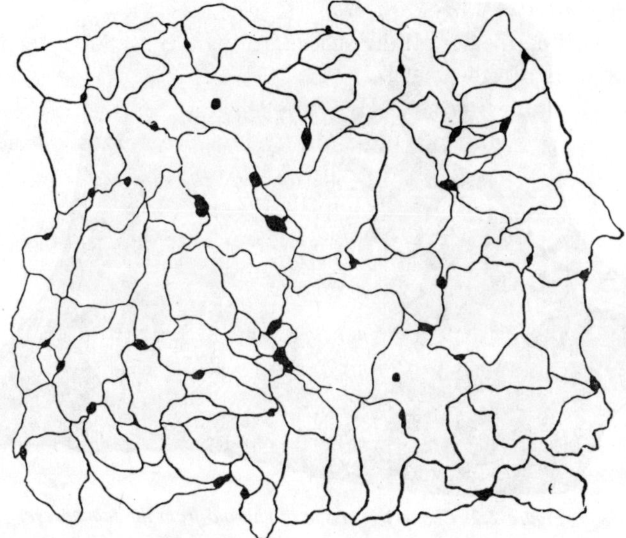

Figure 2.1: Endothelium-like cells of connective tissue from the surface of an aponeurosis. Silver nitrate preparation.

is usually flattened and irregular in shape, often branched; the nucleus is oval. In certain situations, as when they lie upon the surface of an aponeurosis, the lamellar cells are joined edge to edge, like cells of an endothelium. When branched, they come in contact with one another by their branches, as in the cornea.

The formation and maintenance of both collagen and elastic fibres is dependent on these cells. There is still doubt whether the collagen fibres are formed intra- or extracellularly. It seems likely that the material of the collagen fibre is secreted by the fibroblasts into the intercellular spaces. There, under the influence of the fibroblasts, the protein molecules are orientated to form fibres. In scurvy this process is interfered with in its final stages.

Histiocytes or Clasmatocyte

These form part of the reticuloendothelial system which has already been described. Both in filmpreparations and sections these appear as irregularly shaped cells with oval or spherical nuclei and basiphil cytoplasm.

They are most easily identified by their tendency to take up vital stains, and by otherwise displaying active phagocytic properties. Recent work (von Mollendorff) shows that probably the fibroblast can become transformed into the histiocyte, and *vice versa.*

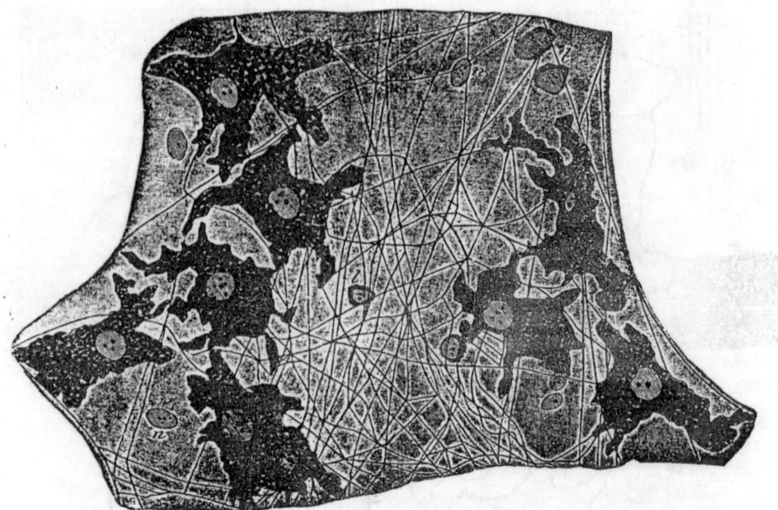

Figure 2.2: Connective tissue of choroid from the human eye.

Basiphil Cells

These are usually *spheroidal* or *ovoidal* and are full of granules staining intensely with basic dyes. In general appearance the connective-tissue basicytes are like the basiphils of the blood, although their relationship to these is *problematic* they are generally much larger than the *blood-leucocytes*.

They are usually common where fat is being laid down. They are always *numerous* in the neighbourhood of the walls of capillaries. According to Jorpes their granules consist of a *mucoprotein* identical with heparin for the production of which they are responsible.

The granules are labile but are well preserved by most fixatives in the tissues of the rat. In many preparations of tissues of other species, the granules are apt to be dissolved by water at some stage prior to mounting.

Plasma-Cells

The plasma-cell is thought to be derived from the lymphocyte, by an increase in size. The nucleus is spherical; the chromatin is often arranged in *irregular* masses like a cart-wheel within it. The cytoplasm, oval or irregular, is *basiphil*, but without granules.

Leucocytes are normally found in small numbers in areolar tissue, whither they have migrated from the blood-stream. They are generally either lymphocytes or polymorphs.

The connective-tissue cells occupy spaces *(cell-spaces)* of correspon-

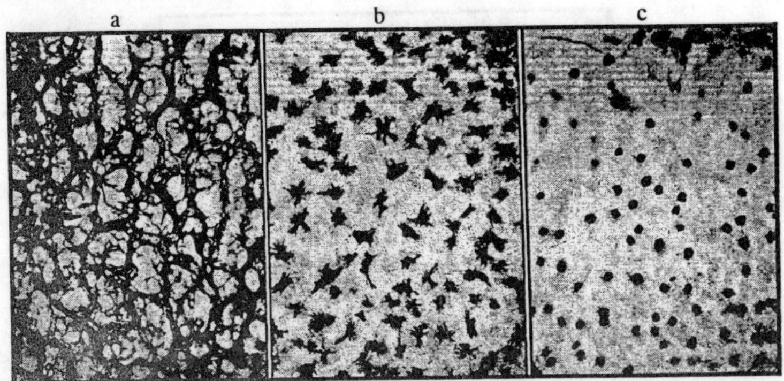

Figure 2.3: Cutaneous pigment-cells (Malanophores) of frog-web. a, from a dark animal, with the pigment spread out over the whole cell; b, with the pigment partially retracted: c, from a pale animal, with the pigment wholly retracted and concentrated around the nucleus of each cell.

ding shape in the ground-substance, lying between the bundles of white fibres. In some parts the white bundles are developed to such an extent as to, pervade the whole of the ground-substance, and then the *connective tissue* corpuscles become squeezed into the interstices; flattened lamellar expansions of the cells extending between the bundles.

Pigment-Cells

In the choroid and iris of the eye in mammals and also in certain parts of the skin, some of the connective-tissue cells are occupied by granules of pigment. Such cells are much more extensively present in lower vertebrates, especially in Amphibia and fishes, where they are either black (melanophores) or of a yellowish colour (xanthophores).

The cells in question exhibit changes which result in the pigment being at one time diffused over a considerable area and at another time restricted to the immediate neighbourhood of the nucleus. The changes are produced by variations in the environment (light, moisture, etc.).

Such variations cause alterations in the general shade and colour of the integument and serve the purpose of protective adaptation of the animals to their surroundings, but all pigment-cells do not exhibit the changes in question.

In those cells in which the alterations occur, the distribution of the pigment within the cell is effected by migration of the pigment-granules in the relatively fixed body, the granules being either heaped round the nucleus (light effect) or scattered throughout the cytoplasm (dark effect).

Not only do the pigment-cells respond to light through the agency of the nervous system, but in some animals also to internal secretions

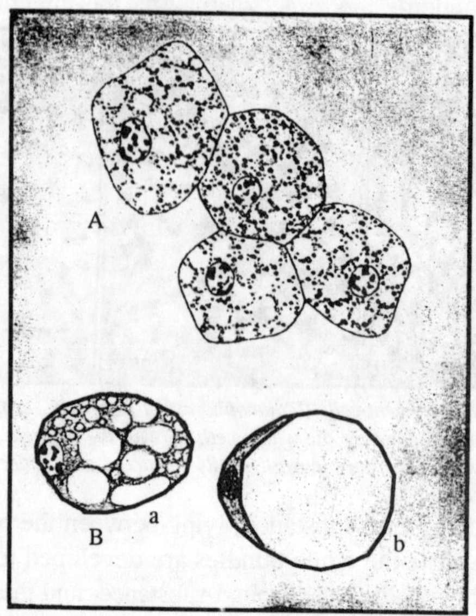

Figure 2.4: Fat-cells, in three stages of development, as seen in the average paraffin section, the fat having been dissolved and only the empty space left.

(hormones) produced within the organism. Thus in the frog's skin the pigment-granules of the melanophores are collected round the nucleus as a result of the action of adrenalin, and cause the integument to appear light; whereas they spread out into all the processes of the cells as a result of the action of an extract of the pars intermedia of the

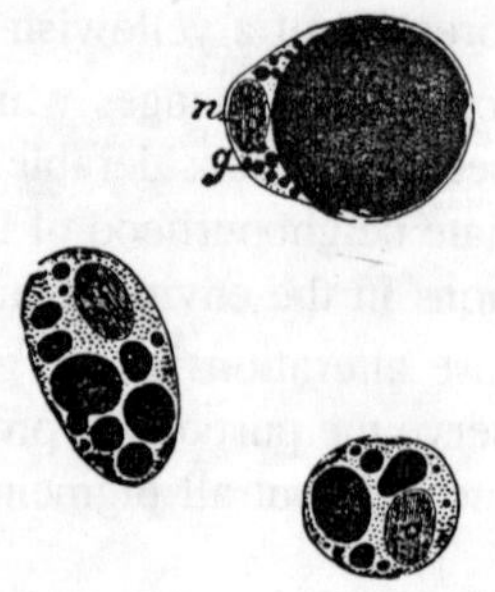

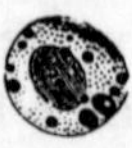

Figure 2.5: Fat-cells from young animal. Osmic acid preparation.

pituitary body, producing the effect of making the integument appear dark.

Fat-cells

Although all cells of the body contain neutral fat, in most this fat cannot be demonstrated histologically, probably because it is in intracellular membranes or granules which are below the limit of visibility, or because it is loosely combined with protein to form lipoproteins. In some cell types, such as the liver, kidney, etc., small fat droplets occur in the cytoplasm.

As a result of degenerative changes, these and many other types of cell may show many and large fat droplets. But it is in certain connective tissue-cells that deposition of fat is normally seen in large amounts. During foetal development and during adult life when fat is being laid down, basiphil granules in these cells, possibly of mitochondrial origin, are transformed into fatty droplets.

As the fat droplets increase in size they run together into a larger drop which gradually fills the cell, swelling it more and more, so that eventually the cytoplasm remains merely as a thin envelope surrounding the fat drop (see figs. 84 and 85). The envelope is thickened at one place where it contains the nucleus, which is oval and flat.

In certain parts of the body, notably the peri-renal region, the fat droplets do not coalesce and the cells retain the appearance of those in figure elsewhere in this chapter, *A*. The same type of cell is also found in the 'yellow fat' laid down in hibernating animals in autumn.

The fat may be stained by one of the Sudan stains or Scharlach R. The dye is more soluble in fat than in the alcohol in which the stain had been dissolved. It may also be stained by osmic acid which is reduced by the unsaturated fatty acids, that are always present, to a lower black oxide of osmium.

These osmium preparations may be embedded in paraffin for section cutting. Otherwise the fat will be dissolved by the xylol used for clearing the tissues and a 'negative ' picture of the fat will be obtained; where there was fat spaces will appear.

FIBRES

These are of three kinds, Collagen, Elastic and Reticular.

Collagen

These are usually broad, 1-20 μ diameter, branch, and impart strength rather than elasticity to tissues. They form the main constituent of tendons, capsules and the dermis. They stain pink with eosin and red

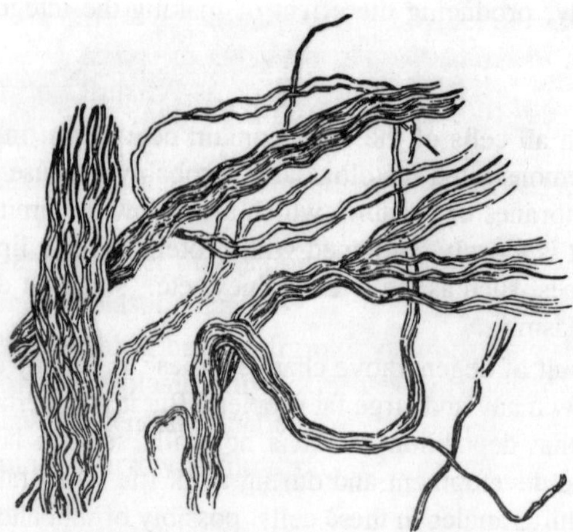

Figure 2.6: White fibres of areolar tissue.

with Van Gieson. In the fresh condition they are doubly refractile. Each fibre is composed of a variable number of fibrils which do not branch but may pass from one bundle to another where the bundles branch. The fibrils are bound together by a clear substance, possibly of a mucoprotein nature.

A similar material in a semi-fluid condition forms the groundsubstance of tissues in which the fibres course and in which the cells of the tissue lie embedded. This ground-substance between the bundles can with difficulty be seen in the fresh tissue on account of its extreme transparency;

Figure 2.7: Areolar tissue impregnated with silver nitrate.

Figure 2.8: Film preparation of subcutaneous connective tissue.

but it can be brought to view by treatment with silver nitrate.

The whole of the tissue is thereby stained a yellowish-brown colour, with the exception of the spaces occupied by the cells, collagen fibrils and elastic fibres.

It is likely that some of the substance that normally binds together collagen fibrils may pass into the tissue spaces when the tissue becomes oedematous. This might account for the altered staining affinities of collagen fibres of oedematous tissues. The increased amount of the ground-substance might explain the water retention.

Collagen is dissolved by boiling water forming a solution of gelatine. It is digested by pepsin but not by trypsin. Acetic acid causes the fibres to swell and become indistinct. In this condition constrictions at irregular intervals may sometimes be seen.

Collagen fibres are formed and maintained by fibroblasts and are related to reticular fibres.

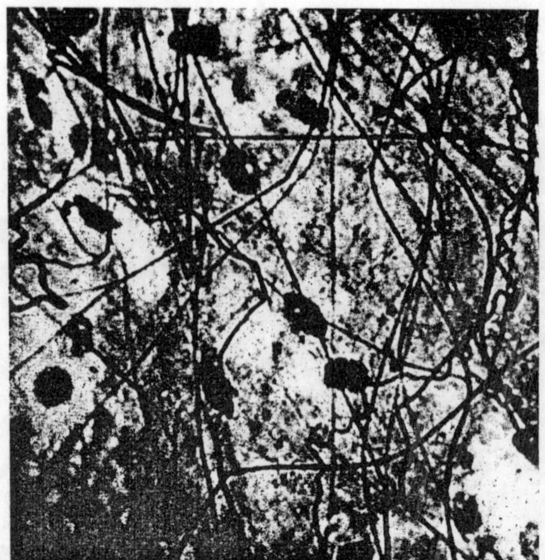

Figure 2.9: Areolar tissue film stained with acid fuchsin.

Elastic Fibres

They are well seen after treatment with acetic acid, and best after specific staining with acid fuchsin or orcein; but they can be detected in fresh preparations mounted in normal saline. They are characterised by their distinct outline, their straight course, the fact that they do not run in bundles, but singly, and that they branch and join neighbouring fibres.

If broken by the needles used in teasing, the elastic recoil causes them to curl up, especially near the broken ends. Elastic fibres stain red with eosin and dark brown with orcein. They resist the action of boiling water and pepsin but are destroyed by tryptic digestion. They appear to have a sheath which is more resistant to reagents than the internal part of the fibre.

They are not doubly refractile. In the fresh condition elastic fibres are faintly yellow in colour whereas collagen fibres are white; hence the names which used to be applied to these two kinds of fibre.

Reticular Fibres

These fibres are of very great importance in the body. They resemble collagen fibres in many ways and are continuous with them. But they are thinner, resist peptic digestion and branch. They are stained by the same acid dyes as collagen fibres but the dye is easily washed out of them, unless it is of very high molecular weight. Further, these fibres

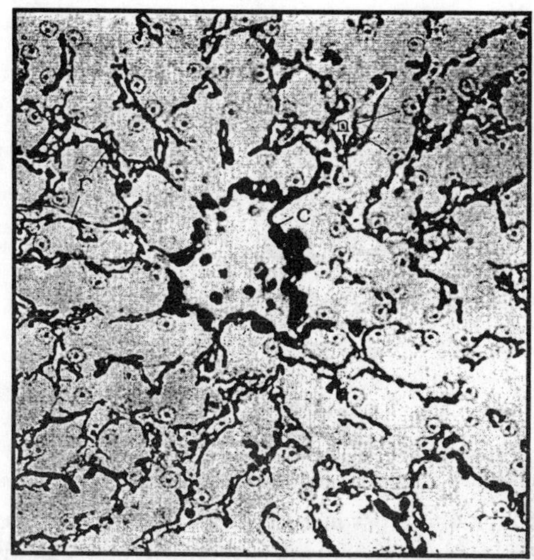

Figure 2.10: Reticular fibres of liver: foot's silver impregnation method.

can be quite specifically stained by colloidal solutions of silver oxide or carbonate; hence the name argyrophil fibres.

Reticular fibres have a very widespread distribution. They form the basement membranes of most epithelia. The basal ends of the cells are often partially enveloped by a basketwork of reticular fibres. But the adherence is effected mainly by a gelatinous condensation of ground-substance.

In mesodermal tissues such as the suprarenal gland they form a delicate basketlike investment which supports and gives mechanical protection to cells which are essentially soft and fragile.

Blood-vessels as in the liver and spleen are supported by reticular fibres. They play a most important role in the maintenance of the patency of the smaller lymphatics. In the spleen, lymph nodes and bonemarrow they are the dominant type of fibre and here form tissues which are called reticular tissues.

In the formation of collagen fibres, reticular fibres are apparently laid down first. Then, provided that vitamin C is available, the reticular fibres are transformed into collagen fibres.

AREOLAR TISSUE

This type of tissue is found between organs which must be loosely bound together. Subcutaneous connective tissue is the type usually studied. To the naked eye it presents an appearance of fine transparent threads

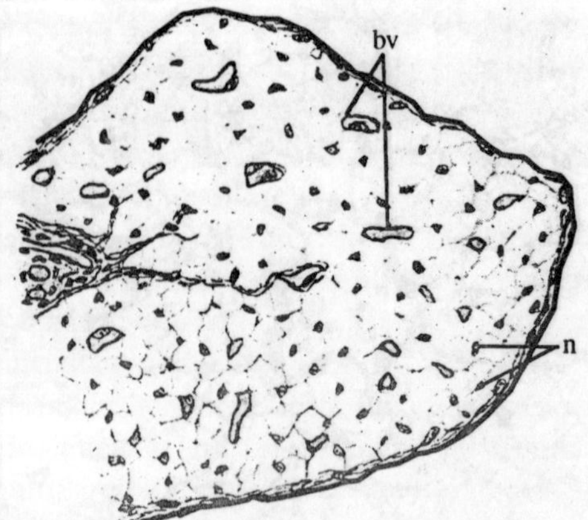

Figure 2.11: Section of lobule of adipose tissue of young cat.

and laminae which intercross in every direction, leaving inter communicating meshes or areolae between them. When examined with a microscope these threads and fibres are seen to be principally collagen fibres.

It is usually assumed that areolar tissue is the most undifferentiated of the connective tissues. Certainly most of the elements of connective tissues may be seen in a preparation of subcutaneous connective tissue and no one element predominates.

Areolar tissue combines a reasonable degree of strength, which prevents undue displacement, with great elasticity which ensures a return to the position occupied before.

ADIPOSE TISSUE

In this type of tissue the dominant cell type is the fat-cell. These may be collected into lobules or masses but often are in small groups alongside nerves and blood-vessels. When not too crowded they are spherical but where densely packed they are seen to be polyhedral.

Supporting the individual cells is a basket-like felt of retitular fibres. Enclosing a lobule by there may be a capsule of collagen fibres. The tissue is well vascularised. This is now under-standable because it is known that there is a constant turnover of the fat present.

Adipose tissue is distributed where its presence as a store will be of least inconvenience. But it also tends to be laid down where its thermal and mechanical insulation will be of greatest advantage. Thus adipose tissue fills up such of the bone-marrow that is not needed for blood formation (yellow marrow).

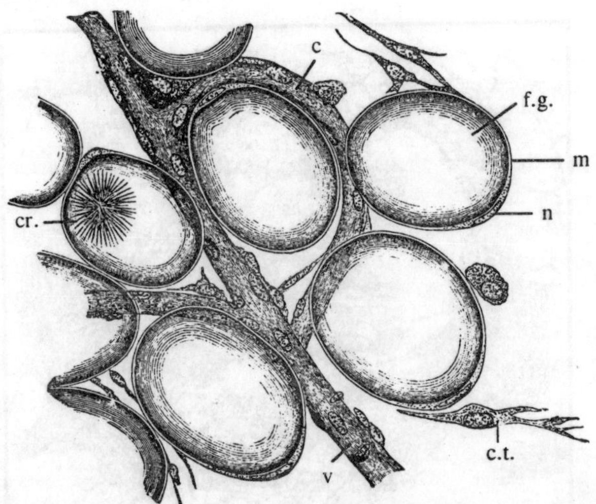

Figure 2.12: Cells from the margin of a fat-lobule. m, membrane of fat-cell consisting of cytoplasm and nucleus (n) and enclosing the large fat-globule er., crystals of fatty acids; c, a capillary joining a venule, v; c.t., a connective-tissue cell.

It is also found round such important organs as the heart and kidney. As the omentum it protects the intestines. Nerves in superficial positions liable to ianjury are often protected by fat (Sunderland).

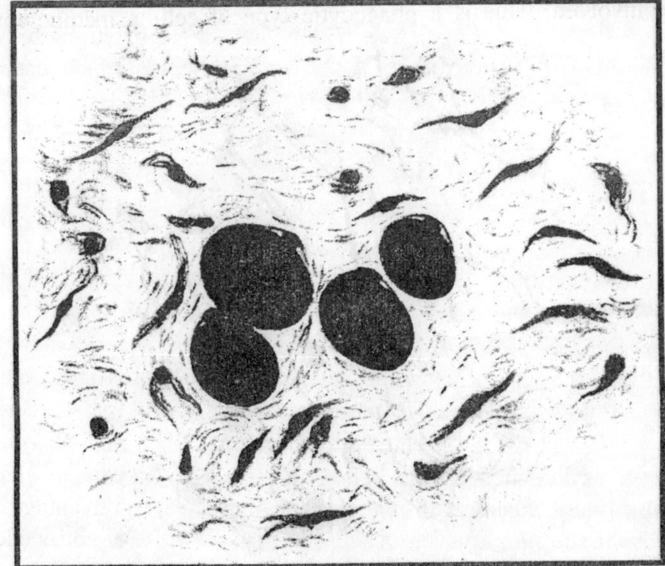

Figure 2.13: Four fat-cells in connective tissue.

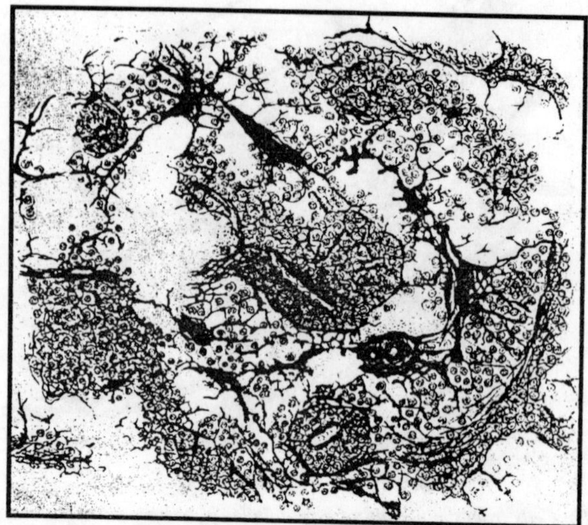

Figure 2.14: Lymphoid tissue of a lymph-gland.

RETICULAR TISSUE

In this type of tissue, the dominant fibre is the reticular fibre. In most tissues the reticular fibre is formed and maintained by fibroblasts. In reticular tissue, it is the reticulo-endothelial cell which would seem to be involved. This is a phagocytic type of cell, a member of the

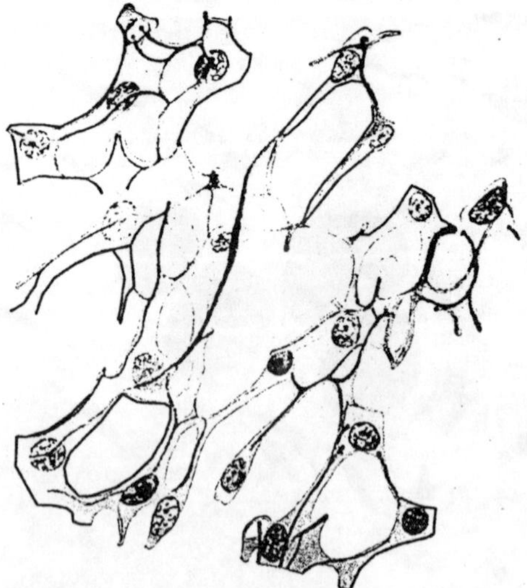

Figure 2.15: Reticulum of a lymph-gland, with its fibres overlaid by endothelial cells.

reticulo-endothelial system. The cells are stretched over the network of reticular, fibres.

In such tissues as the lymph nodes, spleen and bone-marrow, the reticular fibres form a supporting framework for the fragile blood-forming cells, as well as for the reticulo-endothelia l cells. A further description of this will be given in the account of these organs.

ELASTIC TISSUE: FIBROUS TISSUE: DEVELOPMENT OF CONNECTIVE TISSUE

Elastic tissue is a variety of connective tissue in which elastic fibres preponderate. It is found in its most concentrated form in the *ligamentum* nuchle (of quadrupeds) and in the *ligamenta subflava* of the vertebrae, but the connective tissue of other parts may also have a considerable development of elastic fibres, as in subcutaneous and subepidermal connective tissue.

It also occurs in *abundance* in the walls of the bronchi, and uniting the cartilages of the *larynx*. It also enters largely into the formation of the lungs and of the walls of the arteries. In the ligamentum nuchae most of the fibres are large. They often exhibit cross-markings or even transverse clefts.

When dragged asunder they break *sharply* across. They constantly branch and unite, so as to form a network. In transverse section they appear angular, but usually the angles are rounded. They are separated into small groups or bundles by *intervening* areolar tissue.

Elastic tissue does not always take the form of fibres, but also

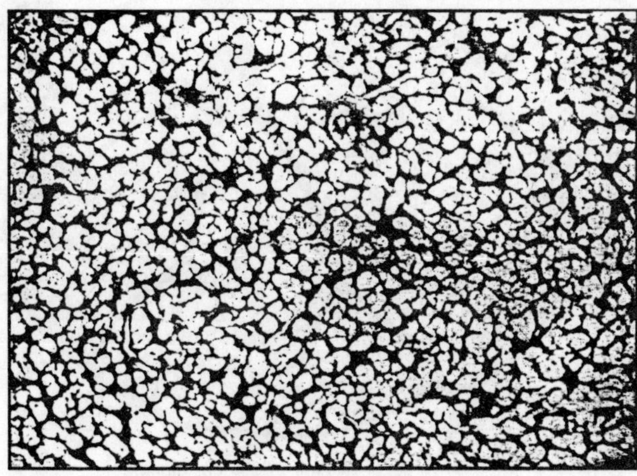

Figure 2.16: Cross-section of elastic fibres from the ligamentum of the ox.

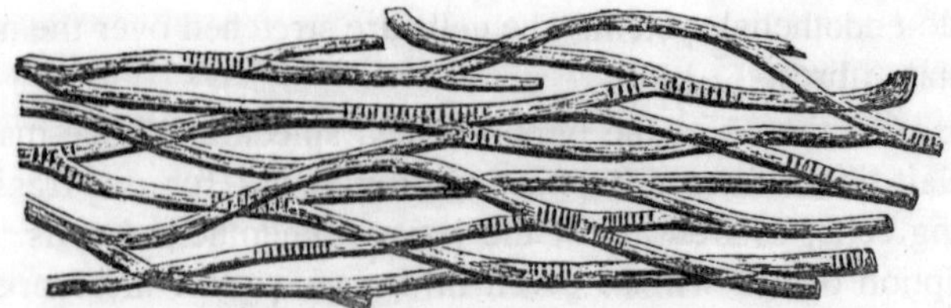

Figure 2.17: Elastic fibres from the ligamentum nuchae of the ox, showing transverse markings.

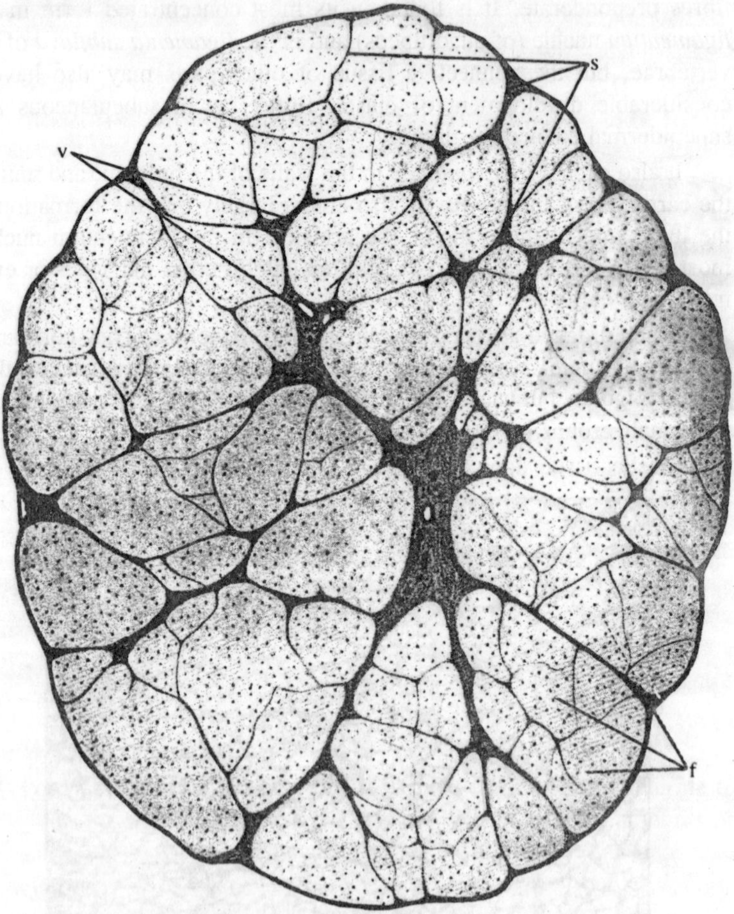

Figure 2.18: Section of tendon, human.

occurs as membranes (e.g., in the internal elastic lamina of blood-vessels). In areolar t issue the elastic fibres may be very fine, but their microscopic and chemical characters are always well marked.

FIBROUS TISSUE

Fibrous tissue is almost wholly made up of bundles of white fibres running in determinate directions. These bundles again are collected into larger bundles, which give the fibrous appearance to the tissue. The bundles are constantly uniting with one another in their course, although their component fibres remain distinct.

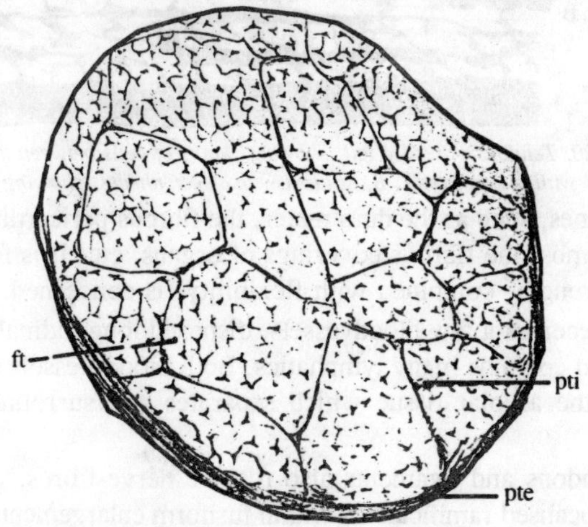

Figure 2.19: Transverse section of tendo achillis of rabbit. pte, sheath of tendon; pti, septa of tendon-bundles; ft, the tendon-bundles between which the darkly staining tendon-cells may be seen.

The interspaces between the larger bundles are occupied by areolar tissue in which the blood-vessels, lymphatics, and nerves of the fibrous tissue are conveyed. The interstices between the smallest bundles are occupied by rows of lamellar connective-tissue corpuscles (*tendoncells*), which, from being squeezed up between three or more bundles, become flattened out in two or three directions.

In transverse section the cells look irregularly stellate, but when seen on the flat they appear lamellar; from this aspect their general shape is square or oblong. They lie, as before said, in rows between the tendon-bundles; the nuclei of adjacent cells are placed opposite one another in pairs. The cell-spaces correspond in figure and arrangement with the cells which occupy them.

Fibrous tissue forms the tendons and ligaments, and also certain

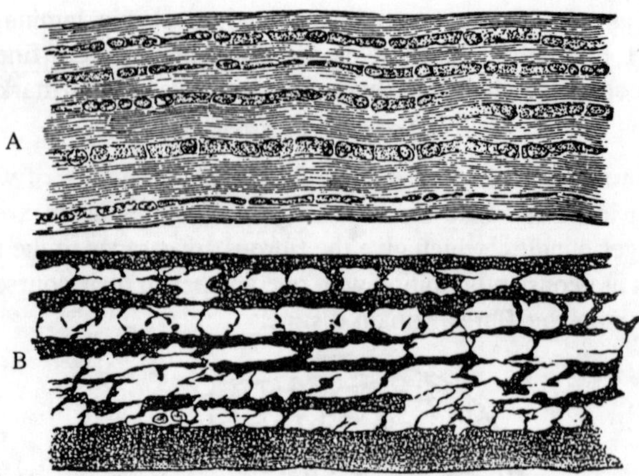

Figure 2.20: Tendons of mouse tail, showing chains of cells between the tendon bundles. A, stained with hwmatoxylln. B, stained with silver nitrate, showing cell-spaces.

membranes, such as the dura mater, the fibrous pericardium, the fasciae of the limbs, the fibrous coverings of organs, etc. It is found wherever great strength, combined with flexibility, is concerned.

It receives a few bloodvessels, disposed longitudinally for the most part, and contains many lymphatics. Both blood-vessels and lymphatics run in the areolar tissue which separates and surrounds the tendon-bundles.

Tendons and ligaments also receive nerve-fibres, many of which end in localised ramifications within fusiform enlargements of the tendon-bundles (organs of Golgi), while others terminate in end-bulbs or in simple Pacinian corpuscles. These will be described with the modes of ending of nerve-fibres.

Basement-membranes or *membrane propria* are homogeneous-looking membranes, which are found forming the surface layer of connective-tissue expansions in certain parts, especially where there is a covering of epithelium, as on mucous membranes, in secreting glands, and elsewhere. They help to anchor the epithelial cells to the underlying connective tissue.

Usually a basement membrane is formed by reticular fibres. But they seem sometimes formed of flattened connective-tissue cells joined together to form a membrane ; in other cases (e.g., front of cornea, trachea) they are evidently formed not of cells, but of condensed ground-substance, and in yet other cases of elastic substance (back of cornea). The name basement-membrane has therefore been used to denote structures of a totally different nature.

Jelly-like connective tissue, although occurring largely in the embryo, is found only in one situation in the adult-viz., forming the vitreous humour of the eye. It is composed mainly of soft, fluid or semi-fluid groundsubstance, with cells scattered here and there through it, and with fibres which interlace throughout the tissue and confine the fluid of the groundsubstance within their meshes, thus conferring upon the tissue its jelly-like character.

All embryonic connective tissue is at one period of this jelly-like nature. It persists until full term in the umbilical cord whereas in the foetus itself collagen fibre formation has already started.

HISTOGENESIS OF CONNECTIVE TISSUE

Connective tissue is developed in connexion with certain cells of the mesoderm of the embryo. In those parts which are to form connective tissue there may frequently be seen a clear space separating the cell-layers which are already formed, this clear space being sometimes permeated with a network of fibres which appear to be in continuity with the cells bounding the space.

Branching mesenchyme cells, which separate off from the bounding cells, are presently found forming a syncytium within the clear space. In the meshes of this syncytium is a semi-fluid intercellular substance.

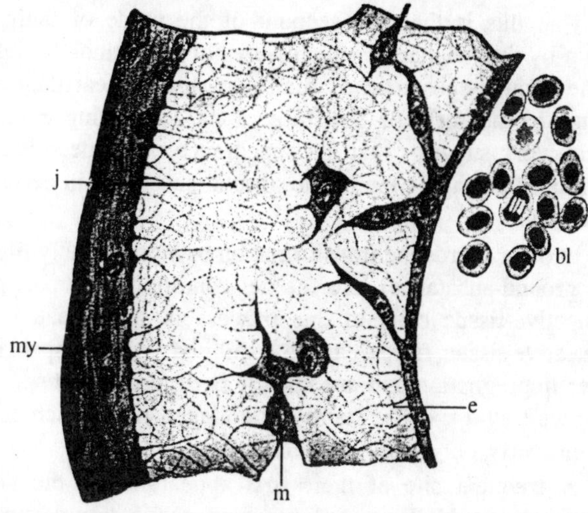

Figure 2.21: Developing connective tissue in heart of chick-embryo of 48 hours. my, cells forming myocardium; j, jelly formed of reticulum with enclosed fluid; e, endothelium; m, mesenchyme cells in jelly; bl, blood-corpuscles.

The connective-tissue fibres, both white and elastic, are deposited in this. The white fibres appear at first as single threads, which soon become numerous and are ultimately collected into fine bundles.

The bundles gradually become larger; so that in some tissues (such as tendon) the whole ground-substance is eventually pervaded by them, and the cells of the tissue become squeezed up into the intervals. Before any considerable development of fibres has taken place, the embryonic connective tissue has a jelly-like appearance; in this form it occurs in the umbilical cord, where it is known as the *jelly of Wharton*.

A jellylike connective tissue is also seen forming the marrow of embryonic bones at a certain stage of development. There has long been a difference of opinion as to the origin of the fibres of connective tissue, some histologists holding that they are formed within the protoplasm of the cells, which gradually lose their cell-characters as fibres become developed within them; others taking the view that the fibres, both white and elastic, are extracellular formations.

While it is certain tat they are produced under the influence of the cells it is probable that both kinds of fibres are deposited in the ground-substance between the cells and not in the cell-protoplasm, so that they are rather to be looked upon, like the ground-substance itself, as formed by a process of secretion rather than by one of direct cell-transformation.

That this is the true account of the mode of their formation is shown by the manner in which fibres of both kinds become developed in the ground-substance or matrix of hyaline cartilage, without any change in the form or structure of its cells being evident. In brief, recent work suggests that the appearance of connectivetissue fibres is essentially a coagulation of the ground-substance in certain planes and directions.

In other words the transformation of a presumably lifeless hydrosol (the ground-substance) into the gel condition. The part played by the connective-tissue cells in this process is still debated. The earliest connective-tissue fibres can be exhibited only by special methods of silver impregnation and are known as *argyrophil fibres*. These do not stain well with specific stains for collagen fibres such as Van Gieson, this property only being acquired later.

A frequent site of their first appearance is the boundary zone between an epithelium and the amorphous groundsubstance of the mesenchyme. It is thus possible that the fibres may be formed without the intervention of connective-tissue cells. In such cases physico-chemical interactions between the epithelium and the groundsubstance must be invoked. In the healing of a wound of the skin the reticular fibres of the basement membrane are sometimes laid down in advance of the growing epithelial cells which can then glide over the relatively smooth surface of the membrane.

It is certainly significant that there appears to be no relation between the number of young fibres and the number of connectivetissue cells (Alfejew). Regeneratio n of tendon is effected by the migration of fibroblasts from the undamaged portions into the crushed or cut segment. New collagen is then laid down. Even a segment of dead formol-fixed tendon may be grafted between two normal segments.

The mode of repair is similar to that described above (Nagrotte). The elastic fibres appear later in the embryo than the collagen fibres. Little is known about their mode of development.

3

MUSCLE

CROSS-STRIATED, VOLUNTARY, OR SKELETAL MUSCLE

Cross-striated muscle is com posed of long *cylindrical* fibres, measuring on an average 50 μ in diameter in mammals, and often having a length of an inch or more. But many fibres are much larger or smaller than the average. Each fibre has an *extensible* sheath, the *sarcolemma*, which encloses the contractile substance and is about 1 μ, in thickness.

The sarcolemma is seldom visible, unless the contained substance becomes broken or has retracted from the sheath as can often be seen in partially autolysed fibres. A *fibrillar* structure has been described in the sarcolemma, but under ordinary circumstances it appears completely *homogeneous*, unless stained to show reticular fibres when it can be seen to consist of a beautiful network of fine fibres which support and protect the muscle fibres.

In addition it provides the means of attachment of the muscle fibre to the *tendon* fibre, which is continuous with the reticular fibres of the sarcolemma. The *contractile* substance is characterised by the alternate dark and light stripes which run across the length of the fibre; hence the term cross-striated.

On focusing, it can be seen that the stripes pass through the whole thickness of the fibre; they have therefore been looked upon as representing alternate disks of dark and light substance. If the *fibre* is very carefully focused, rows of apparent *granules* (dots) are seen lying in or at the *boundaries* of the light streaks, and very fine *longitudinal* lines may,

Table 3.1: Types of Muscle.

	Striated	*Plain*	*Cardiac*
Diameter	About 50 μ	About 5 μ	About 20 μ
Length	Very variable, especially in length, which varies from 50 p to over 40,000 μ, *i.e.*, 40 mm. Branching rare.	Relatively short : 15 to 500 μ. Branching rare.	Length difficult to assess since the fibres branch.
Shape	Filiform.	Filiform, but less pronouncedly so than in striated muscle.	Short and blunt, the ends of the fibres abutting on each other.
Nuclei	Peripheral and very numerous-especially in a long fibre.	Central and single.	Central and usually single, though some times found in pairs.
Striations	Longitudinal and transverse.	Longitudinal only.	Longitudinal and transverse.

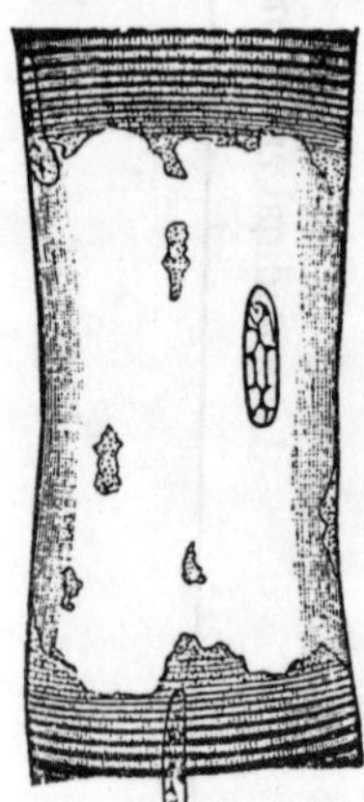

Figure 3.1: Sarcolemma of mammalian muscle.

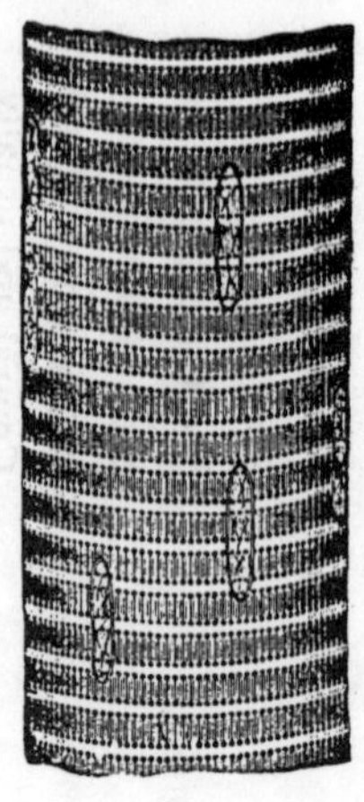

Figure 3.2: Muscular fibre of a mammal examined fresh in-serum, the surface of the fibre being accurately focused.

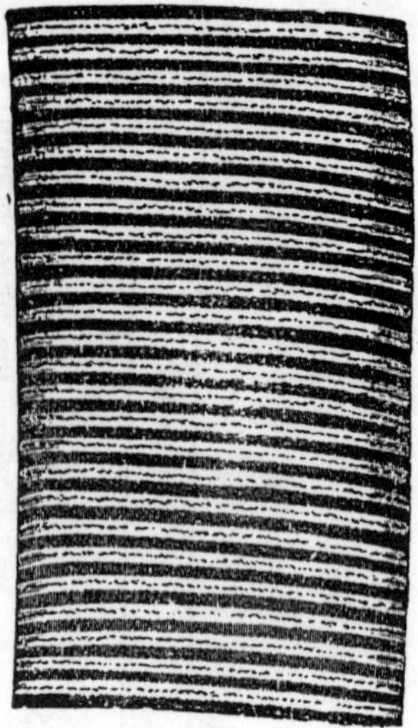

Figure 3.3: Potion of a medium-sized human muscular fibre, showing the intermediated line.

with a good microscope, be detected uniting the dots. These fine lines, with their enlargements the dots, are conspicuous in the muscles of arthropods.

They indicate an interstitial material between the longitudinal elements, the *myofibrils*, which in fixed and stained specimens are seen to compose the fibre. Between the fibrils there is a relatively homogeneous ground-substance, the *sarcoplasm.*

The existence of the myofibrils in the living fibre is open to some doubt since many observers have been unable to detect them in tissue cultures; after fixation, however, they become apparent. The cross-striations, on the other hand, are easily identified in the living fibre.

Nuclei

Besides sarcoplasm and striated substance a muscle-fibre possesses a number of oval nuclei which have the usual structure of cellnuclei; they often show spiral markings. Sometimes there is a little granular substance (protoplasm) at each pole of the nucleus.

But the protoplasm which is adjacent to the nuclei is continuous with the sarcoplasm between the fibrils, both being remains of part of the original protoplasm of the cells from which the muscular fibres are developed. In *mammalian* muscle the nuclei are usually immediately under the sarcolemma, in a frog's muscle they are *scattered* throughout its thickness, in the leg-muscles of insects they lie in the middle of the fibre.

Mitochondria and (probably) *Golgi bodies* are present in the striated muscle fibres.

Red Muscles

In most mammals all the striated muscles have the deep red colour characteristic of the '*flesh*' of animals. In the frog all the muscles are pale in colour. In the rabbit the *muscles* of the ordinary type of structure are pale in colour, but there occur others of a deep red colour. The fibres of this 'red' *muscle* usually contain more granular *sarcoplasm* than the ordinary fibres and also more muscle *haemoglobin*; their blood-vessels have a *peculiarity* of structure which will be afterwards noticed.

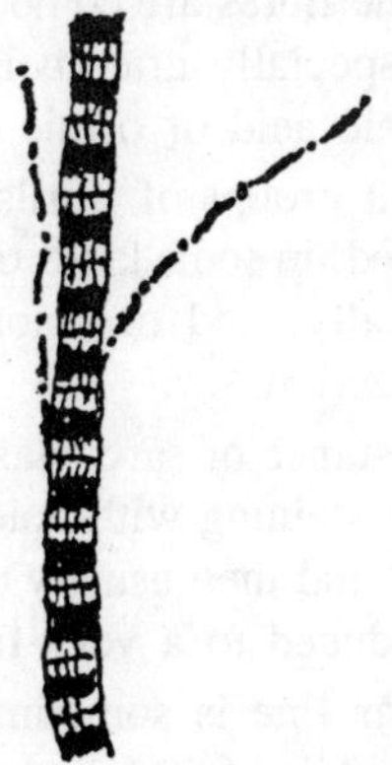

Figure 3.4: Small portion of a muscle-fibre of crab splitting up into fibrils.

They have many more nuclei than the ordinary fibres and occasionally there are nuclei in the substance of the fibre as well as under the sarcolemma; but this is not common, nor is it entirely confined to fibres of the 'red' muscles.

The transverse section of a muscle shows the fibres to be nearly cylindrical, but in places where they are closely set they may be angular in section. Between the fibres is a certain amount of *areolar* tissue, which serves to support the blood-vessels and to unite the fibres into fasciculi; the fasciculi again are united by a large amount of this intramuscular connective tissue, known as the *endomysium*.

On examining the cross-section of a fibre with a high power, it may

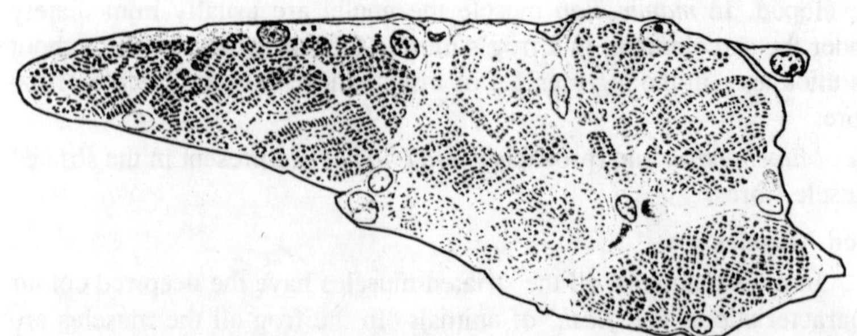

Figure 3.5: Transverse section of four striated muscle fibres from human tongue; the small groups of myofibrils forming the areas fo cohnheim are clearly shown; likewise the peripheral nuclei and the sarcolemma.

be seen subdivided everywhere into small angular fields, *Cohnheim's areas*, which are themselves finely dotted. The dots represent sections of the fibrils of which the fibres are composed, and into which they may be split after death, especially after being fixed in certain reagents, such as alcohol, chromic acid or osmic acid.

The areas represent groups of fibrils, and are usually polyhedral, but they may be elongated; in some kinds of muscle, but not in mammals, they are disposed radially, and occasionally concentrically with the circumference of the section.

The interstitial substance or sarcoplasm lies between the fibrils and can be made visible by staining with gold chloride. It is sometimes in relatively large amount and then usually contains granules, but in most muscula fibres it is reduced to a very fine interstitium.

An ill-defined clear line is sometimes seen running transversely across-the fibre in the middle of each dark band. This is termed *Hensen's line*. If instead of focusing the surface of the fibre it is observed in its depth, an appearance different from that shown in figure elsewhere in this chapter is frequently visible, namely, a fine dotted line *(Dobie's line)*, bisecting each clear stripe.

This appearance is often considered to represent a membrane *(Krause's membrane)*, which subdivides the fibrils at regular intervals. But the membranes of the individual fibrils or sarcostyles are rarely, if ever, visible in an intact mammalian fibre, and it is probable that the appearance known as Dobie's line in the middle of the clear stripe of the intact fibre is due to interference, caused by the light being transmitted between disks of different refrangibility.

Haycraft suggested that the cross-striation of voluntary muscle is due to refractive effects produced by varicosity of the component fibrils;

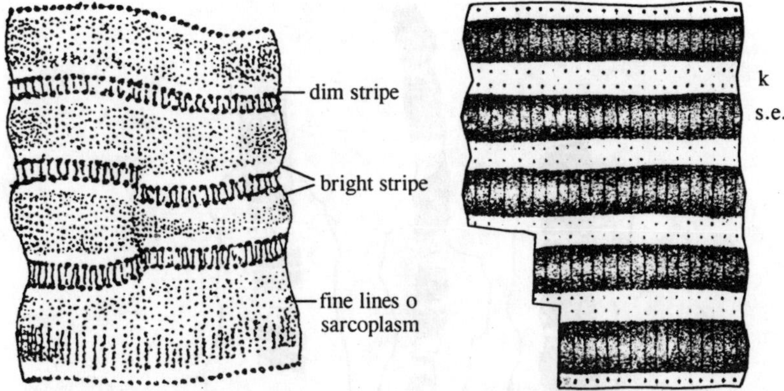

Figure 3.6: Leg-muscle of water-beetle in living conditions.

Figure 3.7: Leg-muscle of insect, stained with gold chloride by Rollett's method.

he based his view upon the fact that in impressions of the fibres made on soft collodion all the crossstriations which are observed in the fibre itself are reproduced.

There is no doubt that a well-marked cross-striated appearance can be produced in homogeneous fibrils by regularly occurring varicosities, and many of the appearances observed in muscle may, as Haycraft contended, be referred to this cause.

Muscles of Insects

In the muscles of insects and crustaceans the stripes are relatively broad, and the structure can be much more readily made out than in mammals. In the living fibres from the muscles which move the legs of insects, the sarcoplasm presents a striking appearance of fine longitudinal lines traversing the muscle, and enlarging within the light stripes into rows of dots.

This is also seen in fibres and portions of fibres which have been treated with acid. The muscular fibres' of the wings of insects are considerably larger than those of the legs and contain a far greater amount of sarcoplasm, in which the fibrils-,.are embedded.. Hence, when a wing-fibre is broken up its fibrils are easily isolated, even' in the fresh tissue.

It can then be seen even in the living muscle, but much more distinctly after fixation and staining, that each fibril or sarcostyle is composed of alternating dark and light portions, which by juxtaposition in adjacent fibrils produce the cross-striated appearance of the fibre. Further, in the middle of each of the clear stria; is a transverse septum,

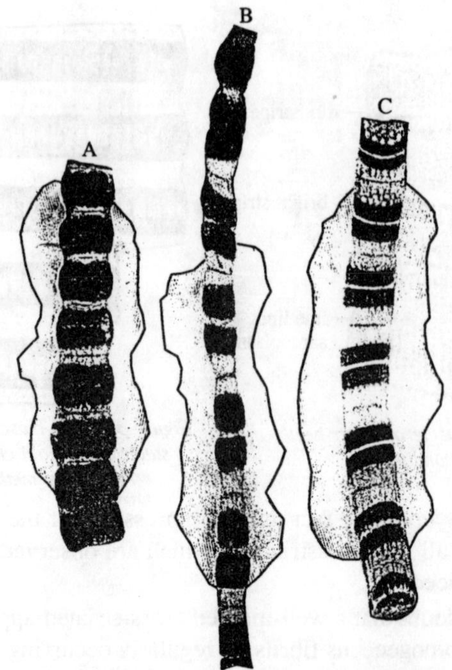

Figure 3.8: Fibrils (Sarcostyles) of the wing muslces of a wasp, prepared by Rollett's method. A, a contracted fibril. B, a contracted fibril which has been forcibly stretched, causing each sarcous element to be separated into two parts at the line of Hensen. C, an uncontracted fibril, showing the porous structure of the sarcous elements.

known as the *membrane of Krause*; by these membranes the fibril is subdivided at regular intervals into serial portions, termed *sarcomeres*. The middle of each sarcomere is occupied by a *sarcous element*; the sarcous elements by their juxtaposition in adjacent fibrils form the dark striae of the fibre.

The sarcous element is really double, as is shown by the fact that in the stretched fibril it separates into two *(line of Hensen)*. At each end of the sarcous element is clear substance (probably watery fluid) separating it from the membrane of Krause: this clear substance is more evident the more the fibril is extended, but diminishes, even to complete *disappearance*, in the retracted (contracted) fibril.

The cause of this change is explained if we study more minutely the structure of the sarcous element. For it can be shown that each sarcous element is pervaded by longitudinal canals or pores, which are open in the direction of Krause's membranes, but closed at the middle of the *sarcous* element.

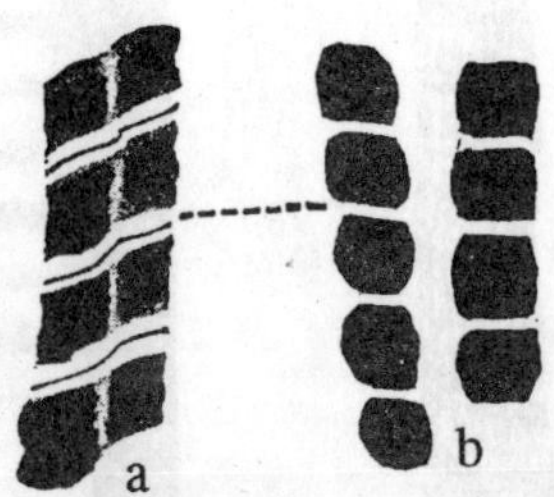

Figure 3.9: Localisation of potassium in sarcous elements of wing-muscle of beetle. a, resting; b, contracted.

In the contracted muscle it can be seen that the clear part of the muscle-substance has nearly dis-appeared, the sarcous element is swollen and the sarcomere is shortened; in the uncontracted muscle, on the other hand, the clear part occupies a considerable interval between the sarcous element and the membrane of Krause, the sarcomere being lengthened and narrowed.

The sarcous element does not lie free in the middle of the sarcomere, but is attached at either end to Krause's membrane by what look like very fine lines, which may represent septa, running through the clear substance; on the other hand, Krause's membrane is attached laterally to a fine membrane which limits the fibril externally.

As already stated, the sarcous elements are set side by side in planes, thus forming the dark stripes or *principal disks* of the striated substance of ordinary muscle-fibres. In the wing-muscles of insects the fibrils are surrounded b so considerable an amount of granular sarcoplasm that the whole fibre is only very indistinctly cross-striated, although each individual fibril is markedly so. The sarcous elements contain a large proportion of potassium salts.

Sometimes in the leg-muscles of arthropods what look like detached dot-like portions of the sarcous element are seen within the clear stripes, lying usually near Krause's membrane. The rows of such dots have been termed *accessory disks*.

Most muscles show no accessory disks, but the dot-like sarcoplasm-enlargements between the fibrils are often mistaken for them.

Muscle in Polarised Light

When muscle-fibres are examined with polarised light between crossed nicols, the sarcous elements (which form the dark stripe) are seen to be doubly refracting (anisotropous), while the clear substance (forming the light stripe) is singly refracting (isotropous). In contracted parts of the muscle the (anisotropous) sarcous elements are seen to have

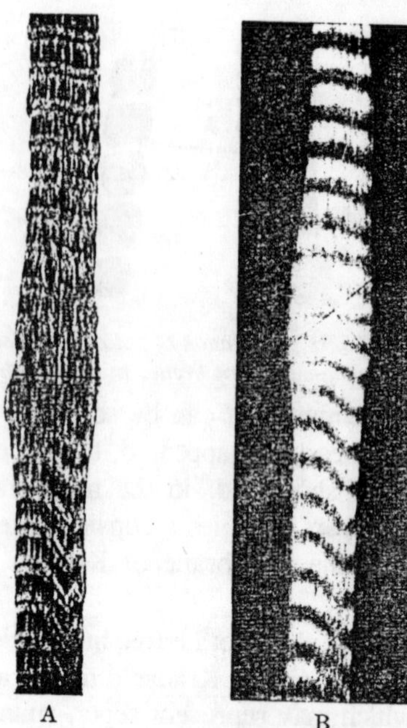

Figure 3.10: Leg-muscle fibre of chrysomela coerulea with (fixed) contraction-wave photographed under polarising microscope. A, with uncrossed nicols; B, with crossed nicols.

Figure 3.11: Wave of contraction passing over a leg-muscle fibre of dysticus.

increased in bulk, while the isotropous substance of the clear stripe has correspondingly diminished.

Merkel imagined that there is a reversal of the stripes during contraction, i.e., *a* transference of the anisotropous substance of the dark stripe from Hensen's line to Krause's membrane, the place of the dark stripes thus becoming occupied by clear material, that of the light stripes by dark.

He further described this condition as being preceded by an intermediate stage in which the fibril shows homogeneity of shading. No doubt in the ordinary muscle-fibres of arthropods, when we observe the so-called 'fixed ' waves of contraction, there is often an apparent blurring of the cross-striation of the fibre just where the muscle is passing from extension to contraction, but this is explicable by the unequal pull of the contracted parts of the fibrils upon those which are not yet contracted.

The contraction in each fibre starts from the nerve ending, which is at one side of the fibre, and spreads first across the fibre and then tends to pass as a wave towards either end. The one side always has a start in the progress of this wave, and the fibrils must thus receive an unequal pull, so that they are shifted along one another and the line of cross-striping is apt to be broken.

That no transference of anisotropous substance really occurs is at once clear from the appearance of the contracting fibre under polarised light, and the study of the isolated fibrils of wing-muscle gives no support to the theory of reversal. That the apparent reversal is not real is also illustrated by figure elsewhere in this chapter, which represents a leg-muscle fibre of an insect in process of contraction.

The dark bands of the contraction-wave are seen to be really due to accumulations of sarcoplasm. Owing to this having a higher index of refraction than the rest of the muscle-substance these accumulations appear as dark lines which not only obscure the continuity of the fibrils, but by contrast cause the whole of the sarcomeres between them to appear light.

CONNEXION WITH TENDON; BLOOD-VESSELS; DEVELOPMENT OF CROSS-STRAITED MUSCLE

Ending of Muscle in Tendon

A small tendon-bundle passes to the conical end of each muscular fibre and becomes firmly united with the sarcolemma which extends over the end of the fibre. Besides this attachment, a further connexion

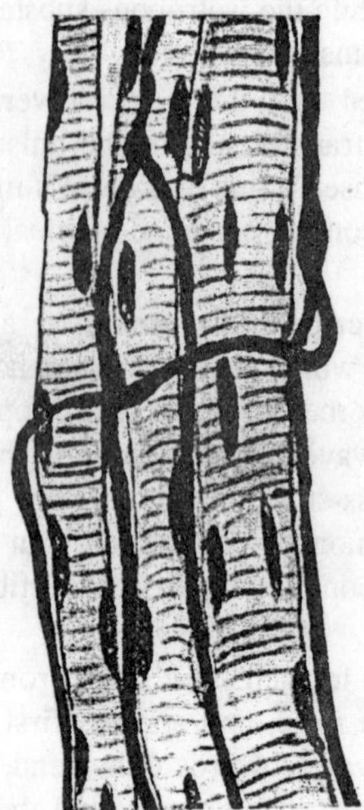

Figure 3.12: Capillaries of striated muscle-fibres.

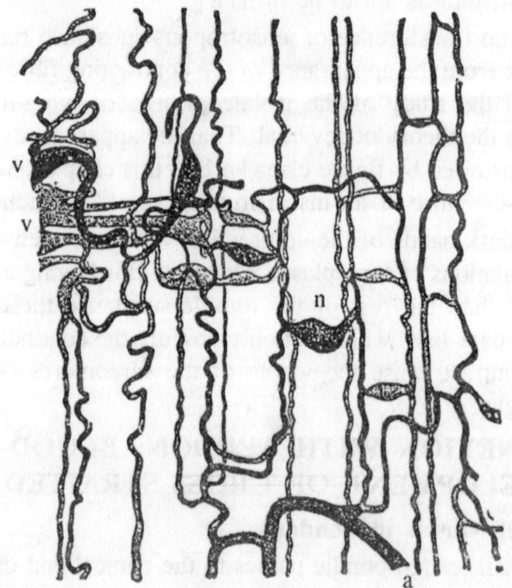

Figure 3.13: Vascular network of a red muscle (semi-tendinosus) of the rabbit. e, arteriole; v, v, venule; n, dilatation on transverse branch of capillaries.

is established by the fact that the areolar tissue between the tendon-bundles is continuous with that which lies between the muscle-fibres. There is probably no actual continuity between contractile substance and tendon.

The muscle-fibre presumably adheres to the sarcolemma and transmits to it the contractile force. The sarcolemma then transmits this force to the tendon-fibre with which it is continuous.

Muscle-fibres are arranged in bundles or fasciculi, which constitute nutritional units with common blood supply, but not functional units, *i.e.* not innervated from the same nerve-fibre. In nearly all muscles, each fibre is connected above and below with the insertions of that muscle by tendon alone.

Hence when any fibre contracts it does not pull on or stretch other muscle-fibres, but exerts the whole of its power in approximating the upper and lower attachments of the muscle belly.

Blood-Vessels of Muscle

The capillaries of muscle are very numerous. They run, for the most part, longitudinally, with transverse branches, so as to form oblong meshes. No blood-vessels penetrate the sarcolemma.

In the red muscles of the rabbit the transverse capillaries sometimes

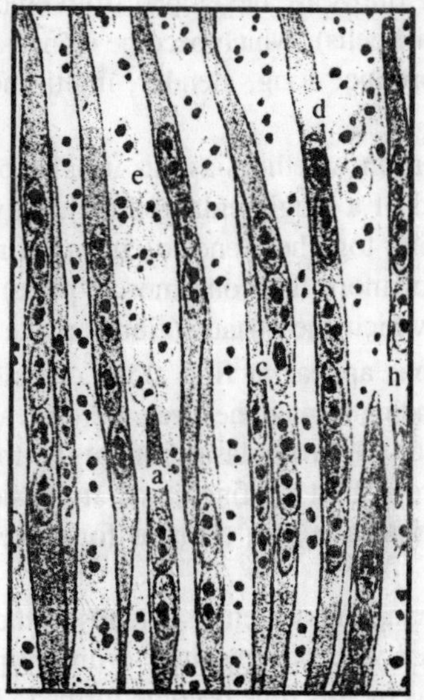

Figure 3.14: Developing muscle of chick, after five days' incubation. longitudinal section.

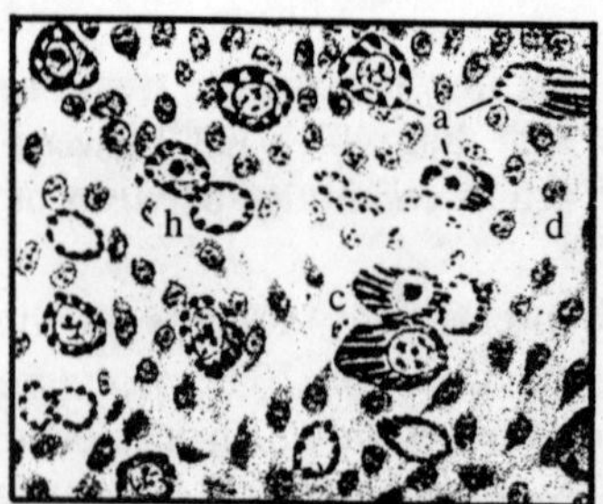

Figure 3.15: Developing muscle of chick, after seven days' incubation transverse section.

have small dilatations upon them. *Lymph-vessels*, although present in the connective-tissue sheath (perimysium) of a muscle, do not penetrate between the component fibres.

Nerves

The motor nerves of striated muscles pierce the sarcolemma and terminate in ramified expansions known as *end-plates* or *motor-end-organs*; the afferent nerves end in groups of specially modified muscle-fibres known as *muscle-spindles*.

Sympathetic fibres are also distributed to striated muscle.

Histogenesis of Striated Muscle

Striated muscular fibres are developed from embryonic cells of the mesoderm (muscle-plate cells), which become elongated, and their nuclei multiplied, so as to produce long, slender, multi-nucleated embryonic fibres.

It is not quite certain whether, as has usually been supposed, the whole fibre is formed of a single enlarged cell, or whether it may be produced by the joining together, end to end, of a number of cells of the muscle-plate (or of more than one muscle-plate), so as to produce a syncytium, within which the striated fibrils make their appearance.

The cross-striations appear at first along one side of the cell, the change gradually extending around the circumference and also penetrating towards the centre; but the protoplasm both at the middle of the fibre, to which the nuclei are at first confined, and at the side opposite to that at which the differentiation began, remains for some time unaltered in character.

Eventually the change in structure extends to these parts also, and the nuclei pass gradually to occupy their ordinary position under the sarcolemma, which has by this time become formed. The young muscle-fibres are at first isolated, but after a time are seen in groups. It is uncertain whether the groups are formed by longitudinal splitting of the original primitive fibre or by the differentiation of adjacent cells to form other muscle-fibres.

CARDIAC MUSCLE

The muscular substance of the heart is composed of transversely striated muscle-fibres, which differ from those of striated muscle in the following particulars, viz., (1) their striations are less marked; (2) they have no distinct sarcolemma, although they may have a thin superficial layer of nonfibrillated substance; (3) they branch, and unite by their branches, and also at the side, with neighbouring fibres; (4) their nuclei lie in or near the centre of the fibres.

In man and many mammals the fibres exhibit transverse markings apparently dividing them into a series of short cylindrical segments,

Figure 3.16: Heart-muscle in longitudinal section: human.

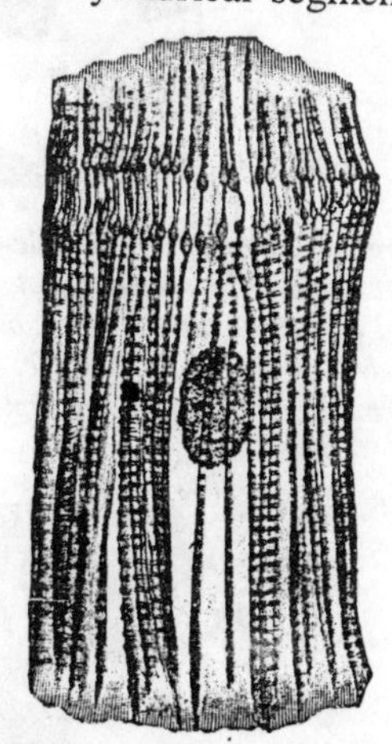

Figure 3.17: Portion of cardiac muscle exhibiting continuity of fibrils across junctional line.

joined together end to end and side to side; often there seems to be a nucleus corresponding to each portion. The transverse markings are evident in longitudinal sections of appropriately stained fixed tissue and are generally known as the *intercallary disks;* they also come distinctly into view in preparations stained with nitrate of silver. They are bridged by the muscle-fibrils, which are thus in continuity from one segment to the next.

These transverse markings were regarded by Schweigger-Seidel, who first described them, as intercellular septa (cell-junctions) for they

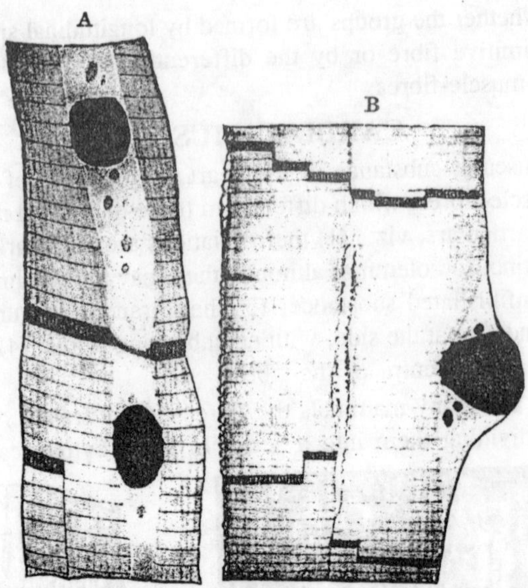

Figure 3.18: Portions of muscle-fibres from the adult human heart. In A one of the so-called septa or intercalary disks traverses the protoplasm which extends between the nuclei as well as the striated substance. A second incomplete septum is also shown. In B a nucleus is seen at the surface, and serves to render the investing membrane apparent. Notice the zigzagging of the septa, an appearance which is not infrequent.

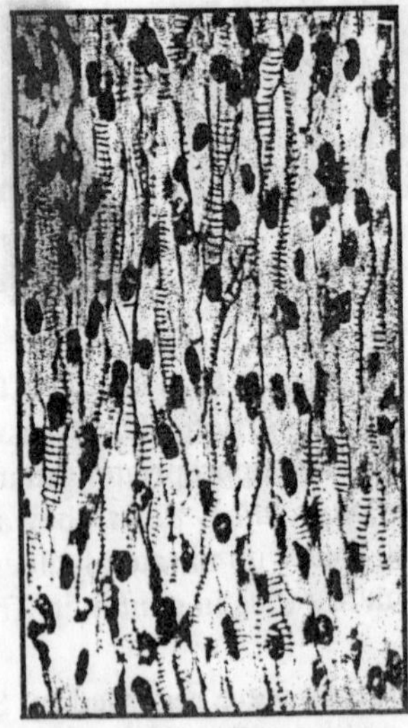

Figure 3.19: Section from heart of five months' embryo: Human.

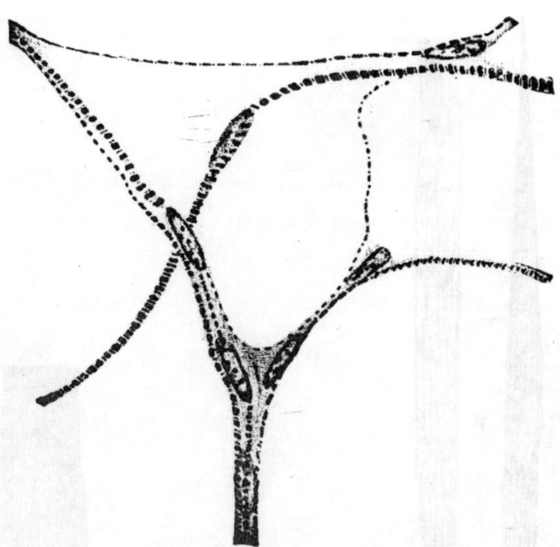

Figure 3.20: Syncytium of heart-muscle of auricle of frog-embryo, showing muslce-fibrils passing form cell to cell.

resemble intercellular substance in staining with silver nitrate. But other authoriti es have taken different views regarding the transverse markings. H. E. Jordan regards them as due to fixed localised contractions, while Martin Heidenhain considers that they represent portions of the fibres at which growth in length occurs (analogous to the suture-lines between the flat bones of the cranium).

As against these views of the transverse septa, and in favour of the original view of Schweigger-Seidel, must be set the silver-staining of the supposed cell-junctions, and the fact that it is easily possible in some animals to separate the fibres after maceration into short uninucleated fragments.

Schweigger-Seidel's view is upheld by v. Palezewska and Werner (working with Zimmermann), who studied the subject in the heart of man and of various mammals. These observers point out, as had been previously done, that the short non-nucleated segments often seen, which Heidenhain regards as fatal to the cell-theory of cardiac muscle, may be parts of cells lying in other planes of the myocardium, which are inserted between those belonging to the plane included in the longitudinal section.

On the other hand, the continuity of the muscle-fibrils within the masses of Purkinje's fibres under the cudocardium in the sheep, the fibrils belonging to one cell being freely continued into those of the

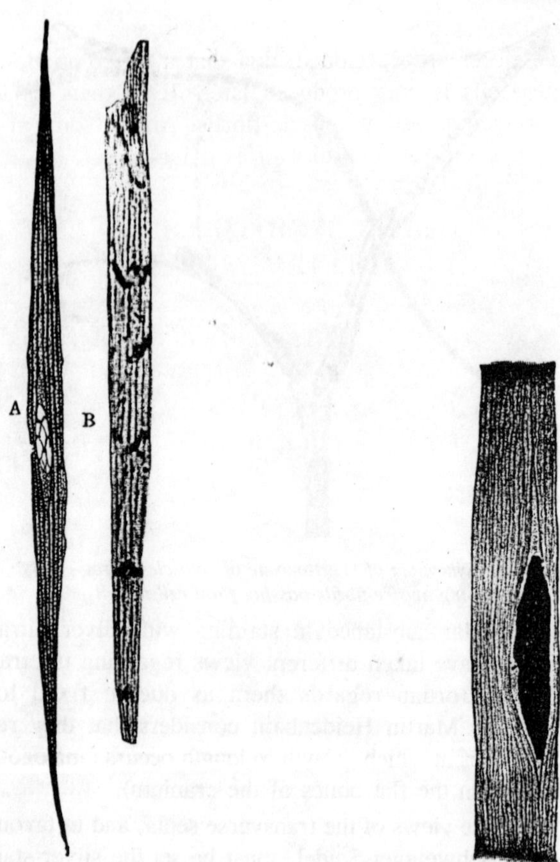

Figure 3.21: Smooth muscle-fibres from intesting of cat. A, a complete cell showing the nucleus and longi tudinal fibrillation visible only after fixation and staining. B, part of a cell showing the nucleus and the coarser fibrils. Photograph.

Figure 3.22: Middle part of a smooth muscle-fibre showing fine longitudinal striation and elongated nucleus.

neighbouring cells, is in favour of a syncytial theory of the structure of heart-muscle. Indeed, in many vertebrates, including some mammals, no cell-territories can be made out in the *myocardium*. It has been concluded (*Marcus*) from high power observations that the myofibrils in man are tubular, consisting of an outer layer containing fluid contents.

Histogenesis of Cardiac Muscle

The explanation of these differences appears to be that heart-muscle at an early period of development is a *syncytium* within which the contractile fibres are developed, and that a differentiation of the syncytium into cells is only produced later. Even then the lines of junction are bridged across by muscle-fibrils. And in some animals a differentiation into separate cell-territories is incomplete or altogether lacking.

PLAIN, SMOOTH OR NON-STRIATED MUSCLE

Plain, smooth or non-striated muscular tissue is composed of elongated fusiform cells, which vary much in length. In cross-section they are usually angular, an appearance due to mutual compression. The cellnucleus is either oval or rod-shaped; it has the usual structure and commonly one or two nucleoli.

There is a centriole-sometimes double-close to the nucleus. *Mitochondria* and a *Golgi* apparatus are also present. The cell-substance is finely fibrillated longitudinally in stained preparations, but does not exhibit cross-striae like striated and cardiac muscle. Very careful observation (E. B. Meigs) of living smooth muscle-fibres failed to reveal any trace of longitudinal fibrils.

These would hence seem to be a fixation artefact. The muscle fibres are supported and attached to one another by a fine network of reticular fibres. It is due to this reticulum that contraction of smooth muscle-fibres around a large hollow viscus can be effective. In the external part of the fibre, in some smooth muscle, there is a layer containing coarser fibrils (boundary fibrils of M. Heidenhain).

Frequently there is seen a series of irregularly placed transverse markings which appear as knot-like condensations of the cell-substance staining somewhat differently from the rest of the cell; these are produced by localised contractions at the moment of death of the cell; the fibrils are enlarged as they run through the knots.

The intercellular substance has been described as being bridged by filaments passing from cell to cell, but these may be artefacts. Plain muscular tissue is found chiefly in the walls of hollow viscera; thus it forms the muscular coat of the stomach and intestines, and occurs abundantly in the muscular coat of the oesophagus, although it is here intermixed with cross-striated muscle; it is found also in the mucous membrane of the whole alimentary canal from the oesophagus downwards in the shape of the muscularis mucosae; in the trachea and its ramifications; in the urinary bladder and ureters; in the uterus and Fallopian tubes; in the prostate; in the spleen and lymphatic glands; forming the muscle of Miller in the orbit, and the ciliary muscle and

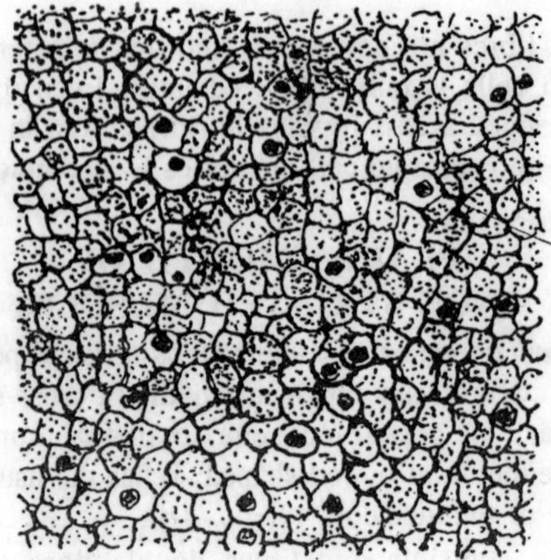

Figure 3.23: Transverse section of plain muscle-fibres of intestine.

iris-musculature. The walls of gland-ducts also contain it; and the middle coat of the arteries, veins, and lymphatics is largely composed of this tissue.

It occurs in the skin, both in the secreting parts of the sweat glands and in small bundles attached to the hair-follicles; in the scrotum it is found abundantly in the subcutaneous tissue (*dartos*); it also occurs in the mammary gland in the *areola* of the *nipple*.

The smooth muscle-fibres of the uterus are remarkable for the *hypertrophy* which they undergo during pregnancy. They are then said to increase their length to 500 μ-an approximate increase to ten times their normal length. They also undergo division to give an increase in the total number present.

Histogenesis of Plain Muscle

C. M'Gill states that the smooth muscle of the alimentary canal (pig) is developed from a *syncytium* of mesenchyme cells which surrounds the endoderm. Some of these cells become elongated and spindle-shaped while retaining their interconnexion. *Myofibrils* are developed in their protoplasm. These need not be confined to the limits of a single cell, but may extend over a number of cells.

The myofibrils are of two kinds, coarse and fine, varying in relative number in different parts. As stated above, an interconnexion of the cells obtains even in the fully formed muscle, which thus retains something of its *syncytial* character.

In certain situations plain muscle is formed from ectoderm; this is the case with the muscular tissue of the *sweat glands* (Ranvier) and with

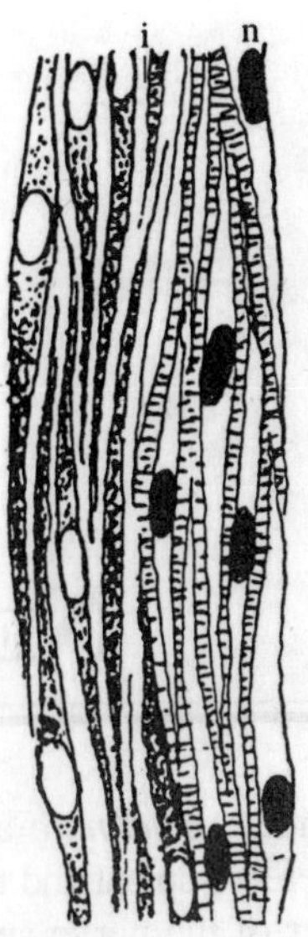

Figure 3.24: Muscle-cells of intestine. The fibres are represented in longitudinal section; the interstices between them are seen to be bridged across by fine fibrils. i, interstice; n, nucleus.

that of the alveoli of the mammary gland. It is also true for the muscular tissue of the iris (Nussbaum).

Smooth muscle-fibres are capable of division and a limited amount of compensatory *hyperplasia* may follow an injury when new non-striated fibres are formed by the division of pre-existing ones.

4

NERVE-FIBRES

Nerve-fibres are of two kinds, *myelinate* and *amyelinate (medullated* and *non-medullated)*. The cerebro-spinal and the *pre-ganglionic* autonomic nerves and the white matter of the nerve-centres are composed chiefly of myelinate fibres; the post-ganglionic autonomic nerves are largely made of amyelinate fibres. The latter are also found in considerable numbers in the *vagus*.

The *myelinate*, *medullated* or *white fibres* are characterised, as their name implies, by the presence of the *myelin sheath* or *white substance of Schwann*. This is a layer of semi-fluid material which encircles the essential part of a nerve-fibre, viz., the *axis-cylinder*. Outside the myelin sheath is a delicate but tough membrane composed of a fine network of reticular fibres, the *neurolemma (sheath of Schwann)*.

Associated with this reticulum are neurolemma cells. The neurolemma is not present in all myelinate fibres, being absent from those within the central nervous system, including the optic nerve. The *myelin sheath is* composed of a doubly refracting lipo-protein material known as myelin, which gives a characteristic double contour and tubular appearance to the nerve-fibre.

It should be regarded as a thickened cell membrane. It affords a continuous investment to the axis-cylinder, except that, as was shown by Ranvier, in peripheral nerve-fibres it is interrupted at regular intervals. At these places the neurolemma appears to produce constrictions in the nerve-fibre, the *nodes of Ranvier,* the latter term having been applied from the resemblance which they bear to the nodes of a bamboo.

It is uncertain whether the constriction is entirely occupied by neurolemma or partly by a special band *(constricting band of Ranvier);*

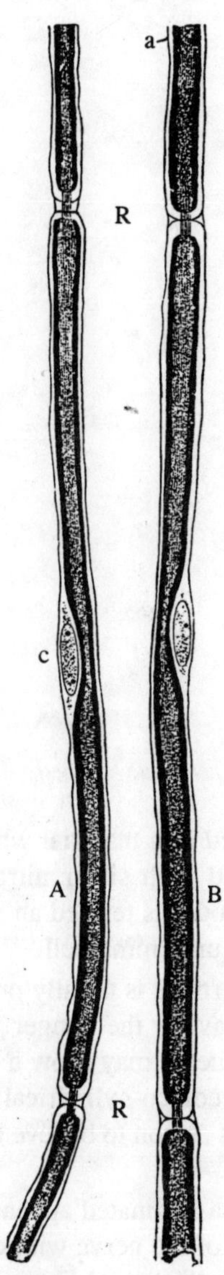

Figure 4.1: Portions of two nervefiberes stained with osmic acid, diagrammatic.

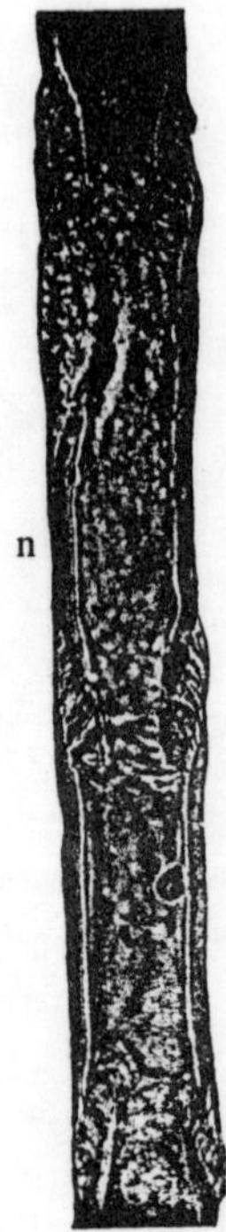

Figure 4.2: A small part of a myelinate fibre, fresh.

Figure 4.3: Myelinate nerve-fibre, fresh, showing a node of ranvier.

if the latter, it is composed *of* a material which resembles intercellular substance in being stained with silver nitrate. The segment of nerve between two successive nodes is termed an *internode* and in the middle of each internode is a neurolemma cell.

The length of the internode is usually proportionate to its diameter, the larger fibres thus having the longer internodes. Besides these interruptions the myelin sheath may show a variable number of oblique clefts, subdividing it into conico-cylindrical portions of variable length *(myelin segments);* there is reason to believe that the clefts are artificially produced.

At the clefts there is a laminated appearance in the myelin sheath, especially after treatment of the nerve with certain reagents; sometimes the clefts look as if they contain spiral fibres. Almost certainly, however, all these appearances are artefacts and do not represent pre-existing structures.

The myelin sheath contains mitochondria, for the most part disposed

Figure 4.4: Longigudinal and transverse section of myelinate nerve-fibre of frog (osmic acid and acid fuchsin).

radially. A reticular appearance has also been described in the myelin sheath after fixation with alcohol, the *neurokeratin network* of Kiihne, but it varies greatly in aspect and is certainly produced by the action of the reagents employed to show it and is almost certainly an artefact.

Osmic acid stains the myelin sheath black owing to the presence of unsaturated fatty substances. The protein part is sometimes preserved in ordinary preparations and appears in the form of an artefact reticulum. The *neurolemma* is a thin sheath of reticular fibres with scattered associated cells.

It closely invests the myelin sheath of the peripheral nerve fibres but is absent from the fibres of the central nervous system. It is the toughest part of the fibre and remains unbroken if the nerve is Biedermann.) pinche, whereby both the myelin sheath and the axis-cylinder may be ruptured.

The oval nuclei the axis-cylinder is shown in seen at regular intervals along the nerve-fibre midway between the nodes partially embedded in the myelin sheath belong to the neurolemma as well as a small amount of protoplasm, containing a Golgi apparatus which adjoins each nucleus.

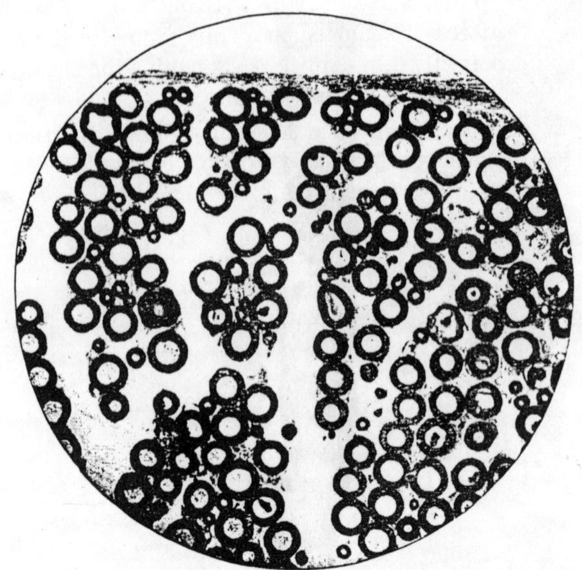

Figure 4.5: Section of the sciatic nerve of a cat, showing the variations in size of its constituent fibres.

The neurolemra dips inwards at the nodes of Ranvier and thus produces the interruptions of the myelin sheath. Nerve-fibres within the Central nervous system, which do not possess a neurolemma, show no interruptions. The *axis-cylinder,* which runs along the middle of the nerve-fibre, is a soft, transparent thread which is continuous from end to end of the fibre.

On account of the peculiar refractive nature of the myelin sheath it is difficult to see the axis-cylinder in the fresh nerve except at the nodes, where it may be observed stretching across the interruptions in the myelin sheath; it may also sometimes be seen projecting from a broken end of a nervefibre.

It often shows after fixation an appearance of extremely fine longitudinal fibrils known as *neuro fibrils*. They are seen isolated at the terminations of nerves, as in the cornea, and are also visible in the section of a nerve-fibre as fine dots, which sometimes appear to have a clear centre, as if the fibrils were tubular.

The axis-cylinder contains delicate rod-like mitochondria, disposed longitudinally. Neither the axiscylinders nor their neuro-fibrils are to be looked upon as solid structures, in spite of the wire-like appearance which the latter exhibit after fixation and staining. For there is no doubt that the whole nerve-fibre, with the exception of the neurolemma, is quite soft; probably of the consistency of a viscous fluid. Observations on the giant nerve-fibres of squids support this. Some of these fibres have axons as much as 200 μ in diameter. On cutting the sheath of the living fibre the substance of the axon streams out.

Another interesting observation is that, although neuro-fibrils cannot be seen in the *uninjured* sheath, section of this causes a longitudinal fibrillation to appear in that part of the axon which is close to the cut surface. But, as the axoplasm flows out, the fibrillations disappear.

Myelinate nerve-fibres vary greatly in size, but may be classified as *large, intermediate,* and *very small.* The largest are those which are passing to the skin and to the striated muscles; the smallest are those destined for viscera and blood-vessels; these constitute the preganglionic autonomic nerves of Langley.

The larger fibres have a diameter of 30 μ or more; the intermediate vary from 10 to 4 μ, while the smallest are only some 2 u in diameter. As shown by W. H. Gaskell, the ventral roots of the last one or two cervical nerves, of all the thoracic, of the first and second lumbar, and of the second and third sacral nerves contain, besides the ordinary large myelinate fibres, bundles of these very small fibres.

Some of the cranial nerves (spinal accessory, vagus, glosso-pharyngeal, facial) contain similar very fine myelinate fibres, intermixed with the larger fibres. About a dozen amyelinate fibres are included in the *photograph.* Besides these one ordinary myelinate fibre and three fine and probably intermediate fibres are seen.

The term 'autonomic' was introduced by Langley to include both the fibres of the sympathetic system and the analogous fibres (parasympathetic) proceeding from the cranial and sacral regions. All autonomic nerves consist (1) of fine myelinate 'preganglionic fibres' arising in the central nervous system and ending in ganglia, and (2) 'postganglionic fibres' arising in the ganglia and passing thence to their peripheral distribution. Most bat not all of these are amyelinate.

Although amyelinate and myelinate fibres are usually treated in textbooks as quite distinct ink, haracter, this probably is not the case. Work indicates that the birefringence characteristic of the myelinated fibre is only found in fibres of about 2 μ in diameter and upwards. Further, this birefringency can be correlated with the gradual increase in the lipoid content of the sheath as the size of the fibre increases. Thus all nerve-fibres have a thickened cell membrane.

But it is only the thicker fibres that have a membrane that is thick enough and contains enough unsaturated fatty substances to be visible when stained with osmic acid.

Amyelinate (non-medullated) Fibres

Intermingled with the myelinate fibres there may always, in peripheral nerves, be found a certain number of fibres devoid of the distinct double contour which is characteristic of the presence of a myelin sheath. These are the *grey* or *amyelinate fibres,* also called, after their discoverer, *fibres of Remak*.

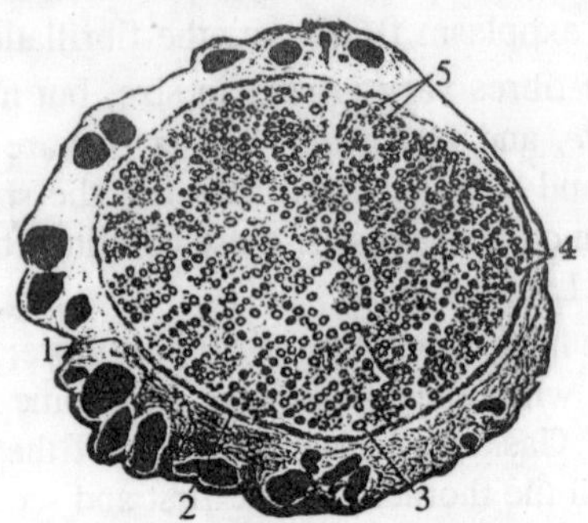

Figure 4.6: section of thoracic sympathetic cord of cat.

They are beset with numerous nuclei which have usually been regarded as belonging to a delicate sheath, although it must be admitted that the nuclei often appear to lie in the substance of the fibres rather than at their surface. A reticular apparatus of Golgi is closely related to each nucleus.

As just stated all the autonomic nerves, when they approach their peripheral distribution, are chiefly made up of fibres of this nature (the so-called post-ganglionic fibres); whereas the pre-ganglionic fibres, both of sympathetic and of other autonomic nerves, always possess a thin myelin sheath, and have the usual structure of myelinate fibres.

By the pyridine silver method of staining, it can be shown that the ordinary nerves of the limbs contain a very large number of amyelinate fibres-which, according to S. W. Ransom, are derived only in, part from the sympathetic but mainly from the small cells of the spinal ganglia.

Microscopic Anatomy of a Nerve-Trunk

In their course through the body the nerve-fibres are gathered up into round bundles or *funiculi* and these are again united to form the nerves met with in dissection.

The connective tissue which connects the funiculi and invests the whole nerve, uniting it to neighbouring parts and conveying to it blood-vessels, lymphatics, and even nerve-fibres destined for its coats, is

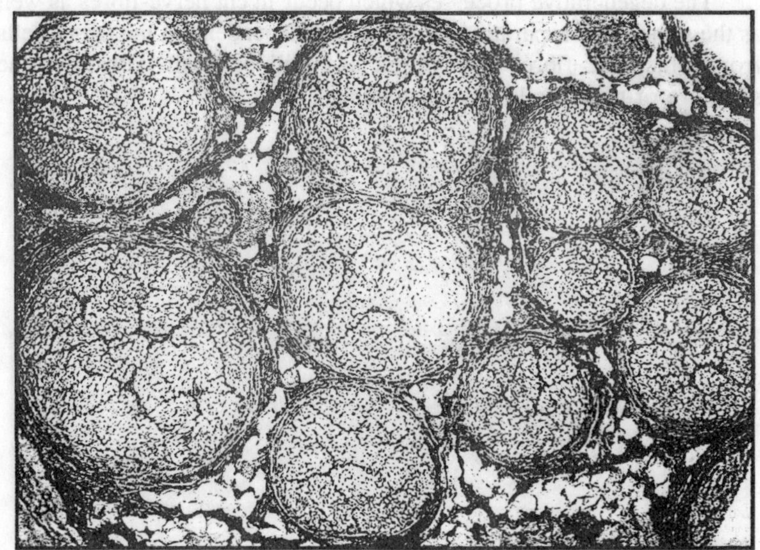

Figure 4.7: Section of part of sciatic nerve of man.

termed the *epineurium*; it frequently contains fat-cells. That which ensheathes the funiculi is known as the *perineurium*.

It has a lamellar structure, the lamellae being composed of connective tissue covered by flattened endothelial cells. Between the lamellae are clefts which convey lymph from the interior of the funiculus to the lymphatics of the perineurium.

The delicate connective tissue which lies between the nerve-fibres of the funiculus is termed *endoneurium*. The longitudinally arranged meshwork of blood-capillaries is conveyed in it; its interstices communicate with the lymph-clefts of the perineurium.

The vacuolated appearance which the·' dullated fibre presents in sections fixed and stained by ordinary methods is due to the myelin having been dissolved.

All the branches of a nerve, and even single nerve-fibres which are passing to their distribution, are invested with a prolongation of the perineural sheath, often of considerable thickness, known as the *sheath of Henle*.

The nerve-trunks themselves receive afferent nerve-fibres (*nervi nervorum*) which ramify chiefly in the perineurium and terminate within this in end-bulbs. Nerves contain few blood-vessels, from which it may be inferred that their metabolism is not active.

The degenerative processes which occur in cut nerve-fibres as well as the subsequent reparative processes are dependent on the nerve-cells from which the fibres take origin and will be dealt with after the structure of nerve-cells has been studied.

5

The Integument

The *epidermis*, or scarf skin, is a stratified epithelium. It is composed of a number of layers of cells, the deeper of which are soft and protoplasmic, and form the *rete mucosum* of Malpighi, while the superficial layers are hard and horny, this horny portion sometimes constituting the greater part of the thickness of the epidermis. The deepest cells of the *rete mucosum,* which are set on the surface of the cutis vera, are columnar in shape, those immediately above the basal layer are polyhedral (prickle-cells).

Many of the deeper cells show mitoses, an indication that the epidermis is regenerated from these cells. The deepest cells of the rete mucosum, especially in the darker parts of the skin, exhibit granules of the pigment *melanin*. These are particularly abundant in the darker races of mankind.

Pigment may also be found in the branched cells which are often seen lying in the cutis vera, especially where there is much pigment in the epidermis. Between all the cells of the rete mucosum there are fine intercellular clefts separating the cells from one another, but bridged across by fibres which pass from cell to cell, and also through the substance of the cells.

The intercellular channels probably serve for the passage of tissuefluid to maintain the nutrition of the cells. In addition to the cells described there is present, in the deeper layers of the rete mucosum, a third type of element. This is the *melanoblast* or cell of Langerhans. This cell has branching processes which ramify between the other cells, and it can be clearly defined by means of a procedure known as the 'dopa' reaction, which stains it black.

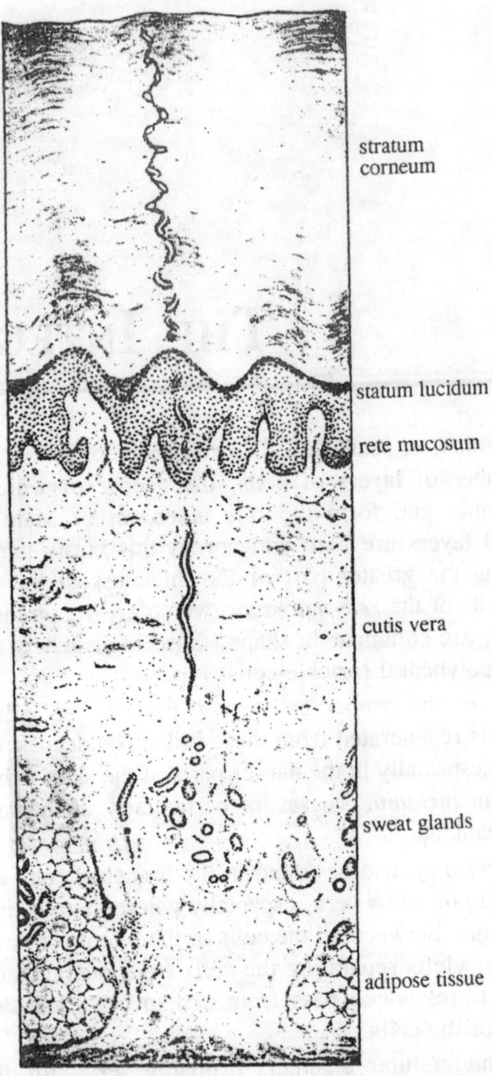

Figure 5.1: Vertical section through th e skin of the sole of the foot. The spiral course of the duct of a sweat gland is well shown.

Although unpigmented there is reason to believe that the melanoblast is in some way responsible for the appearance of melanin in the cells of the stratum Malpighi. Melanin appears to be one of the blackest pigments known. The total content of melanin in the skin of an adult negro has been estimated at not more than 1 gram.

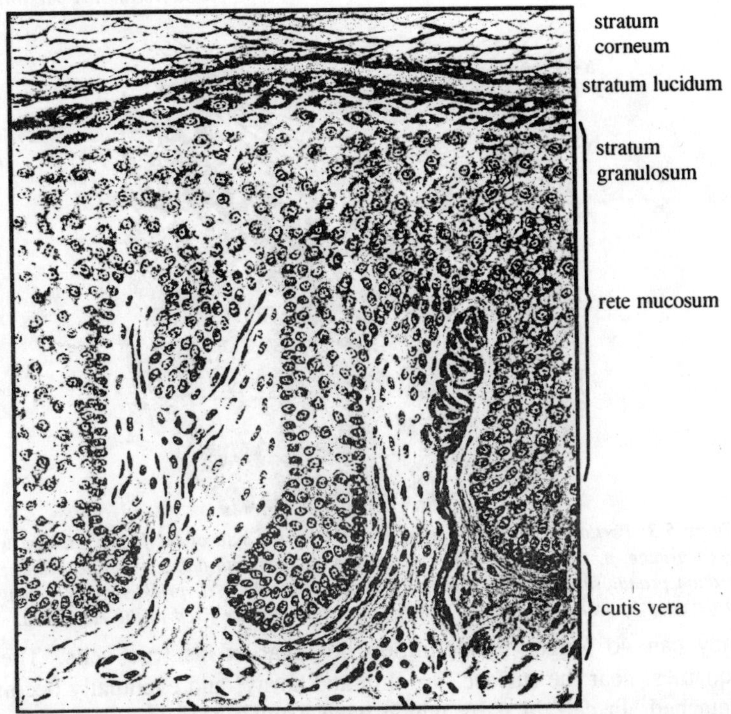

Figure 5.2: Vertical section throgh the skin of the palmar side of the finger, showing two or three papillie and the deeper layers of the epidermis.

The superficial layer of the rete mucosum is formed of somewhat flattened cells filled with granules or droplets of a material *(eleidin)* staining -deeply with carmine and hzematoxylin. These cells form an irregular layer termed the *stratum granulosum*. This is not sharply marked off from the rete mucosum next to it, for many of the cells of this show similar granules, although they fill the cells less completely.

Superficial to the stratum granulosum is a layer in which the cell-outlines are indistinct and the cells contain flakes or larger droplets of a hyaline material, *kerato-hyalin,* staining less intensely than the granules in the last layer, and tending to run together.

This layer has a clear appearance in section, and is known as the *stratum lucidum*. The cells in this layer are devoid of nuclei and are apparently dead. Immediately superficial to the stratum lucidum is the *horny part* or *stratum corneum* of the epidermis.

It is composed of a number of layers of epithelium-cells, to which the term epithelial *squames* is more appropriate since, being anucleate,

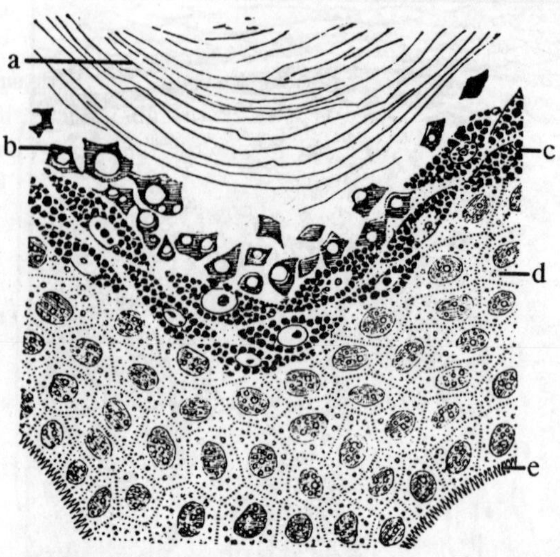

Figure 5.3: Portion of epidermis from a section of the skin of the finger, stained with picrocarmine. a, stratum corneum ; b, stratum lucidum with flakes of kerato-hyalin ; c, stratum granulosum, the cell filled with drops of eleldin ; d, prickle-cells; e, dentate projections by which the deepest cells of the epidermis are fixed to the cutis vera.

they can no longer by definition be regarded as true cells. These squames, near the surface, are thin and horny, and eventually become detached. In certain parts which have a thick epidermis and are not covered with hair (e.g., the palms and soles), the superficial part of the epidermis is a layer mainly formed by a number of greatly swollen squames, forming collectively what has been termed the *epitrichial layer*. In the embryo in the second and third months of intrauterine life it covers the whole body, but is thrown off where hairs are developed.

Table of Layers of Skin

Stratum corneum	Thin, anucleate, squamous ; nearly all cellular structure lost; thickest on palmar and plantar surfaces; thinnest on outer aspect of lips.
Stratum lucidum	Cell outlines indistinct and nuclei usually lacking ; presents a hyaline and band-like appearance in sections due to presence of flakes of kerato-hyalin.
Stratum granulosum (often included under IV)	A thin and irregular layer; nucleated; cell outlines clear; the name due to presence of abundant granules of eleidin.

Rete mucosum or Malpighian layer Majority of cells polyhedral with well-marked cell-bridges and fibrils. Cells of basal layer columnar and often showing mitoses.

Dermis Composed of collagen and elastic fibres and containing blood-vessels, lymphatics, nerves, sense organs, sweat glands, etc.

The growth of the epidermis takes place by a multiplication of the cells of the deeper layers. The newly formed cells, as they grow, push towards the surface those previously formed, and in their progress the latter undergo a chemical transformation, their protoplasm being converted into horny material: this change seems to occur just at and above the stratum granulosum.

The granules of eleidin occupying the cells of the stratum granulosum are chemically transformed into the *keratin* of the more superficial strata. The thick epidermis, which has been described, only occurs on the plantar and palmar surfaces. Over the rest of the body both the Malpighian layer and the stratum corneum are much thinner.

The stratum granulosum and stratum lucidum may be absent, because the transformation process, which they represent, is a rhythmical one occurring infrequently and lasting a short time.

The *cutis vera* or *dermis* is composed of dense connective tissue, which becomes more open and reticular in texture in its deeper part, where it merges into the subcutaneous tissue. It is thickest over the posterior aspect of the trunk, whereas the epidermis is thickest on the palms of the hands and soles of the feet.

The superficial or vascular layer of the corium is com posed mainly of fine reticular fibres which form a dense network (basement membrane) to which the epithelial cells adhere. It bears microscopic *papillae;* these project into the epidermis, which is moulded over and attached to them; they contain abundant elastic fibres.

Most of the dermic papillae have looped capillary vessels projecting into them from the network in the cutis vera, but some, especially those of the palmar surface of the hands and fingers, and the corresponding parts in the foot, contain tactile corpuscles, to which myelinate nerve-fibres pass.

In some parts of the body (scrotum, penis, nipple and its areola) smooth muscular tissue occurs in the deeper portion of the cutis vera ; and, in addition, wherever hairs occur, small bundles of this tissue are attached to the hair-follicles. The blood-vessels of the skin are distributed almost entirely to the surface, where they form a close capillary network, sending up loops into the papillae as already noted.

Special branches are also sent to the various appendages of the skin, viz., the sweat glands and hair-follicles, with their sebaceous glands and muscles. Numerous vessels also pass to the adipose tissue which is usually present in the deeper parts of the cutis.

No blood-vessels pass into the epidermis, but it receives nerves which ramify between the cells of the rete mucosum in the form of fine varicose fibrils. In some parts these are enlarged at their extremity and along their course into menisci lying between the deeper epidermis cells. Such terminations are seen in the skin over the pig's snout and in the rootsheaths of hairs.

They also occur in the neighbourhood of the entrance of sweat-ducts into the epidermis. The lymphatics originate near the surface in a network of vessels, placed a little deeper than the blood-capillary network. They receive branches from the papilla, and pass into larger vessels, which are valved, and run in the deeper or reticular part of the corium.

From these the lymph is carried away by still larger vessels, coursing in the subcutaneous tissue.

Skin Patterns

The criminological importance of these is well known. The original pattern remains constant, for each finger, throughout the life of the individual.

The ridges and depressions of the finger-print are probably caused by the similar underlying interpapillary pattern of the dermis. This explains why superficial removal of the epidermis is eventually followed by re-establishment of the original pattern.

DEVELOPMENT OF THE SKIN

The cutis vera is entirely formed from mesoderm, but the epidermis and the nails, hairs and cutaneous glands are all ectodermic in origin. The ectoderm is at first single-layered but differentiates into two layers during the first month of feetal life. The inner becomes many-layered and develops into the future epidermis.

The outer layer is known as the *epitrichium.* It also thickens and its cells become vesicular, persisting in this condition until the sixth month of intra-uterine life. Most of the cells are then shed and mingle with the secretion of the sebaceous glands.

A waxy covering-the *vernix caseosa*—is thus formed. This covers the embryonic epidermis until birth and serves to protect it against maceration by the amniotic fluid. But in some situations the epitrichium persists as a superficial layer which covers the epidermis.

The *appendages* of the skin are the *nails,* the *hairs,* the *sebaceous glands,* and the *sweat glands.* They are all developed as thickenings and downgrowths of the Malpighian layer of the epidermis.

THE NAILS

The *nails* are thickenings of the deeper part of the stratum corneum developed over a specially modified portion of the skin, which is known as the *matrix* or *bed of the nail*; the depression at the posterior part of the nail-bed from which the nail grows forward being known as the *nail groove.*

The distal part of the nail projects beyond the rest of the *free border*; this is the thickest part of the nail, the thinnest being at the bottom of the nail grove. The substance of the nail is composed of clear horny cells, somewhat like the cells of the stratum lucidum of the rest of the epidermis, except that they are much more keratinised.

Each contains the remains of a nucleus. The horny nail proper rests immediately upon a Malpighian layer or rete mucosum similar to that found in the epidermis generally, but destitute of a defined stratum granulosum. Nevertheless, the more superficial cells of the rete mucosum contain a large number of special granules which appear to represent those of the stratum granulosul of the epidermis.

The granules, however, are not composed of eleidin, but of a material known as the *onychogenic substance* of Ranvier which stains brown instead of red with carmine ; a similar material occurs in the cells which form the fibrous substance and cuticula of the hairs.

The cutis of the nail-bed is beset with longitudinal ridges instead of the papillae which are present over the remainder of the skin ; these ridges, like the rest of the superficial part of the cutis, are extremely vascular, whence the pink colour of that part of the nail which is in contact with the nail-bed.

The nail-bed receives many nerve-fibres. The deeper of these end in Pacinian corpuscles, while others ramify in the ridges of the cutis, and some penetrate among the epithelium-cells of the Malpighian layer.

The growth of the nail is usually estimated at about 0.1 mm. *per diem*; it is accelerated in warm weather and often considerably retarded by illness. Arterio-venous anastomoses of a special type are found in the foot and the hand and exist in great numbers in the digits-especially beneath the nails.

The histology of such anastomoses has been studied by P. Masson. The artery breaks up into two or more branches: of these, one supplies the *capillary system* in the usual manner; the *other* or *others* (there may be as many as six) form a short, thick-walled segment opening into the vein by a funnel-shaped junction.

This segment between the artery and the vein is surrounded by a specialised type of smooth muscle-cell; it is also richly supplied with myelinate and amyelinate nerve-fibres.

It would appear that the reaction of the extremities to cold by increased blood-flow is largely due to the opening up of these anastomoses.

DEVELOPMENT

The nails show in the foetus at about the third month, a groove being formed at this time in the corium, and the nail-rudiment appearing in it as a development of onychogenic substance in some of the cells of the epithelium which lies over the bed.

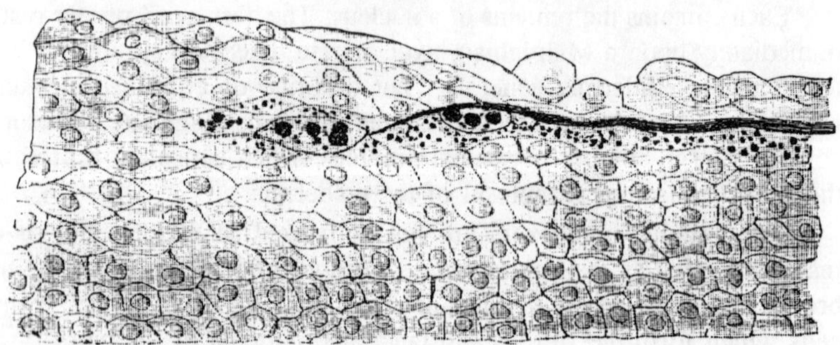

Figure 5.4: First appearance of nail substance in the form of granules of onychogenic material in some of the cells covering the nail-bed.

The nail becomes free in the sixth month, its end being at first thin ; but as it grows forward over the bed it receives additions on its under surface, so that after a time the distal end becomes thicker. The epitrichial layer of the cuticle which originally covered the developing nail becomes detached after the fifth month ; all that represents it afterwards being the narrow border of cuticle, the *eponychium,* which overlies the root.

HAIRS

The *hairs* are growths of the epidermis, developed in deep pits—the *hair-follicles*—which extend downwards into the thickness of the cutis vera and even in the subcutaneous tissue. The hair grows from the bottom of the follicle, the part which lies within the follicle being known as the *root*.

Structure of Hair

The substance of a hair is mainly composed of a pigmented, horny, *fibrous material* which.can be separated by the action of sulphuric acid into long tapering fibrillated cells, the nuclei of which are still visible. The fibrous substance of the hair is covered by a layer of delicate imbricated scales, termed the *hair-cuticle*.

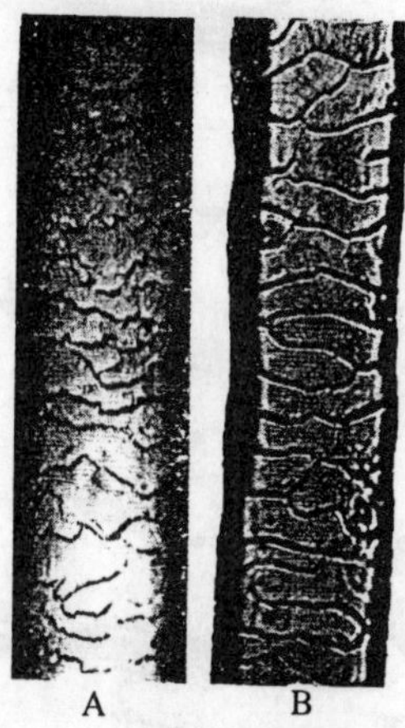

Figure 5.5: Cuticular pattern of hairs as seen from contact film of Amyl Acetate. a, Adult human; b, Newborn human and animal.

In many hairs, but not in all, the centre is occupied by an axial substance, formed of angular cells which contain granules of eleidin, and frequently have a dark appearance from the presence of minute air-bubbles. The latter may also occur in interstices in the fibrous substance. When air is present, the hair looks dark by transmitted, white by reflected, light; but when a dark appearance is due to pigment, the hair looks dark by both transmitted and reflected light.

Hair, however, may appear white by reflected light and yet contain pigment if the medulla contains much air. The *root* has the same structure as the body of the hair, except at its deep extremity, which is enlarged to form the hair-bulb; this enlargement is composed mainly of soft growing cells, and fits over a vascular *papilla*, which projects up into the bottom of the follicle.

The diameter of human hairs is very variable; those of the beard are the thickest and may attain 200 μ, while the finest (lanugo) hairs

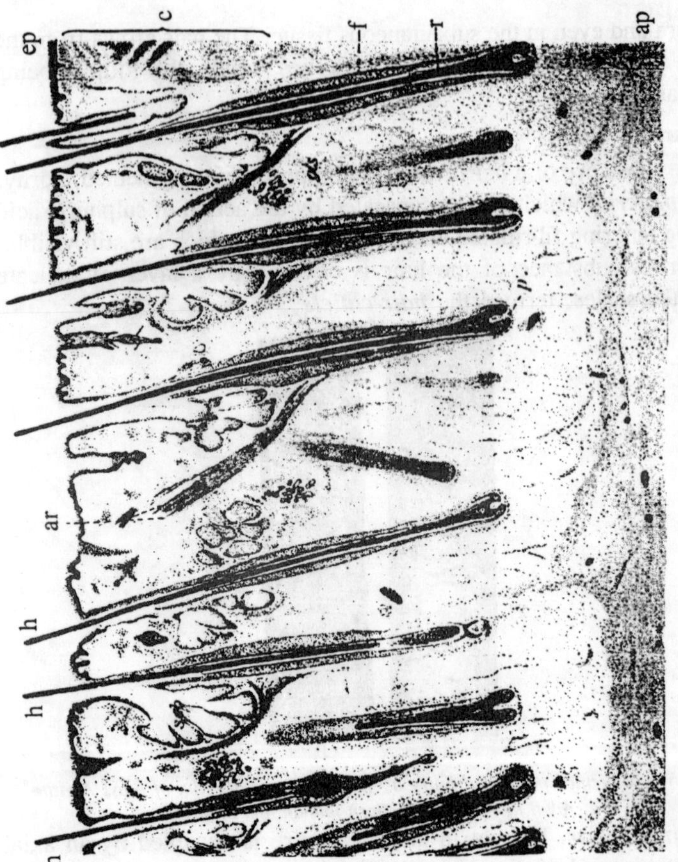

Figure 5.6: Section of human scale. h, h, ordinary or bulb-hairs; h', club-hair; ar, arrector pill muscle; f, nair-follicle; r, root of hair; p, papilla; ep, epidermis; c, cutis vera; ay, aponeurosis below subcutaneous tissue; gls, sweat glands; seb, sebaceous glands.

are often only 5 μ in diameter. The lanugo hairs and the hairs which immediately succeed them (primary hairs) have no medulla. Some hairs which are found throughout life are also destitute of medulla. These are termed 'non-medullary' or 'lanugo' hairs.

Structure of Hair-Follicle

The follicle, like the skin itself, of which it is a recess, is composed of two parts: one epithelial, the other connective tissue. The epithelial or epidermic part of the follicle closely invests the hair-root, and is often dragged out with it; hence it is known as the *root-sheath*.

It consists of an outer layer of soft columnar and polyhedral cells, like the Malpighian layer of the epidermis, but without stratum granulosum-the *outer root-sheath*; and of an inner, thinner, horny stratum next to the hair-the *inner root-sheath*.

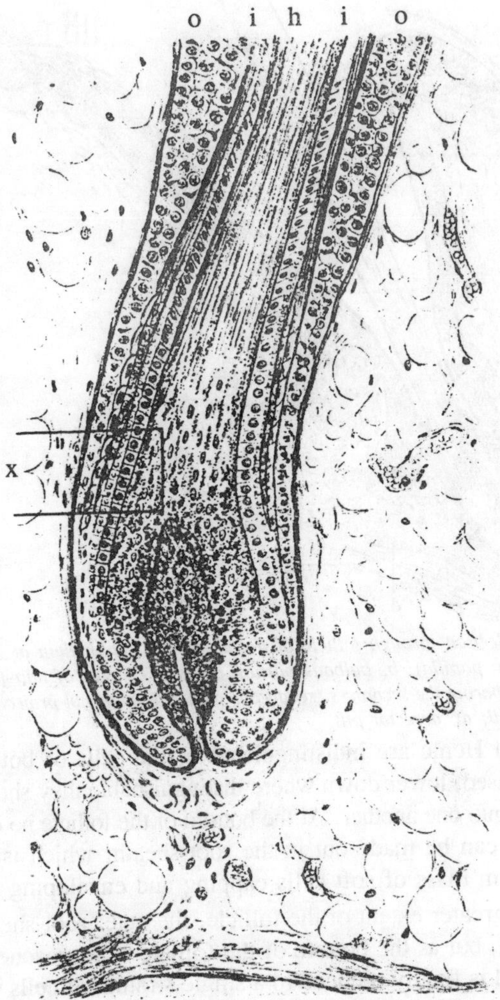

Figure 5.7: Lonoitudinal section of a hair follicle.o, outer root-sheath; i, inner root-sheath; h, hair; x.

The inner root-sheath itself consists of three layers, the outermost being composed of horny, fibrillated, oblong cells the nuclei of which are obscure (*Henle's layer*), the next of polyhedral nucleated cells containing eleidin (*Huxley's layer*), and the third—the *cuticle of the root-sheath*—a layer of downwardly imbricated scales, which fit over the upwardly imbricated scales of the hair itself.

In the more superficial part of the hair-follicle. the layers of

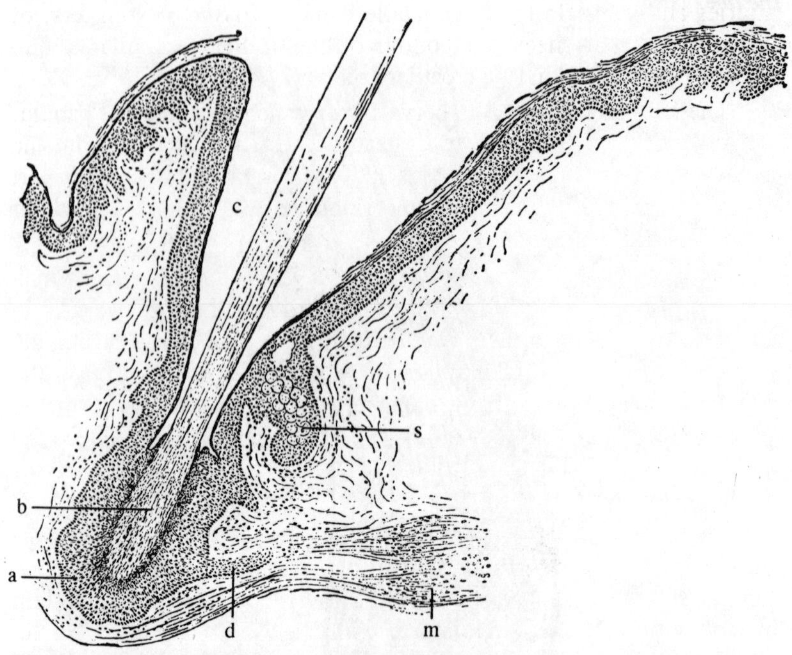

Figure 5.8: Section through follicle of a club-hair. a, epithelium at bottom of follicle (which has no papilla); b, bulbous portion of hair; c, neck of hair-follicle somewhat opened in preparing the section; s, sebaceous gland; d, epithelial projection at attachment of arrector pili; m, arrector pili.

Huxley and Henle are indistinguishable, the cells of both being clear and keratinised; lower down where distinguishable they show a tendency to dovetail into one another. At the bottom of the follicle no differentiation into layers can be made out in the root-sheath, which is here formed by a uniform mass of soft cells capping and enveloping the papilla.

In the greater extent of the follicle, the outer root-sheath is several layers thick, but as the bottom of the follicle is approached it becomes thinner, and is finally reduced to a single stratum of cells which, in the papillary part, becomes flattened out into a very thin layer.

The connective tissue or dermic part of the hair-follicle is composed internally of a *vascular layer,* which is separated from the root-sheath by a basement-membrane termed the *hyaline layer* of the follicle. The vascular layer corresponds to the superficial layer of the cutis vera.

Its fibres and cells have a regular circular arrangement around the follicle, the cells being flattened against the hyaline layer. Externally the dermic coat of the follicle has a more open texture, corresponding to the deeper part of the cutis, and contains the larger branches of the arteries and veins. In the large tactile hairs, *vibrissae* or whiskers, of animals the veins near the bottom of the follicle are dilated into sinuses, forming a kind of erectile structure.

The hair-follicle receives nerve-fibres which pass into the papilla, and others which enter the root-sheath. These are derived from the nerves of the corium and form ring-like arborisations in the upper part of the hairfollicle; while below the rings there is usually a sheaf of vertical palisadelike endings.

The terminations between the cells of the outer root-sheath may take the form of tactile disks. Nerves are especially well developed in connexion with the whiskers of animals. The hair grows from the bottom of the follicle by multiplication of the soft cells which cover the papilla, these cells becoming elongated and pigmented to form the fibres of the fibrous substance, and otherwise modified to produce the medulla (when present) and cuticle of the hair and the several layers of the root-sheath.

The cells which form the medulla of the hair and the inner root-sheath are filled with granules of eleidin, but those which form the fibrous substance and cuticle of the hair have granules which stain brown with carmine, and appear similar to the granules in the corresponding cells of the nail-matrix.

Besides the hairs which have been described, and which are provided with a vascular papilla, from the cells covering which the hair and its inner root-sheath grow *(growing* or *bulbhairs, papillated hairs),* there are other hairs unprovided with a papilla and the follicle of which ceases at the level of attachment of the arrector pili muscle (*non-growing* or *club-hairs, nonpapillated hairs*).

These are hairs which have become detached from their papilla and have ceased to grow; they are more easily pulled out than the growing hairs, and after a time tend to fall out spontaneously. In their follicles the whole of the lower part of the hair, including the original papilla and the soft growing cells which cover it, may entirely disappear, the hair being now attached at its sides and below to the root-sheath.

A hair which has thus ceased to grow is eventually lost, but its place is presently supplied by a new hair, which becomes developed in a down-growth from the old follicle, a new papilla being formed at the extremity of the down growth. If not previously detached the old hair drops out from the follicle as the new one grows up to replace it.

The detachment of the non-papillated hairs is preceded by an absorption of the root of the hair and of the investing inner root-sheath.

This absorption appears to be effected by the cells of the outer sheath, which multiply at the expense of the keratinised parts of the hair-root and undermine its attachment to the follicle. The root of such a hair when pulled out is of less diameter than the shaft.

Human hairs grow at the rate of about 2 mm. a day. When a hair is pulled out, the new hair is not apparent at the surface for some weeks after. During this period active karyokinesis occurs among the cells at the bottom of the follicle some of which gradually arrange themselves to produce the new hair.

Hair that has been recently cut may be identified by the straight and usually finely serrated end ; after fourteen days the frayed edge is straight and smooth, while, in about a month, the distal end is rounded. Uncut hair, on the other hand, has a fine, filiform end or is finely frayed. The above points are of medico-legal importance.

Hairs are found all over the body except on the palms of the hands and the soles of the feet (including the fingers and toes), the dorsal surface of the distal phalanges of the fingers and toes, the glans penis and some other parts of the external sex-organs.

They usually slant. In the negroid races the hair-follicles are even considerably curved and the hairs are oval or flattened in section. In other races differences also occur both in their shape in section and in size, the straight-haired races usually having the thickest hairs. On the scalp the hairs are set in groups, as is seen in a horizontal section, being most numerous here (200 to 300 per square centimetre).

On the side to which the hair slopes a small patch of thickened epidermis is usually to be found, developed over an enlarged papilla of the cutis vera: while on the opposite side of the hair is a flat area of skin with thickened scale-like epidermis, which may represent a vestige of the reptilian scale (Pinkus).

The hair-rudiments when they first appear are singularly like certain tactile patches which are found in the skin of amphibia and some reptiles, and it is possible that hairs have become developed phylogenetically from these patches.

It is well known that the tactile sensibility of many parts of the skin is intimately associated with the hairs, although parts devoid of hairs also have a highly developed sense of touch.

Muscles of the Hairs

A small muscle composed of bundles of plain muscular tissue is attached to each hair-follicle; it passes from the superficial part of the corium, on the side to which the hair slopes, obliquely downwards, to be attached near the bottom of the follicle to a projection formed by a localised hypertrophy of the outer root-sheath.

When the muscle contracts, the hair becomes more erect, and the follicle is dragged upwards so as to cause a prominence on the general surface of the skin, while the part of the corium from which the little muscle arises is correspondingly depressed ; the roughened condition known as '*goose skin*' being in this *way* produced.

There is always a sebaceous gland in the triangle formed between the arrector pili and its points of attachment to the hair-follicle and the epidermis, so that the contraction of the arrector pili generally causes the secretion of the gland to be extruded. These small muscles are supplied by nerve-fibres derived from the sympathetic.

DEVELOPMENT

The hairs are originally developed in the embryo as small solid downgrowths from the Malpighian layer of the epidermis. The hair-rudiment, which gives rise not only to the hair proper but also to the epithelium-cells of the hair-follicle, is at first composed entirely of soft growing cells, the outermost and deepest having a columnar shape; but presently those in the centre become differentiated, so as to produce a minute hair invested by the inner root-sheath, its base resting upon a papilla which has become enclosed by the extremity of the hair-germ and which is formed by the connective tissue of the cutis.

As the minute hair grows, it pushes its way through the layers of the epidermis, which it finally perforates, the epitrichial layer being thrown off. During the whole process the follicle is growing more deeply into the cutis vera, carrying the papilla down with it.

The hair-rudiments begin to appear at the third or fourth month of fcetal life; their growth is completed about the fifth or sixth month, and the fine hairs which they form constitute the hairy covering termed the *lanugo*. This is shed within a few months of birth, the new hairs being formed in down growths from the old hair-follicles in the manner already mentioned.

GLANDS OF THE SKIN

Sebaceous glands are small saccular glands, the ducts of which open into the mouths of the hair-follicles. They are also found in a few situations which are devoid of hairs (such as the margin of the lips, the external auditory meatus and parts of the external sex-organs). The Meibomian glands of the eye-lid are modified sebaceous lands. Both the

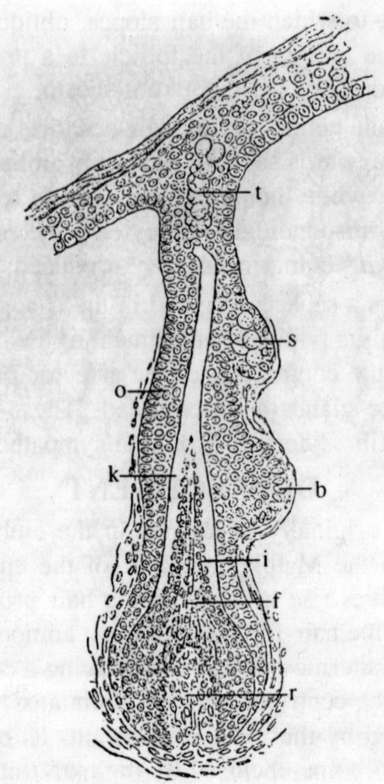

Figure 5.9: Developing hair from human embryo of four and a half month. p, papilla; f, hair-rudiment; i, cells from which the inner root-sheath is beocming formed; k, keratinised part of inner root-sheath, uncoloured by carmine; o, outer root-sheath; b, epithelial projection for insertion of arrector pili; s, sebaceous gland; t, sebaceous tranformation of cellsin the part which will become the neck of the follicle. This forms a channel for the passage of the hair-point through the malpighian layer.

duct and the saccules are lined, and sometimes filled, by epithelium-cells which become charged with fatty matter.

There may be two or more sebaceous glands attached to each hair-follicle. The mode of secretion is remarkable : the secretory product is formed by the actual disintegration of the epithelium-cells themselves, on which account they are termed *holocrine glands*. In the mammary and apocrine glands, only the free ends of the cells break down ; such glands are therefore known as *apocrine glands*.

The sebaceous glands are developed as outgrowths from the outer rootsheaths of the hairs.

Sweat glands are abundant over the whole skin, but are most numerous on the palm of the hand and on the sole of the foot. They are composed of coiled tubes, which lie in the deeper part of the integument and send their ducts up through the cutis to open on the surface by corkscrew-like channels in the epidermis.

The *secreting* part of the gland is formed of a convoluted tube composed of a basement-membrane lined by a single layer of cubical or columnar epithelium-cells, and with a layer of· *longitudinally* or obliquely disposed plain muscle-fibres between the epithelium and basement-membrane. The secreting tube is considerably larger than the duct, which begins within the gland and usually makes several *convolutions* before leaving the gland to traverse the cutis vera.

The duct has an epithelium consisting of two or three layers of cells, within which is a well-marked cuticular lining; there is no muscular coat. The passage through the epidermis has no proper wall, but is merely a channel excavated between the epithelium-cells.

The *apoerine glands* are very large sweat glands occurring in the axilla and round the anus. In these secretion is effected by the *disintegration* of the free ends of the cells, which project into the lumen of the alveolus.

In type they are intermediate between the smaller sweat and the sebaceous glands, resembling the mammary gland in the mode of secretion. They are said to undergo cyclical changes in structure during the menstrual cycle. According to Kuno, their secretion has a sexual significance.

The sweat glands receive nerve-fibres, and each gland has a special cluster of capillary blood-vessels. The *eeruminous glands* of the ear are also modified sweat glands, but the secretion is of a fatty nature, instead of being watery like that of the ordinary *sweat glands*. Closely associated with the ceruminous glands "are large sebaceous glands. Their secretion is said to act as an insect-repellant.

DEVELOPMENT

The sweat glands are developed, like the hairs, as downgrowths of the Malpighian layer of the epidermis into the corium. They are distinguishable from the hairrudiments by the fact that the cells of the outermost layer are not columnar in shape, but spheroidal or polyhedral. The sweat-gland rudiments which are thus formed become eventually coiled up at their extremities and converted into hollow tubes. The muscular fibres of the tubes are peculiar in that they are derived from the ectoderm.

THE MAMMARY GLANDS

The *mammary glands* are large compound racemose glands serving

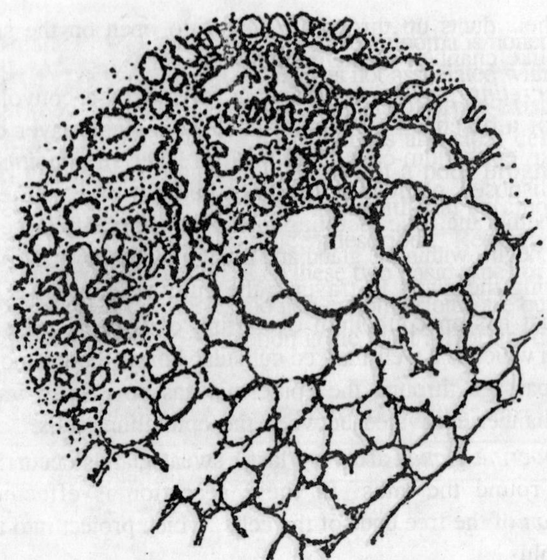

Figure 5.10: Section of two adjacent alveoli in mammary gland of lactating cat, one of which is full of milk, whilst. The other is emptied of its secretion.

for the secretion of milk. Each mamma actually represents a group of glands, which open by numerous ducts upon the apex of the nipple. Each duct is dilated into a small reservoir, the *sinus lactiferus,* just before reaching the nipple.

The nipple contains a considerable amount of plain muscular tissue, lying between and around the ducts. Traced backwards, the ducts are found to commence in groups of saccular alveoli, the walls of which are lined by a single layer of epithelium which is columnar when the milk is being produced within the cells, but becomes flattened out as it is discharged and fills the alveolus.

Milk globules may be seen forming within the columnar cells and also lying free within the alveoli. The distal part of each cell disintegrates during lactation, the nucleus and the rest of the cytoplasm remaining attached to the wall of the alveolus. The contrast between alveoli distended with milk and those which have been emptied of the secretion is striking.

The emptying is brought about by contraction of plain muscle-cells in the alveolus lying just inside the basementmembrane (as in the sweat glands). The muscle is stimulated to contract by intravenous injection of pituitrin. According to Ely and Petersen pituitrin is liberated by reflex stimulation from the nipple during suckling or by emotional stress; this is known as the 'let down ' reaction.

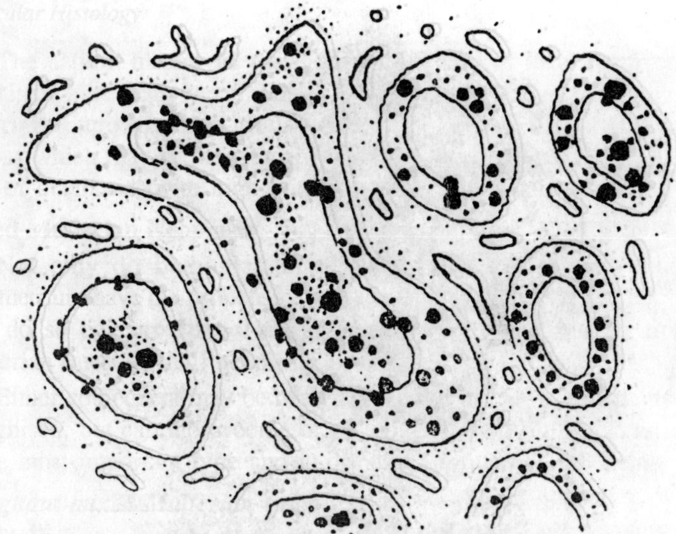

Figure 5.11: Sectionof human mammary gland during lactation. The section shows droplets stained by osmium tetroxide both within the cells and discharged into the lumen.

At the commencement of lactation large pbagocytic cells containing fatparticles appear in the secretion, the *colostrum corpuscles*. These are either detached portions of the secreting epithelium-cells or, as some believe, leucocytes. Recent work (Bratianu and Guerriero) indicates that these corpuscles are derived from the epithelium.

In the resting gland in the human female there is a large amount of dense fibrous or adipose tissue between the groups of acini, but in most mammals the whole organ is mainly formed of the secreting alveoli.

Vessels and Nerves

The blood is distributed to a capillary network which surrounds the alveoli. There are numerous lymphatics within the gland ; most of these, in man, carry their lymph to the axillary lymph-glands. The mammary glands also receive many nerves, mainly from the intercostals, but these do not appear directly to influence the outpouring of the secretion.

DEVELOPMENT

The mammary glands are developed in the same manner as the sweat glands, excepting that the secreting part does not become convoluted and tubular. In the virgin mamma they show very few and small groups of alveoli, scattered in abundant, thick connective tissue, but as pregnancy

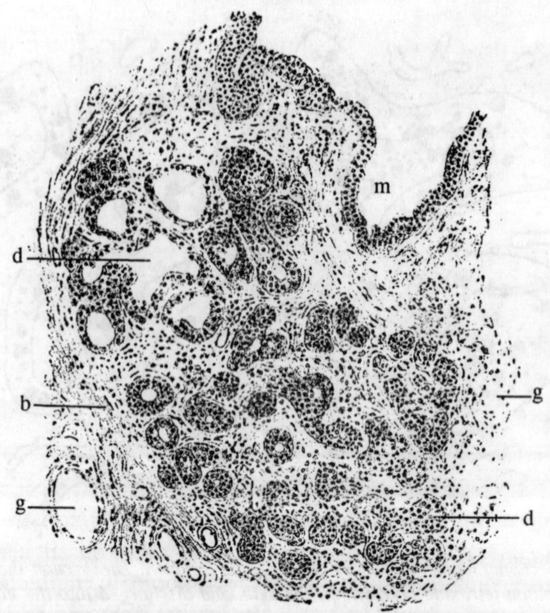

Figure 5.12: Section showing developing alveoli in lactating human mammary gland. m, part of a large duct; d, undeveloped alveoli: d, partially developed alveoli; g, g, blood-vessels; b, connective tissue of gland.

advances the gland-ducts bud out extensively, and many more alveoli are formed and undergo enlargement, until the greater part of the connective tissue in the mammary region is permeated by them.

Growth of the duct system is caused by the action of the oestrogens. Development of the alveoli is brought about by progesterone. Liberation of the lactogenic hormone from the pituitary gland after parturition initiates secretion. In most animals the whole mamma becomes occupied by secreting alveoli during active lactation.

In the human subject, however, there are, even during full lactation, considerable portions of the mamma between the groups of alveoli, composed of connective tissue, generally with a large amount of adipose tissue, and even in sections of the lactating gland alveoli maybe seen in various stages of development. After lactation is over, the alveoli undergo a process of retrogression.

In the male, the mammary gland consists of scanty ducts embedded in dense fibrous tissue. There are no alveoli, but under some circumstances development of glandular tissue and secretion of milk may occur as in the female.

After the gland has ceased to secrete, the alveoli atrophy, becoming reduced to mere excrescences on the endings of the ducts; the calibre of the ducts also diminishes. As a consequence the fibrous tissue of the gland becomes very apparent, and this is particularly the case in the human subject.

6

Liquid Connective Tissue

Blood is a unique organ: it is fluid and comes into contact with almost all other tissues. The blood cells are noncohesive and supported in the fluid medium of blood-the plasma. The blood cells comprise the non-nucleated *erythrocytes* and *platelets*, and the nucleated cells or *leukocytes*.

In addition to primary disease of the blood-forming organ-the bone marrow-many disease states produce secondary changes in the blood. For this reason, the counting and *morphological* examination of blood cells is routine in the clinical assessment of disease, frequently providing valuable diagnostic information.

CELLULAR COMPONENTS

The *peripheral* blood is investigated by microscopy of a droplet spread evenly over the surface of a glass slide the blood film. Routinely, the blood film is treated with a combination of stains which allow identification of nuclear and *cytoplasmic* detail.

Quantitation of blood cells is essential; in modern laboratories this is routinely performed by automated cell-counting equipment. The size and concentration of erythrocytes, and the leukocyte and platelet concentrations are measured.

Haemoglobin is automatically measured. Also, the proportion of leukocytes of each *category*—the differential white cell count—is measured from cell size and granule content.

Erythrocytes

Erythrocytes (red blood cells) are deformable, non-nucleated and biconcave discs. They are the most abundant blood cell. When blood is separated, by centrifugation, into cellular and plasma components, the red cell portion is approximately 45% of the total volume: this is the 'packed cell volume' or *haematocrit*.

The erythrocyte is a special oxygen-carrying cell because it is rich in haemoglobin. The cell membrane is composed of a phospholipid bilayer with integral proteins. The shape of the cell is maintained by structural proteins, such as spectrin, which form a cytoskeleton.

Enzyme systems protect the haemoglobin from irreversible oxidation. The mature erythrocyte has no nuclear material, so new protein cannot be synthesised.

Absolute Values

The absolute values are measures of red cell size and haemoglobin content which provide valuable information in the assessment of anaemia, as they provide diagnostic clues as to the likely cause. Absolute values are calculated from the red cell concentration, haemoglobin concentration and haematocrit as follows:

Mean corpuscular volume (MCV) in femtolitres (fl) =

$$\frac{\text{Haematocrit (g/l)}}{\text{Red cell concentration (per litre)}}$$

Mean corpuscular haemoglobin (MCH) in picograms (pg) =

$$\frac{\text{Haematocrit (g/dl)}}{\text{Red cell concentration (per litre)}}$$

Mean corpuscular haemoglobin concentration (MCHC) (g/dl) =

$$\frac{\text{Haemoglobin concentration (g/dl)}}{\text{Haematocrit (l/l)}}$$

In the modern laboratory, automated cell counters provide these data on each blood sample analysed.

Morphology

The biconcave erythrocyte shape provides a large surface area for oxygen diffusion. By light microscopy erythrocytes appear as uniform round cells with central pallor. Up to 1% of cells stain with a purplish tinge and are of rather greater diameter. These are polychromatic cells; this purple staining is due to the residual ribonucleic acid (RNA) of the immature erythrocyte.

Pathological basis of hatmatoi,ogical signs and symptoms

Sign or Symptom	*Pathological Basis*
Tiredness, dyspnoea	Reduced oxygen-carrying capacity of blood due to anaemia
Mucosal pallor	Anaemia
Glossitis (sore mouth, smooth tongue)	Mucosal effects of haematinic deficiency
Spoon-shaped nails	Due to iron deficiency
Jaundice	Bilirubin accumulation from haemolysis
Abnormal tendency to infections	Neutropenia, e.g. in leukaemia or hypoplastic anaemia
	Immune deficiency, e.g. in myeloma, and due to chemotherapy in leukaemia and lymphoma
Splenomegaly	Due to expansion of haemopoiesis in myeloproliferative disorders, red cell pooling and destruction in haemolytic anaemias, infiltration in leukaemias and lymphomas
	Also non-haematological causes, e.g. portal hypertension
Lymphadenopathy	Infiltration with leukaemia or lymphoma
	Non-neoplastic causes, e.g. infectious mononucleosis
Bone pain and fractures	Osteoclast activation in myeloma
Purpura, bruising, mucosal or traumatic bleeding	Thrombocytopenia or platelet dysfunction
Bruising, muscle and joint bleeding and traumatic bleeding	Coagulation factor deficiency

These young cells become *indistinguishable* from the mature red cell population after 48 hours in the blood. When stained with a supravital stain (such as methylene blue) polychromatic cells are more easily identified by the presence of characteristic inclusions; they are then termed *reticulocytes*.

The inclusions are remnants of RNA. When bone *marrow* production of *erythrocytes* is increased, the proportion of *polychromatic* cells, or reticulocytes, in the peripheral blood becomes greater than 1% or 100 $\times 10^9/1$. This occurs most commonly in recovery from acute haemorrhage or when there is an increased rate of destruction of red cells, which is called haemolytic anaemia.

Changes in disease

Anaemia is present when the haemoglobin concentration is less than approximately 13.0 g/dl in a male or 11.5 g/dl in a female; the haematocrit is also reduced. Conversely, *polycythaemia* describes an increased red cell concentration; it is usually accompanied by a raised haemoglobin concentration and haematocrit. Anaemias may be simply classified according to red cell size (MCV) and haemoglobin content (MCH). This classification is of great diagnostic value in most common types of anaemia.

Further diagnostic information is obtained by the microscopic examination of the red cell morphology on a blood smear. Disease of the blood is frequently associated with increased variation in red cell sizeanisocytosis-and the presence of erythrocytes of abnormal shape *poikilocytosis*.

Increased erythrocyte anisocytosis and poikilocytosis are non-specific abnormalities present in many haematological and systemic disorders. An example is the marked aniso-poikilocytosis which occurs in the absence of a functioning spleen, due to surgical removal or secondary to disease. In this situation there are also inclusions in red cells. They are called Howell Jolly bodies and are remnants of nuclear material which would normally be removed when newly formed erythrocytes

Table 6.1: Normal red cell values.

Value	*Male*	*Both sexes*	*Female*
Haemoglobin (g/dl)			
Adult	13.0-17.0		11.5-16.0
Newborn		13.5-19.5	
3 months		9.5-13.5	
12 months		10.5-13.5	
Haematocrit (l/1)	0.39-0.50		0.34-0.47
Red cell count ($\times 10^{12}/l$)	4.3-5.7		3.9-5.1
MCH (pg)		26-33	
MCV (fl)		78-98	
MCHC (g/dl)		30-35	

Table 6.2: Morphological classification of anaemia.

Morphology	*Absolute values*	*Common causes*
Microcytic	MCV <78	Iron deficiency
Hypochromic	MCH <26	Thalassaemia
Macrocytic	MCV >98	Megaloblastic anaemias, myelodysplasias
		Acute blood loss
Normocytic	MCV	Most haemolytic anaemias
Normochromic	MCH	Anaemia of chronic disorders
		Bone marrow failure

released from bone marrow circulate for the first time through the spleen.

In addition to Howell Jolly bodies, red cells may contain other inclusions under certain circumstances. The basophilic stippling of the 'stipple cell' is due to the presence of residual RNA; stipple cells may be present in several anaemias, especially thalassaemia.

Siderotic granules contain iron and may occur in states of iron overload, for example in chronically anaemic subjects who have received treatment by frequent transfusion of red cells. Occasionally, nucleated red cell precursors may escape into the peripheral blood; when these normoblasts are accompanied by immature neutrophil leukocytes the film is described as *leukoerythroblastic*.

A leukoerythroblastic blood film results from gross marrow disturbance such as infiltration by malignancy, or fibrous tissue (myelofibrosis) or in severe anaemia due to deficiency of vitamin B_{12} or folate (megaloblastic anaemia).

Supravital staining is used to detect the presence of reticulocytes, as described above. This technique also identifies another type of red cell inclusion-Heinz bodies. These inclusions represent denatured haemoglobin and are seen typically in certain haemolytic anaemias, especially those due to a deficiency in the protective enzyme systems such as glucose-6-phosphate dehydrogenase deficiency.

Leukocytes

The nucleated cells of the peripheral blood are termed white blood cells or leukocytes. Their primary role is protection against infection or infestation of the body. Morphologically, on a stained blood film, five varieties of leukocyte are identified.

The normal concentrations of these are:

- neutrophil granulocytes 2.0-7.5 × 10^9/1
- lymphocytes 1.0-3.0 × 10^9/1
- monocytes 0.15-0.6 × 10^9/1
- eosinophil granulocytes 0.05-0.3 × 10^9/1
- basophil granulocytes 0.01-0.10 × 10^9/1.

These are typical values for healthy adults and older children. The normal counts differ in infants, who have a higher proportion of lymphocytes, for example.

Also, it is important to appreciate how such laboratory normal ranges are established in order to avoid misinterpretation. Cell counts are performed on a large number of healthy subjects and the range determined from the population mean and 2 standard deviations above and below the mean.

This dictates that, for a particular measurement, 2.5% of healthy subjects have a count just below the lower limit of 'normal' and a further 2.5% just above. The granulocytes and monocytes are phagocytic leukocytes produced from precursor cells in the bone marrow.

The lymphocytes are part of the immunologically competent series, which includes *immunoglobulin*—producing plasma cells; they are produced initially in the bone marrow and thymus, and later develop in the lymphoid tissue of the body. Plasma cells are not seen in the blood in health.

Neutrophil granulocytes

Neutrophils are the most numerous leukocytes in the blood of the healthy adult. The *nucleus* of the neutrophil *granulocyte* is characteristically segmented into up to five lobes and the nuclear chromatin stains densely. The *abundant cytoplasm* stains pink and contains *characteristic* granules. Within the granules are enzymes, including myeloperoxidase and alkaline phosphatase, and lysozyme. *Neutrophils* have a scavenging function and are of particular importance in the defence against bacterial infection.

Neutrophil precursors and neutrophils spend 14 days in the bone marrow, whereas the half-life of neutrophils in the blood is only 6-9 hours. Peripheral blood counts therefore measure less than 10% of the total body neutrophils. Within the circulation the cells move between a circulating and a 'marginatiog' pool, margination being attachment to vascular endothelial cells.

To perform their scavenging function, granulocytes irreversibly enter the tissues by penetrating *endothelial* cells modified by inflammatory mediators. Cytokine-stimulated endothelial cells present adhesion molecules which interact with neutrophils and facilitate their passage: one such is ICAM-1 (intercellular adhesion molecule 1).

Lymphocytes

The peripheral blood lymphocytes are small leukocytes with a round or only slightly indented nucleus and scanty sky-blue-staining cytoplasm which may contain an occasional pink- or red-staining granule. A small proportion of lymphocytes may be larger with abundant cytoplasm, sometimes referred to as 'activated' lymphocytes.

These are believed to represent cells which have been stimulated, perhaps by foreign antigen. A more complete description of the classification and role of lymphocytes is to be found in other chapter of this book.

Monocytes

Monocytes are the largest blood cells. The nucleus is oval or reniform but not lobed. The abundant cytoplasm stains pale blue and often contains pink granules; vacuoles are often present. The function of monocytes is similar to that of neutrophil granulocytes: they enter the tissues and, as tissue macrophages, are responsible for the phagocytosis and digestion of foreign material and dead tissue.

Eosinophil granulocytes

Eosinophil granulocytes have much larger red-staining granules. They contain enzymes, including a peroxidase. The nucleus is lobulated, but usually only two or three lobes are seen. The eosinophil is important in the mediation of the allergic response and in defence against parasitic infestation.

Basophil granulocytes

Basophil granulocytes are the least frequent leukocytes in normal blood. The granules are large, blue-black and obscure the bilobed nucleus; they contain heparin and histamine. Basophils are closely related to tissue mast cells but their function has not been determined precisely. They appear to be key mediators of immediate hypersensitivity reactions, involving release of histamine.

Changes in disease

Changes may be *quantitative* or *qualitative;* the former are more important and often of diagnostic value. A knowledge of the causes of increased numbers of the various leukocytes in the peripheral blood is useful clinically.

Quantitative changes

Leukocytosis means an increase in numbers of circulating white blood cells. Depending on the cause, there may be a polymorphonuclear leukocytosis (neutrophilia-increased neutrophil leukocytes), monocytosis, eosinophil leukocytosis (eosinophilia), basophil leukocytosis (basophilia) or lymphocytosis.

Causes of reactive neutrophil leukocytosis include:

- sepsis (e.g. acute appendicitis, bacterial pneumonia)
- trauma (e.g. major surgery)
- infarcts (e.g. myocardial infarction)
- chronic inflammatory disease (e.g. systemic lupus erythematosus (SLE), rheumatoid disease)
- malignant neoplasms
- steroid therapy
- acute haemorrhage or haemolysis.

Monocytosis may be reactive to:

- sepsis
- chronic infections (e.g. tuberculosis)
- malignant neoplasms.

Eosinophil leukocytosis may be reactive to:

- allergy (e.g. asthma)
- parasites (e.g. tapeworm infestation)
- malignant neoplasms (e.g. Hodgkin's disease)
- miscellaneous conditions (e.g. polyarteritis nodosa).

Lymphocytosis is most commonly associated with an infection such as infectious mononucleosis, tuberculosis, etc.

In some disorders the leukocytosis may be extreme (for example $100 \times 10^9/l$), particularly in children. There may also be a tendency for immature leukocytes, particularly myelocytes and metamyelocytes, to appear in the peripheral blood.

Severe bacterial infection may result in such an extreme reactive picture, which has in the past been referred to as a 'leukaemoid reaction' because of the similarity of the blood picture, with immature forms present, to that of chronic myeloid leukaemia.

Occasionally, the lymphocyte series may be involved in such an extreme reactive process, especially during childhood viral infection. A characteristic leukocytosis composed of 'atypical' lymphocytes is a feature of *infectious mononucleosis* (glandular fever). The infection is common in young adults and often manifests as a sore throat with enlarged lymph nodes and spleen and skin rash. It is due to infection with EpsteinBarr (EB) virus and is common between 15 and 25 years of age. The major additional features are:

- infection of B-lymphocytes with EB virus
- T-lymphocytosis with morphologically atypical forms in the blood
- hepatitis often present
- development of antibodies reactive with non-human erythrocytes (heterophile antibodies)
- development of antibodies to EB virus.

The atypical cells in peripheral blood are recognisable as lymphocytes but are much larger and have abundant cytoplasm and nuclear irregularities. They are probably reactive T-lymphocytes responding to Blymphocytes containing the virus, are detectable in blood about 7 days after the onset of illness and may persist for 6 weeks or more.

Apparently fortuitously, but usefully, antibodies reactive against horse, sheep and ox red cells (heterophile antibodies) typically develop during the second week and may persist for a few months; they are detected in the Paul-Bunnell test or by more convenient commercial screening slide tests such as the 'Monospot' test, and are of diagnostic value.

A very similar clinical and haematological (but not serological) picture can develop as a result of other infections, especially with human immunodeficiency virus (HIV), cytomegalovirus and toxoplasma. All of the above are examples of reactive leukocytosis. Increased white cell counts in peripheral blood, often with immature forms present, are also a typical feature of some malignant disorders of the bone marrow, especially leukaemias and myeloproliferative disorders.

A reduction in circulating leukocytes is termed *leukopenia*. Most important is a deficiency of neutrophil granulocytesneutropenia. Neutropenia is commonly seen in association with a reduction in other blood cells, that is, as part of a pancytopenia. Important causes of pancytopenia are:

- bone marrow failure (e.g. hypoplastic anaemia; marrow infiltration with leukaemia or carcinoma; due to cytotoxic drug therapy; due to irradiation)
- megaloblastic anaemia (in which deficiency of vitamin B_{12} or folate impairs DNA synthesis and thereby slows cell replication)

- hypersplenism (in which an enlarged spleen in disease causes pooling of blood cells within the splenic vasculature, e.g in portal hypertension due to liver disease).

Important causes of selective neutropenia are:

- overwhelming sepsis (e.g. septicaemia, miliary tuberculosis)
- racial (in African races the normal neutrophil count is lower)
- autoimmune (e.g. due to auto-antibody, often in association with other autoimmune disease such as rheumatoid arthritis)
- drug-induced (as an idiosyncratic reaction)
- cyclical.

In cyclical forms the neutropenia is temporary and recurrent, often with a periodicity of 3-4 weeks. It is an uncommon condition.

Neutropenia with counts of less than $0.5 \times 10^9/1$ may result in severe sepsis, especially of the mouth, pharynx and perianal regions, and also in disseminated infection. This clinical picture is now most commonly seen in patients receiving drug or irradiation therapy for malignant disorders.

Qualitative changes

Qualitative leukocyte changes are less important than quantitative abnormalities. Defects of phagocytic cell function resulting in an increased tendency to bacterial infection are recognised, particularly as acquired defects after splenectomy, in leukaemic disorders and due to corticosteroid therapy.

Congenital abnormalities of leukocyte function are uncommon. Atypical' lymphocytes in infectious mononucleosis have been described earlier. Other abnormalities of neutrophil morphology are also recognised. Deficiency of lymphocytes in blood is termed lymphopenia. It is often due to medication with immunosuppressive or cytotoxic drugs, for example. Lymphopenia is an important feature of infection with HIV.

Platelets

On a stained blood film platelets appear as non-nucleated fragments of granular cytoplasm, approximately one-fifth the diameter of erythrocytes and in a concentration of $150\text{-}400 \times 10^9/1$. Platelets are contractile and adhesive cells, the function of which is the maintenance of vascular integrity.

Exposure of vascular subendothelial structures results in rapid adhesion of platelets to the exposed area and aggregation of platelets to each other in the formation of a primary haemostatic plug. Platelets are rich in intracellular granules, which are released during stimulation.

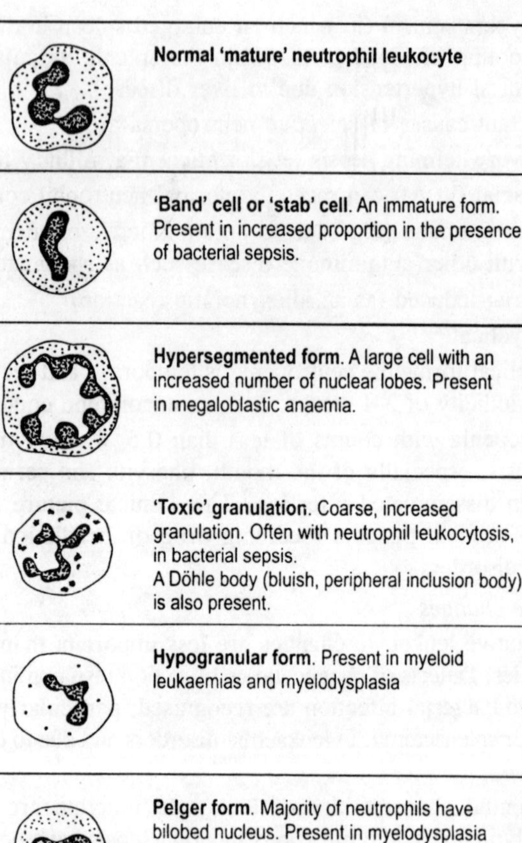

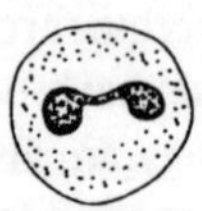

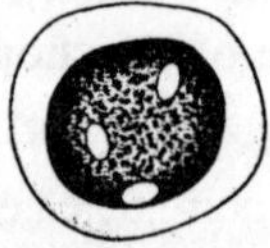

Figure 6.1: Abnormalities of neutrophil morphology.

The most abundant granules, alpha granules, contain proteins and peptides, including von Willebrand factor, some clotting factors and growth factors. Platelets deliver these to sites of vascular injury, where they contribute to clot formation and the repair process. Dense bodies are-less abundant platelet granules and are rich in calcium, serotonin and adenine nucleotides.

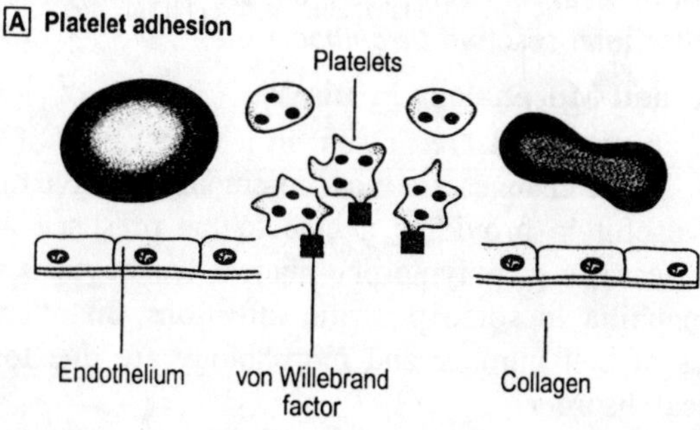

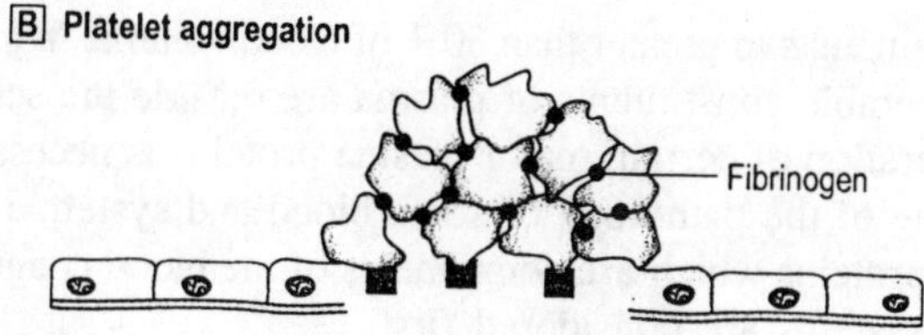

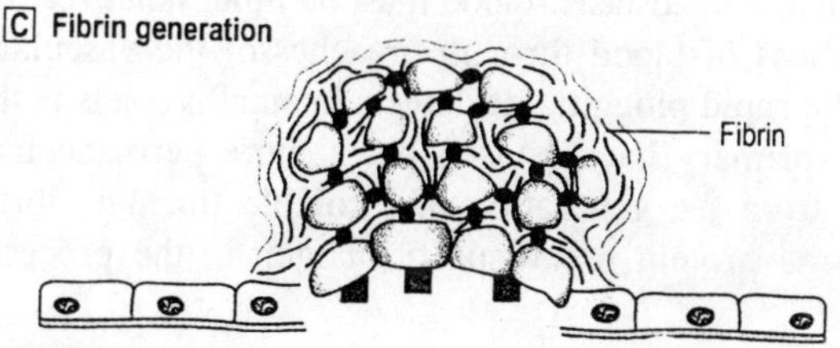

Figure 6.2: The physiology of primary haemostasis.

A deficiency of blood platelets is termed *thrombocytopenia,* the causes and consequences of which are described anywhere else in this chapter. *Thrombocytosis,* or increased platelet numbers, is usually reactive to:

- acute or chronic blood loss (e.g. from peptic ulcer, menorrhagia)
- iron deficiency (e.g. dietary deficiency, chronic blood loss)
- chronic inflammatory disease (e.g. rheumatoid arthritis)
- neoplastic disease (e.g. bronchial carcinoma, lymphoma)
- tissue trauma (e.g. post-operative state, especially splenectomy).

Thrombocytosis may also occur in primary disorders of bone marrow-the *myeloproliferative* diseases. Morphological platelet abnormalities are of minor importance, although '*giant*' platelets, with a diameter exceeding that of an *erythrocyte*, are a feature of the myeloproliferative disorders rather than reactive *thrombocytosis*.

Blood Count and Morphology in Disease

Changes in the blood are present in a wide range of diseases of other organs. These changes are most commonly reactive or secondary but may be useful in providing a clue to the presence and type of underlying disease, e.g. polymorpho-nuclear leukocytosis in bacterial sepsis; eosinophilia in some parasitic infections. In other cases the abnormalities of cell number and morphology are due to a primary haematological disorder.

BLOOD PLASMA

Plasma amounts to greater than 50% of blood volume. While changes in the innumerable constituents of plasma are outside the scope of this text, consideration of certain major plasma proteins is necessary for an understanding of the pathology of some blood and systemic disorders. The plasma proteins which are components of the blood coagulation and fibrinolytic systems are considered first.

Blood coagulation

For normal homeostasis, blood must be fluid; however, the capacity to minimise loss of blood through breaches of the vascular system is essential. The rapid plugging of defects in small vessels is the function of platelets (primary haemostasis) but a more permanent and secure seal results from the generation of insoluble fibrillar fibrin from its soluble plasma protein precursor fibrinogen in the process of blood coagulation.

Failure of primary haemostasis, due to platelet disorders, or of coagulation due to clotting factor deficiency or presence of a coagulation inhibitor, can each result in life-threatening haemorrhage. In contrast, inappropriate activation of platelets or blood clotting may result in vascular occlusion, ischaemia and tissue death.

A complex system of activators and inhibitors in plasma has therefore evolved in order to allow localised clot formation at sites of injury but minimise the risk of undesirable clotting, that is thrombosis. These are the coagulation and fibrinolytic factors and their inhibitors.

Important features of the haemostatic mechanism include:

- The components interact in a biological amplification system.
- Thrombin is a key enzyme in coagulation because it acts in a feedback loop to activate several of the other coagulation factors and is therefore pivotal in the amplification system.

- Almost all of the coagulation factors and inhibitors are synthesised in the liver. Liver disease is therefore a cause of abnormal bleeding.
- Factors II, VII, IX, X, XI and XII are serine proteases, that is enzymes in which the presence of serine at the active site is necessary for their action in hydrolysing peptide bonds.
- Factors II, VII, IX and X require vitamin K for synthesis in their completed form. This is clinically important: vitamin K inhibitors known as coumarins are among the main anticoagulant drugs used in clinical practice; warfarin is an example.
- Many of the interactions involved in coagulation require assembly of the components on a surface, for example the generation of thrombin from prothrombin by activated factor X. In vivo, this surface is provided by platelet membranes which become reconfigured during platelet activation to promote the binding of coagulation factors.

Coagulation inhibitors limit unwanted clotting and protect against vessel occlusion, especially in veins:

- In common with clotting factors, the principal inhibitors are synthesised in the liver. Proteins C and S require vitamin K for their complete synthesis.
- Antithrombin acts at several sites to inhibit activated coagulation factors. Inhibition of the key coagulation enzymes thrombin and activated factor X are most important. Antithrombin requires glycosaminoglycan 'heparans', present on the vascular endothelial cell surface, for full inhibitory activity. In clinical practice the glycosaminoglycan heparin is a widely used antithrombotic which enhances the inhibitory activity of antithrombin several thousandfold.
- Protein C requires a co-factor, protein S, for full activity. When activated, protein C inhibits activated factors V and VIII.
- Protein C requires thrombin bound to an endothelial protein, thrombomodulin, for its activation. Thrombin therefore acts to promote fibrin formation but also has a crucial role as part of a negative feedback loop to inhibit clot formation.
- Another inhibitor, tissue factor pathway inhibitor, acts early in the process of coagulation activation.
- The fibrinolytic mechanism acts as a further check on uncontrolled clot formation. The enzyme plasmin rapidly digests fibrin.

Several components of the fibrinolytic system also originate in the liver; tissue plasminogen activator is, however, a product of vascular endothelial cells.

Although the scheme for the initial stages of coagulation activation can be conveniently divided into extrinsic and intrinsic pathways, this is a simplification. Coagulation activation in vivo is initiated through tissue factor, an integral cell membrane protein which is not expressed by vascular endothelial cells in an unstimulated state but is expressed by subendothelial cells and smooth muscle as well as other cells.

As soon as blood leaks from a vessel it is exposed to tissue factor. Tissue factor activates factor VII. The much slower pathway for fibrin generation through activation of factor XII on contact with subendothelial components is of minor importance. This explains the absence of any increased tendency to haemorrhage in subjects who are congenitally deficient in factor XII.

It is the tissue factor-activated factor VII complex which rapidly activates factors X and IX, leading to thrombin generation. When the procoagulant stimulus is sufficiently strong, the degree of amplification through thrombin activation of factors V and VII overcomes inhibition by activated protein C and fibrin generation proceeds.

The final step in clot formation is the stabilisation of fibrin by cross-linking through the activity of factor XIII. In the laboratory, the function of the components of the coagulation system can be assessed by the time required for clotting of recalcified plasma prepared from a blood sample anticoagulated with sodium citrate.

The citrate binds calcium ions, which are required at several points in the mechanism. Recalcification allows fibrin formation to take place. The two principal screening tests are:

- Activated partial thromboplastin time (APTT). In the APTT, the intrinsic pathway is activated by contact activation, for example by addition of kaolin (chalk powder, which provides a massive surface area for contact). Phospholipid is added to substitute for the role of platelets in coagulation. The APTT therefore involves all clotting factors other than factor VII and factor XIII.
- Prothrombin time (PT). In the PT, tissue factor ar phospholipid are added. The PT therefore assessi factors VII, V, X, II and fibrinogen only.

The pathology and consequences of deficiency of tl components of the coagulation and fibrinolytic system ai described anywhere else in this chapter.

Rheological considerations

Blood is a viscous fluid and changes in its physical proper ties accompany some diseases. The major determinant blood viscosity is the *haematocrit*. The plasma *fibrinogen* concentration is the major determinant of red cell aggregation and is second only to haematocrit as a factor in determination of blood viscosity. Other plasma protein molecules tend to be smaller and more symmetrical than fibrinogen and consequently have a much lesser effect on viscosity.

However, when they are present in increased concentrations, blood viscosity may be affected. This may result in *a hyperviscosity syndrome,* in which there is stasis within the microcirculation and tissue anoxia. Cerebral dysfunction, with headache, visual disturbance and drowsiness progressing to coma may result.

Very high plasma immunoglobulin concentration, which is a common feature of the malignant *disorders* multiple myeloma and macroglobulinaemia, is a common cause of the *hyperviscosity* syndrome. Numbers of leukocytes and platelets have little influence on blood flow in health. However, when leukocyte counts exceed $300 \times 10^9/1$, usually in *leukaemia*, flow may be adversely affected, resulting in clinical features similar to those described above.

The hyperviscosity syndrome represents an extreme abnormality of blood flow producing organ dysfunction. However, epidemiological studies suggest that even minor increases in blood viscosity, due to increased haematocrit or fibrinogen concentration, may result in a tendency to vascular occlusion, manifesting as an increased incidence of myocardial infarction and cerebral infarction.

The concentration of plasma fibrinogen is a risk factor for atherosclerosis and arterial thrombosis which is at least as potent as the level of serum cholesterol. The interplay between rheological and haemostatic changes in thrombotic disease is not yet fully understood.

Erythrocyte sedimentation rate

The erythrocyte sedimentation rate (ESR) measures the rate at which red cells sediment by gravity in plasma in 1 hour and is a widely used laboratory test. Increased aggregation and sedimentation occur in the presence of high concentrations of immunoglobulin and fibrinogen. As the latter is an acute phase reactant, the ESR is increased in a wide variety of inflammatory and neoplastic conditions.

It is an entirely non-specific test and a normal value for ESR can never be used to exclude the presence of significant disease. Direct measurement of plasma viscosity provides equally useful data and has replaced ESR measurement in some diagnostic laboratories.

HAEMOPOIESIS AND BLOOD CELL KINETICS

Haemopoiesis is the formation of blood cells.

Sites of Haemopoiesis

In the adult, all blood cells are produced in the red marrow, which is restricted to the bones of the axial skeletonvertebrae, ribs, sternum, skull, sacrum, pelvis and proximal femora. In these regions the bone marrow is composed of approximately 50% fat, within adipocytes, and 50% blood cells and their precursors.

The fatty marrow of other bones is capable of haemopoiesis when requirements for blood cells are increased in some diseases. In the infant and young child, practically all of the bones contain haemopoietically active marrow.

In fetal life, the liver and spleen are the major haemopoietic organs between about 6 weeks and 6-7 months gestation; the yolk sac is the main site before 6 weeks. In disease, the liver and spleen can again become haemopoietic organs, even in adult life; this development is referred to as *extramedullary haemopoiesis* and is particularly associated with the progressive fibrosis of bone marrow seen in the myeloproliferative disorders.

The bone marrow is examined histologically in two ways. Marrow can be aspirated through a needle inserted into a marrow cavity (usually sternum or pelvis), smeared on a slide and stained in a method similar to that for peripheral blood.

Further information, particularly on the structure and cellularity of the marrow, can be obtained by preparation of sections of a marrow trephine biopsy: this is a core of tissue obtained using a wide-bore needle.

Haemopoietic Stem Cells

Studies of bone marrow in culture lead to the conclusion that erythrocytes, leukocytes (including lymphocytes) and platelets are derived from a common, self-replicating precursor cell or 'pluripotential stem cell'. By a series of cell divisions, cells committed to each line are produced and further divisions result in mature cells-erythrocytes, granular leukocytes, megakaryocytes and T- and Blymphocytes.

The pluripotential stem cells possess the ability to renew, in addition to the capacity to differentiate. It is now clear that bone marrow also contains mesenchymal stem cells which can give rise to connective tissues such as fat cells, fibroblasts, bone and cartilage.

The development and preferential survival of a malignant clone of haemopoietic cells, derived from mutated bone marrow stem cells, explains the pathological features of the leukaemias and myelodysplastic syndromes.

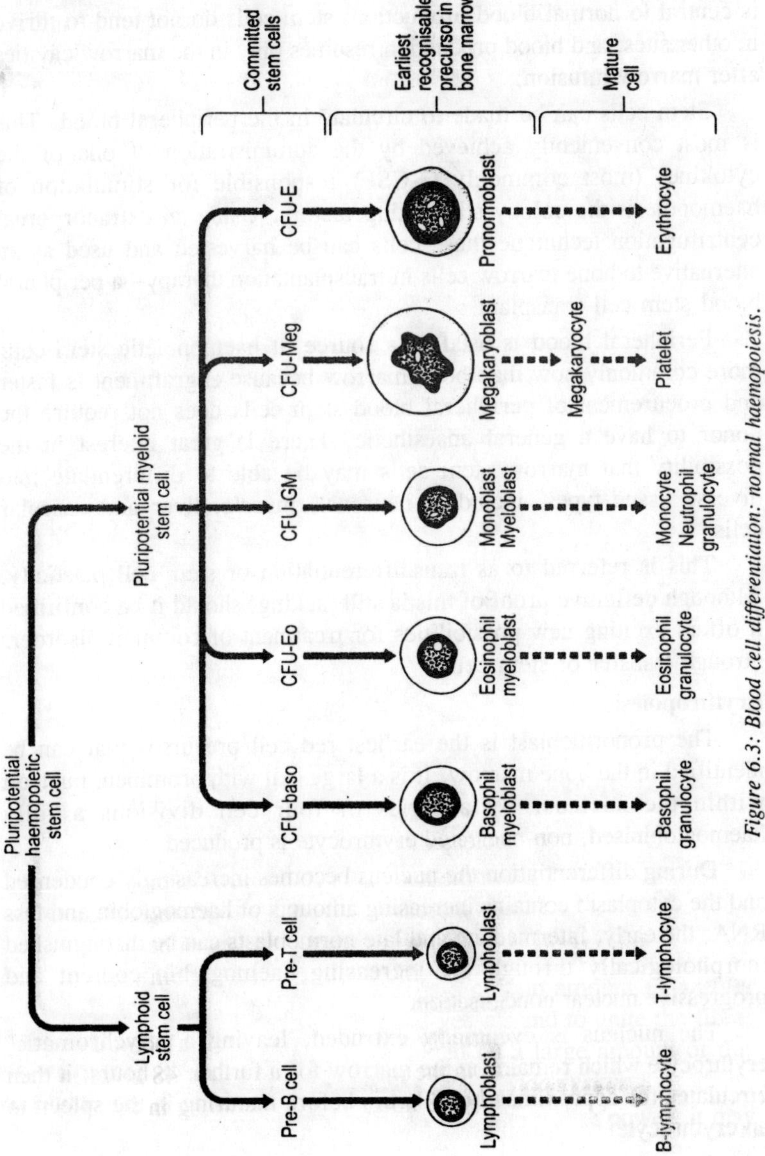

Figure 6.3: Blood cell differentiation: normal haemopoiesis.

If human bone marrow is infused intravenously into a subject without functioning marrow, as during bone marrow transplantation treatment, normal blood cell production returns after a period of several weeks. This finding confirms the presence of pluripotential stem cells in bone marrow and also indicates that the microenvironment of the bone marrow is central to normal blood production; stem cells do not tend to thrive in other sites, and blood production resumes only in the marrow cavities after marrow infusion.

Stem cells can be made to circulate in the peripheral blood. This is most conveniently achieved by the administration of one of the cytokines (most commonly G-CSF) responsible for stimulation of haemopoiesis-the colony stimulating factors. Using an extracorporeal centrifugation technique these cells can be harvested and used as an alternative to bone marrow cells in transplantation therapy—a peripheral blood stem cell transplant.

Peripheral blood is used as a source of haemopoietic stem cells more commonly now than bone marrow because engraftment is faster and procurement of peripheral blood stem cells does not require the donor to have a general anaesthetic. There is great interest in the possibility that marrow stem cells may be able to differentiate into diverse tissue types, including neuronal, muscle, liver and vascular cells.

This is referred to as transdifferentiation or stem cell plasticity. Although definitive proof of this is still lacking, should it be confirmed it offers exciting new possibilities for treatment of common disorders through transfer of stem cells.

Erythropoiesis

The pronormoblast is the earliest red cell precursor that can be identified in the bone marrow. It is a large cell with prominent nucleoli within the nucleus. By a series of four cell divisions a fully haemoglobinised, non-nucleated erythrocyte is produced.

During differentiation the nucleus becomes increasingly condensed and the cytoplasm contains increasing amounts of haemoglobin and less RNA; the early, intermediate and late normoblasts can be distinguished morphologically through the increasing haemoglobin content and progressive nuclear condensation.

The nucleus is eventually extruded, leaving a'polychromatic' erythrocyte which remains in the marrow for a further 48 hours; it then circulates for approximately 48 hours before maturing in the spleen to an erythrocyte.

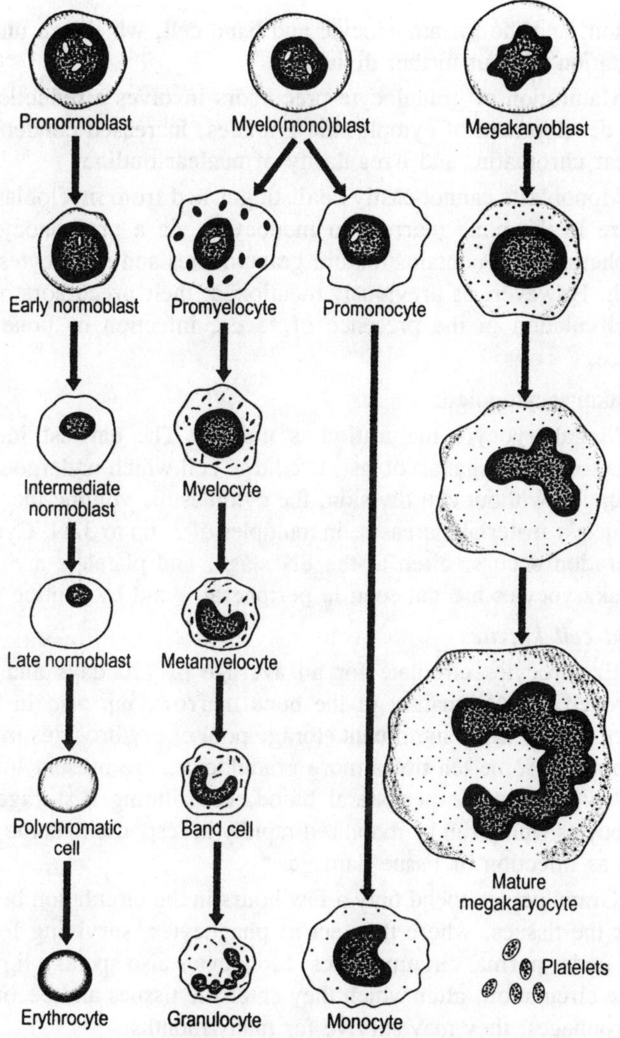

Figure 6.4: Haemopoiesis.

Only polychromatic erythrocytes and mature erythrocytes normally circulate. However, nucleated red cell precursors are present in the peripheral blood in the presence of some marrow disorders.

Leukopoiesis

The normal bone marrow contains many more myeloid than nucleated erythroid cells (around 5:1). In the granulocyte series these include the myeloblast, promyelocyte and myelocyte, which are capable of cell division, and the metamyelocyte and band cell, which are undergoing maturation without further division.

Maturation of granulocyte precursors involves a reduction in cell size, development of cytoplasmic granules, increased condensation of nuclear chromatin, and irregularity of nuclear outline.

Monoblasts cannot easily be distinguished from myeloblasts. They mature in the bone marrow to monocytes via a promonocyte stage. Peripheral blood contains mature granulocytes and monocytes only, in health. However, as previously mentioned, their precursors may enter the circulation in the presence of severe infection or bone marrow disease.

Megakaryocytopoiesis

Megakaryocyte maturation is unique. The earliest identifiable precursor, the megakaryoblast, is a large cell which undergoes nuclear replication without cell division, the cytoplasmic volume increasing as the nuclear material increases, in multiples of 2, up to 32N. Cytoplasmic maturation occurs, often at the 8N stage, and platelets are released. Megakaryocytes are not seen in peripheral blood by routine methods.

Blood cell kinetics

Erythrocytes circulate for an average of 120 days and are then destroyed, predominantly in the bone marrow, but also in liver and spleen. There is no significant storage pool of erythrocytes in humans. In contrast, some ten times more granulocytes are present in the bone marrow than in the peripheral blood, constituting a storage pool of leukocytes which can be mobilised rapidly in response to some stimulus, such as infection or tissue damage.

Granulocytes spend only a few hours in the circulation before they enter the tissues, where they act as phagocytes, surviving for several days under normal circumstances. Monocytes also spend a limited time in the circulation, after which they enter the tissues and become tissue macrophages; they may survive for many months.

Platelets circulate for approximately 10 days. The spleen acts as a reservoir of reserve platelets; some 30% are present in the spleen at any time.

Control of haemopoiesis

Peripheral blood cell counts are normally maintained within close limits. However, the ability of each cell line to respond appropriately to increased requirements is exemplified by the increased red cell production after haemorrhage, the granulocyte leukocytosis in response to sepsis and the enhanced platelet production which results from chronic bleeding.

Erythropoietin is a glycoprotein hormone, produced by the kidney, which increases erythropoietic activity. The production of erythropoietin is increased in response to a reduced oxygen tension in the blood reaching the kidney. It results in an increase in the number of cells committed to the erythroid line, reduced maturation time and early release of erythrocytes from the bone marrow.

Erythropoietin mediates the physiological response of the bone marrow to anaemia or hypoxia. In pathological states, failure of erythropoietin production is a major contributor to the anaemia of chronic renal failure and this can be corrected by erythropoietin administration; inappropriate excessive erythropoietin production results in polycythaemia secondary to some renal cysts and tumours.

Numerous growth factors have been found to govern production of leukocytes in the bone marrow. They are synthesised mainly by T-lymphocytes, monocytes/macrophages, endothelial cells and fibroblasts of the bone marrow stroma. Examples are interleukins 1, 3 and 6 and the *colony stimulating factors*. GM-CSF increases stem cell commitment to granulocyte and monocyte production, GCSF to granulocytes and M-CSF to monocytes.

Recombinant forms of some of these cytokines are now in therapeutic use, particularly in cancer chemotherapy, where the duration of drug-induced neutropenia can be limited by cytokine administration. *Thrombopoietin*, capable of the stimulation of platelet production, has recently been identified. It is synthesised principally in the liver. Its role in treatment of disease is not yet clear.

Haemoglobin

Structure, synthesis and metabolism

Some knowledge of haemoglobin structure and metabolism is necessary for an understanding of the pathology of the anaemias. Haemoglobin is the oxygen-carrying pigment. The haem group of haemoglobin is responsible for oxygen carriage and is composed of a protoporphyrin ring structure with an iron atom.

By 1 month of age red cell precursors synthesise predominantly haemoglobin A, composed of four haem groups and four polypeptide (globin) chains, of which two molecular forms are present: α and β chains. Haemoglobin A thus has the structure $\alpha_2\beta_2$. Up to 2.5% of the haemoglobin in adults has δ chains ($\alpha_2\delta_2$)-haemoglobin A_2; and up to 1%

of the haemoglobin in adults has γ chains ($\alpha_2\gamma_2$)-haemoglobin E Adult blood therefore has predominantly haemoglobin A with some A_2 and F.

In later fetal and early neonatal life haemoglobin F predominates. In early fetal life three other haemoglobins are present: Gower 1, Gower 2 and Portland.

Table 6.3: Human haemoglobins.

Type	*Chains*	*Nomenclature*	
Adults	$\alpha_2\beta_2$	A	
	$\alpha_2\delta_2$	A_2	
Fetal	$\alpha_2\gamma_2$	F	
Embryonic	$\alpha_2\varepsilon_2$	'Gower 2'	Present in early fetal life only
	$\zeta_2\varepsilon_2$	'Gower 1'	
	$\zeta_2\gamma_2$	Portland	

The whole haemoglobin molecule is thus composed of a tetramer of globin chains, each with a haem group. The complex structure of the molecule is responsible for its oxygen (O_2) binding characteristics, the globin chains moving against each other during transfer of O_2. The affinity of the haemoglobin molecule for O_2 is also controlled by its ability to bind the metabolite 2,3-diphosphoglycerate (2,3DPG).

When 2,3-DPG enters the haemoglobin molecule as the β chains pull apart during release of O_2, the affinity for O_2 of the haemoglobin-2,3-DPG complex is reduced, allowing O_2 to be given up more readily. Haemoglobin F cannot bind 2,3-DPG and thus has a relatively high O_2 affinity, facilitating O_2 transfer from maternal blood across the placenta.

At the end of the erythrocyte life-span haemoglobin is metabolised, with conservation of iron and amino acids. Iron is carried by plasma transferrin to the bone marrow and utilised in the synthesis of haem. Globin is degraded to its constituent amino acids, which enter the general pool. Liver, gut and kidneys are all involved in excretion of products of haem breakdown as derivatives of bilirubin.

In the congenital disorders collectively known as *haemoglobinopathies,* the rate of synthesis of one globin chain type is defective (the *thalassaemias)* or an abnormal chain is synthesised (the *sickle haemoglobinopathies* and other haemoglobin variants).

Functions of the Blood

From a consideration of the preceding sections the functions of blood and the major pathological consequences of blood and marrow disease will be apparent.

Oxygen transport is the primary function of the red blood cells. Failure of red cell production, or loss or dysfunction thereof, results in tissue hypoxia affecting the metabolism of all organs.

The cells responsible for host defence against infection are carried, in the blood, from the bone marrow to sites of infection. Infections with bacteria, viruses and fungi are the predictable results of a failure to produce normal leukocytes in adequate numbers.

The primary haemostatic and coagulation mechanisms allow the transport functions of blood to operate without risk of exsanguination from breaches of the vascular compartment. Failure of these leads to spontaneous haemorrhage, whereas a defect in the control mechanisms can result in thrombosis and vascular occlusion.

The diseases which interfere with the function of the blood and their pathological consequences are now described.

ANAEMIAS

Anaemia is present when the haemoglobin falls below around 13.0 g/dl in a male or 11.5 g/dl in a female. The different lower limits of normal haemoglobin concentration for neonates, infants and children should be noted.

The consequences of anaemia are dependent upon the speed of onset. Thus the rapid loss of 10% or more of the circulating blood volume through haemorrhage will result in shock, that is the failure of adequate perfusion of all tissues and organs, with consequent hypoxia.

In this situation the subject may not initially be anaemic, as both red cells and plasma are lost through haemorrhage. The plasma component is more rapidly replaced, however, and anaemia will be present after several hours have elapsed.

Anaemia which develops more gradually is better tolerated. A haemoglobin concentration as low as 2 g/dl may be consistent with survival if it develops over a protracted period. The inevitable result of anaemia, however, is a reduction in the oxygen-carrying capacity of the blood and thus chronic tissue hypoxia.

The general consequences of anaemia are due to the tissue hypoxia, which can result in fatty change, especially in the myocardium and liver, and even infarction. Lethargy and increased breathlessness on exertion are typical clinical features. Breathlessness at rest implies the development of heart failure, a result of severe anaemia.

Expansion of the red marrow is present in those anaemias where a marrow response is possible-generally the haemolytic anaemias. Other features are specific to anaemias resulting from a particular mechanism, such as the jaundice of haemolytic anaemias, or are specific to anaemia of a particular type, such as the nail changes of iron deficiency anaemia. Such pathological features are described in the relevant sections.

A low haemoglobin concentration usually reflects a reduction in the body red cell mass. An important exception is pregnancy, when both red cell mass and plasma volume increase, but the latter to a greater degree. This process results in a haemoglobin concentration in blood which is lower than in the non-pregnant state in the presence of a relatively increased red cell mass and overall oxygencarrying capacity; this condition is often referred to as the physiological 'anaemia' of pregnancy.

The increased red cell mass during pregnancy is necessary to support the increased metabolic requirement of the mother and fetus. The reason for the expansion of the plasma compartment is obscure, but it may be explained in part by a need for increased skin perfusion for heat loss due to the increased metabolic rate.

Expansion of the plasma volume, resulting in dilutional anaemia, may also occur when the spleen is pathologically enlarged. (The spleen appears to exert a controlling influence on plasma volume.) Other mechanisms also operate in this situation, however, as described under hypersplenism.

Classification

Table elsewhere in this chapter outlines a classification of anaemias. Anaemias are divided into two categories: those where anaemia is due to failure to produce erythrocytes, and those in which erythrocyte loss is increased but production is normal (or usually increased, in response to the anaemia). While useful, this categorisation is an oversimplification, as both mechanisms are present in some anaemias.

Thus, in the megaloblastic states, cell production is defective due to lack of vitamin B_{12} or folic acid for nucleic acid synthesis but, in addition, the erythrocytes which are produced are abnormal and of diminished survival. In thalassaemia, cell production is not optimal due to abnormal haemoglobin synthesis, and there is also increased erythrocyte destruction.

The myeloid and megakaryocytic lines are also involved in some anaemias due to failure of haemopoiesis (megaloblastic anaemia, hypoplastic anaemia) but not others (iron deficiency anaemia).

Despite these qualifications, the classification described is useful as an aid to determining the cause of the anaemia.

Table 6.4: A classification of anaemias.

Type	*Cause*
Production failure anaemia	
Haematinic deficiency	Insufficiency of iron, vitamin B_{12} or folic acid
Anaemia of chronic disorders	Infection, inflammation and neoplasia
Dyserythropoiesis	Sideroblastic anaemia 'Refractory' anaemias
Hypoplasia	
Marrow infiltration	Leukaemias Myeloproliferative states Non-haematological malignancies Miscellaneous infiltrates
Increased red cell loss, lysis or pooling	
Acute blood loss	
Haemolysis due to red cell abnormality	Membrane defects, e.g. hereditary spherocytosis Enzyme defects, e.g. pyruvate kinase deficiency Haemoglobinopathies, e.g. thalassaemia, sickle disorders Paroxysmal nocturnal haemoglobinuria
Haemolysis due to abnormality outside the red cell	Immune haemolytic anaemias Microangiopathic haemolysis Drugs, toxins and chemicals Parasites
Hypersplenism	

Production Failure Anaemias

The most commonly encountered anaemias are in the production failure group.

Haematinic deficiency

Haematinics are dietary factors essential for either haemoglobin synthesis or erythrocyte production.

Iron deficiency

Iron deficiency is the commonest cause of anaemia worldwide. It is also the commonest cause of a microcytic hypochromic blood picture, the others being thalassaemias and (rarely) sideroblastic anaemias.

Iron metabolism

Iron is an essential requirement. It is also one of the commonest elements present in the earth's crust. Excessive iron deposited in the tissues is, however, toxic, causing damage to the myocardium, pancreas and liver in particular.

As the body has no active method for iron excretion, iron status is controlled largely by its absorption; the capacity to absorb iron is, however, limited and any tendency to increased loss of iron, due to haemorrhage, is highly likely to result in a negative iron balance and iron deficiency.

These factors explain the high prevalence of iron deficiency. Normally, at least 60% of the body iron is in the haemoglobin of erythroid cells. Approximately 30% is stored within the reticulo-endothelial system, especially in the bone marrow, as *ferritin* and *haemosiderin*. A small proportion of total body iron is present in other tissues, especially muscle and iron-containing enzymes.

This tissue iron is relatively conserved during states of iron deficiency. Only a small fraction of the total body iron is in transport, attached to the carrier protein *transferrin*. Ferritin is a protein-iron complex. The protein, apoferritin, is a shell made up of 22 subunits. The core is composed of ferric oxyhydride.

Haemosiderin consists of partially degraded ferritin aggregates. Ferritin is present in all tissues, but especially in the macrophages of the bone marrow and spleen and in hepatocytes. A small amount is detectable in plasma and, as it is derived from the storage pool of body iron, its concentration is an accurate indicator of body iron stores. Low serum ferritin concentration is a useful confirmatory test for iron deficiency, therefore.

However, because ferritin is an acute phase response protein, the concentration in plasma is not a reliable guide to body iron stores in the presence of infection, inflammation and neoplasia. In those situations serum ferritin may be normal or high despite tissue iron depletion.

Ferritin is water-soluble and not visible by light microscopy; haemosiderin is insoluble and forms yellow granules. When exposed to potassium ferrocyanide (Perls' stain) the granules are blue-black. Examination of aspirated bone marrow stained with Perls' stain can therefore be used to assess body iron stores reliably.

When iron stores are normal, haemosiderin is visible, mainly in the reticulo-endothelial cells of the bone marrow. In iron overload, most of the iron is in the form of haemosiderin and can be easily identified.

Transferrin is an iron-binding β-globulin responsible for iron transport and delivery to receptors on immature erythroid cells. Each molecule of transferrin can bind two atoms of iron, but normally the transferrin is only one-third saturated (thus the serum iron concentration is normally one-third of the total serum iron-binding capacity). Transferrin is reutilised after delivering its iron.

In order to maintain iron balance, sufficient iron must be absorbed to replace that lost from the urinary and gastrointestinal tracts as shed cells and in sweat, together with any extra requirements.

Daily iron requirements are:

- adult male 1.0 mg
- child 1.5 mg
- pregnant female 1.5-3.0 mg
- menstruating female 2.0 mg.

Thus, requirements vary with circumstances, extra iron being required for growth during childhood, for the fetus and placenta and expansion of maternal red cell mass during pregnancy, and to compensate for menstrual loss of women of child-bearing age.

As a Western diet contains only 10-20 mg of iron per day and only a maximum of one-third of this can be absorbed, excess losses of iron of just a few milligrams will inevitably result in negative iron balance and eventual depletion of iron stores. One millilitre of blood contains 0.5 mg iron.

Thus, loss of 10 ml of blood daily will inevitably exceed the capacity to absorb sufficient iron, even from a good diet. This explains the finding of some degree of iron depletion in 25% or more menstruating women. Iron absorption takes place in the duodenum and upper jejunum. Haem iron is present in meat and readily absorbed, with little effect from other dietary components.

Inorganic iron in vegetables and cereals is mostly trivalent and may be complexed to amino acids and organic acids, from which it must be released and reduced to the divalent state for absorption. HCl produced by the stomach and ascorbic acid in food favour its absorption. In contrast, phosphates and phytates in some foods form precipitates and prevent absorption.

Mechanisms controlling the rate of iron absorption are incompletely understood. Major influences are the total body iron stores and rate of erythropoiesis. Thus, if iron stores are replete a smaller proportion of available iron is absorbed; when erythropoiesis is more active, due to premature red cell destruction for example, extra iron is absorbed even though total stores may be high.

This is a feature in thalassaemia, and iron overload may ensue. At the cellular level some control is exerted at the brush border of the mucosal cell by an unknown mechanism. In addition, excess iron entering the cell is not absorbed but becomes bound to apoferritin and remains within the mucosal cell as ferritin, being subsequently shed with the cell into the gut lumen when the tip of the villus is reached.

Mechanisms of iron deficiency

In developed countries, iron deficiency in the nonmenstruating and non-pregnant adult most frequently results from chronic blood loss, often from the gastro-intestinal tract. As it is possible to lose several millilitres of blood daily into the gut lumen without marked change in appearance of the stool, such blood loss is frequently occult.

Iron deficiency anaemia is thus commonly a presenting feature of lesions within the gastrointestinal tract. In clinical practice, when iron deficiency anaemia occurs in the face of a reasonable diet and no excessive menstrual loss it is mandatory to perform a careful assessment of the gastrointestinal tract.

Causes of iron deficiency are:

- chronic blood loss (e.g. peptic ulcer; carcinoma of stomach, caecum, colon or rectum; menorrhagia)
- increased requirements (e.g. in childhood and pregnancy)
- malabsorption (due to gastrectomy, coeliac disease)
- malnutrition.

More than one factor may operate. Thus a poor-quality vegetarian diet is highly likely to result in iron deficiency in a menstruating female. In a male or post-menopausal female, failure to ingest or absorb any iron would result in complete depletion of iron stores only after 3 or more years (1 mg/day).

Malnutrition or malabsorption is thus rarely the sole cause of iron deficiency, although it may be an important contributory factor. The microcytic hypochromic anaemia is a late stage in iron deficiency; it does not occur until iron stores are severely depleted. The microcyte results from an extra cell division, in addition to the normal four, during red cell production.

Increasing cytoplasmic haemoglobin concentration normally acts as an inhibitor of normoblast division. The failure of haemoglobin synthesis which results from iron deficiency therefore allows extra mitoses to occur, with the production of small erythrocytes.

The same mechanism is responsible for the microcytes in thalassaemia, another disorder of haemoglobin synthesis.

Blood and bone marrow changes

The typical blood picture is one of microcytic, hypochromic red cells, with increased anisocytosis and poikilocytosis; elongated 'pencil' or 'cigar' cells are typically present. The proportion of polychromatic cells (or reticulocytes) is low for the degree of anaemia, indicating an inability of the bone marrow to respond due to lack of iron for haemoglobin synthesis.

The platelet count is often raised, especially if chronic bleeding is present. The leukocytes are typically normal. Occasionally, a mixture of microcytic, hypochromic erythrocytes and macrocytic cells is seen. This is termed a dimorphic picture and occurs in mixed deficiency of iron and folic acid or vitamin B_{12}. The MCV and MCH may be misleadingly normal.

A mixture of microcytic, hypochromic cells and normocytes is present in iron deficiency responding to iron replacement or after transfusion of a subject with iron deficiency anaemia (Fig. 23.16). In the former circumstance, mildly increased polychromasia (and reticulocytosis) may be present.

Abnormalities are also present in the bone marrow. The nucleated red cell precursors are small in diameter and the cytoplasm is frequently ragged-micronormoblastic erythropoiesis. Staining for haemosiderin (Perls' stain) reveals its absence from macrophages and normoblasts.

Important biochemical changes in the blood are a fall in serum iron and increase in total iron-binding capacity (representing a compensatory increased transferrin concentration). Saturation of iron-binding capacity is thus reduced to 10% or less, from the normal 33%.

The serum ferritin is generally markedly reduced, corresponding to severely depleted body iron content. This situation contrasts with the anaemia associated with chronic inflammatory disease or neoplasia ('anaemia of chronic disorders'), where red cells are often normocytic but may be mildly microcytic.

The serum iron may also be low but this is misleading as iron stores are normal. In contrast to iron deficiency, total iron-binding capacity is usually reduced in anaemia of chronic disorders, and serum ferritin is often raised due to the presence of inflammation or malignancy.

Changes in other organs and tissues

In addition to the manifestations of chronic anaemia, a variety of epithelial changes may be present in chronic iron deficiency:

- angular cheilitis

- gastric achlorhydria
- atrophic glossitis
- brittle nails
- oesophageal web
- koilonychia.

The cause is unknown. Angular cheilitis, painful fissuring of the mouth corners, is common but not specific: it occurs in dental malocclusion, most often due to poorly fitting dentures. Smooth tongue is also common. Gastric achlorhydria appears to be an occasional result, as well as a contributory cause, of iron deficiency.

Dysphagia (difficulty in swallowing) due to the presence of a web or fold of mucosa in the post-cricoid region is an uncommon association of iron deficiency. The combination has been termed Paterson-Kelly or Plummer-Vinson syndrome and is important mainly because the mucosal abnormality is premalignant, carcinoma occasionally developing at the site.

Koilonychia (spoon-shaped nails) of chronic tissue iron depletion is typical but only rarely seen. The pathological changes of iron deficiency are reversed by adequate replacement therapy by the oral route.

Vitamin B_{12} and Folate Deficiency

Vitamin B_{12} and folic acid are essential co-factors for blood cell production. Deficiency of either results in macrocytic anaemia with characteristic pathological appearances in the bone marrow described as *megaloblastic haemopoiesis*.

Megaloblastic anaemias are common, being second in incidence only to iron deficiency and the so-called anaemia of chronic disorders among production failure anaemias. Some other disorders may be associated with macrocytosis but megaloblastic haemopoiesis is most commonly due to deficiency of vitamin B_{12} or folate.

Vitamin B_{12} Deficiency

Vitamin B_{12} metabolism

Vitamin B_{72} is necessary for DNA synthesis. Deoxyadenosylcobalamin is the main form of vitamin B_{12} in tissues and methylcobalamin is the main form in plasma. These forms differ only in the type of chemical group (deoxyadenosylor methyl-) attached to the cobalt atom which is located at the centre of a corrin ring, to which a nucleotide portion is attached. (The corrin ring is similar to the porphyrin ring of haem.) The vitamin is known to be a coenzyme in the methylation of homocysteine to methionine and also in conversion of methylmalonyl

CoA to succinyl CoA. During the former reaction, methylcobalamin loses its methyl group and this is replaced from methyltetrahydrofolic acid, the principal form of folic acid in plasma.

The tetrahydrofolic acid is essential for the generation of deoxythymidine monophosphate, a precursor of DNA. Metabolism of vitamin B_{12} and of folate are thus closely related and essential for nucleic acid production. Vitamin B_{12} is present in foods of animal origin. It cannot be synthesised by higher animals but is produced by micro-organisms. Animals obtain the vitamin from bacterially contaminated foods.

Cereals, fruit and vegetable foods contain no vitamin B_{12} unless they have undergone bacterial contamination. Milk and eggs contain sufficient vitamin B_{12} for human needs (1-2 mg daily) and thus dietary deficiency can occur only if a strictly vegetarian (vegan) diet is consumed. Nutritional vitamin B_{12} deficiency (in contrast to dietary folate deficiency) is thus rarely encountered.

Vitamin B_{12} released from food in the stomach becomes bound to a glycoprotein produced by gastric parietal cells—*intrinsic factor*. The complex of cobalamin and intrinsic factor binds to receptors on the mucosal cells of the terminal ileum, where vitamin B_{12} is absorbed and intrinsic factor remains in the lumen of the bowel. In the absence of intrinsic factor, cobalamin cannot be absorbed.

Vitamin B_{12} is transported to the tissues attached to a plasma-binding protein-transcobalamin II. Another transcobalamin (transcobalamin

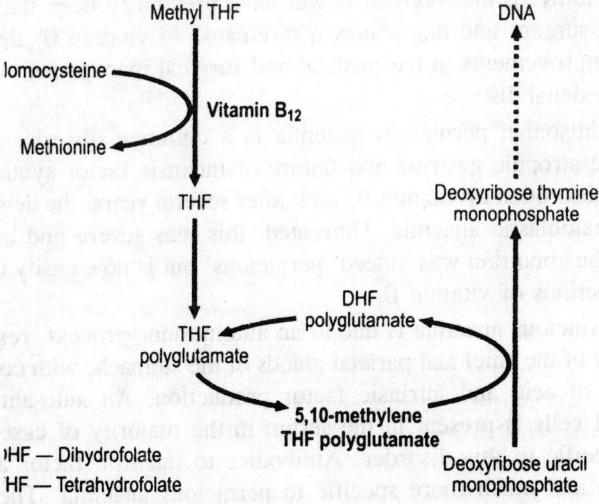

Figure 6.5: The roles of vitamin B_{12} and folate in DNA synthesis.

I), synthesised by neutrophil granulocytes, binds the greater proportion of plasma vitamin B_{12} but does not liberate it efficiently. The function of transcobalamin I-bound vitamin B_{12} is unknown.

Body stores of vitamin B_{12} amount only to some 2-3 mg. However, only 1.sg daily is required for normal DNA synthesis. Several years must therefore have elapsed before a deficiency state develops, even in the absence of absorption of the vitamin. Twenty micrograms or more per day is available in a mixed diet.

Mechanisms of vitamin B_{12} deficiency

Causes of vitamin B_{12} deficiency are:

- pernicious anaemia due to lack of intrinsic factor
- gastrectomy resulting in lack of intrinsic factor
- congenital due to lack of intrinsic factor
- blind-loop syndrome due to bacterial overgrowth competing for vitamin B_{12}
- ileal resection resulting in lack of absorption site
- Crohn's disease resulting in lack of absorption site
- tropical sprue
- malnutrition (e.g. dietary deficiency of vitamin B_{12} in veganism).

Addisonian pernicious anaemia accounts for by far the most cases of megaloblastic anaemia due to deficiency of vitamin B_{12}. Other causes are uncommon. Some cases occur after gastric resection, usually total gastrectomy. Blind loops of bowel have previously been the result of gastric surgery and this is now a rare cause of vitamin B_{12} deficiency, with improvements in the medical and surgical management of gastric and duodenal disease.

Addisonian pernicious anaemia is a common disorder in which chronic atrophic gastritis and failure of intrinsic factor synthesis lead to malabsorption of vitamin B_{12} and, after several years, the development of megaloblastic anaemia. Untreated, this was severe and eventually fatal; the condition was indeed 'pernicious' but is now easily corrected by injections of vitamin B_{12}.

Pernicious anaemia is due to an autoimmune process, resulting in atrophy of the chief and parietal glands of the stomach, with consequent failure of acid and intrinsic factor production. An auto-antibody to parietal cells is present in the serum in the majority of cases, but is not specific to this disorder. Antibodies to intrinsic factor are often present and much more specific to pernicious anaemia. These latter antibodies are of two types: one inhibits binding of vitamin B_{12} to intrinsic factor, and the second inhibits binding to ileal receptors.

The disease is rather more common in females and rarely presents before 30 years of age, although an uncommon childhood form is occasionally seen. The patient may have another autoimmune disorder such as thyroid disease or vitiligo. There is an association with blue eyes and premature greying of hair.

Blood and bone marrow changes

In contrast to iron deficiency, the defect in DNA synthesis affects all cell lines, and pancytopenia is frequently present. The MCV is high, and oval macrocytes are visible on the blood film. In megaloblastic anaemia, a reduction in the number of mitoses during red cell development, due to impaired DNA synthesis with normal RNA and protein synthesis, results in the production of macrocytes.

The degree of polychromasia on the blood film is not appropriate to the severity of anaemia, because the marrow is unable to respond. A proportion of neutrophil leukocytes have exaggerated lobulation of the nucleus and are often large (neutrophil hypersegmentation). Rarely, the blood picture is leukoerythroblastic.

The bone marrow is hypercellular and the stained smears reveal the characteristic megaloblastic change of the developing red cells: the red cells are larger than normal at each stage of development; nuclear chromatin has a very open appearance, with little condensation, and nuclear development lags behind that of the cytoplasm; thus well-haemoglobinised cells with an immature nucleus are a feature.

Multilobed *polymorphonuclear* leukocytes may be seen, as well as particularly large metamyelocytes and band cells. Megakaryocytes may also appear abnormal. Biochemical abnormalities detectable in the serum include unconjugated *hyperbilirubinaemia* and increased concentration of lactic dehydrogenase.

These changes are due to increased cell breakdown within the marrow, called ineffective erythropoiesis, and the premature removal of macrocytes, in the reticulo-endothelial system. The serum concentration of vitamin B_{12} is reduced.

Changes in other organs and tissues

Lesions of the nervous system are a frequent feature of vitamin B_{12} deficiency from any cause. Myelin degeneration of the posterior and lateral columns of the spinal cord is typical and often associated with a peripheral neuropathy affecting sensory neurones. This *subacute combined degeneration of the cord* causes spasticity, reduced coordination and impaired sensation in the lower limbs and may be present despite normal haemoglobin levels, although the megaloblastic erythropoiesis is always detectable.

Conversely, extreme megaloblastic change and profound pancytopenia may be present without evidence of damage to the nervous system from vitamin B_{12} deficiency. Optic atrophy and cerebral changes resulting in psychiatric disease are less common accompaniments of deficiency of vitamin B_{12}. The cause may be failure of synthesis of S-adenosyl methionine necessary for myelin formation.

Deficiency of folate is *not generally* associated with the neurological features seen in cobalamin deficiency, although psychiatric abnormalities may occur.

Mucosal abnormalities may be present. Atrophic glossitis is a common feature. In pernicious anaemia there is atrophy of the glands of the gastric body affecting chief cells and parietal cells; there is replacement by mucus-secreting goblet cells. The intestinal epithelial cells are often larger than normal, reflecting megaloblastic change akin to that in the bone marrow.

In addition to the above, changes may be present in the heart and elsewhere due to the chronic hypoxia of severe anaemia. Cardiomyopathy is a particularly important feature; transfusion is tolerated badly due to volume overload and may result in fatal cardiac failure.

The clinical features of B_{12} deficiency are explained by the pathology, although it is unusual for all features to be present together:

- lethargy, breathlessness and cardiac failure due to megaloblastic erythropoiesis with anaemia
- bruising and mucosal haemorrhage due to thrombocytopenia in severe cases
- weight loss due to malabsorption resulting from mucosal changes
- sore mouth due to mucosal changes
- sensory impairment in the feet, altered gait, visual disturbance and dementia due to demyelination and axonal degeneration.

Treatment is by parenteral (intramuscular) administration of vitamin B_{12}. Oral replacement is ineffective in pernicious anaemia due to the deficiency of intrinsic factor.

The haematological abnormalities are completely reversed by vitamin B_{12} replacement; however, the neuropathology and associated clinical features may only be partly corrected. The gastric atrophy and achlorhydria are primary features in pernicious anaemia, not secondary to the deficiency state, and as such do not reverse on treatment of the deficiency.

There is a life-long slightly increased risk of carcinoma of the stomach. The haematological response is manifested by marked increase in the reticulocyte count from 2-3 days after administration of vitamin B_{72} and maximal at 7 days; the rise is proportional to the severity of the anaemia.

White cell and platelet count recover within several days and haemoglobin increases at about 1 g/dl each week, with an accompanying fall in the MCV to normal values. Erythropoiesis is already normoblastic within 48 hours of starting replacement therapy.

Folic acid Deficiency

Deficiency of folic (pteroylglutamic) acid, the parent compound of folates, causes a macrocytic anaemia with megaloblastic haemopoiesis identical to that resulting from deficiency of cobalamin.

Folate metabolism

Folates are required for DNA synthesis. Folate polyglutamates (pteroylglutamic acid with extra glutamic acid residues) are the main intracellular forms. However, all dietary folates are metabolised to the monoglutamate methyltetrahydrofolate during absorption from the gut and are transported in this form.

Folates are necessary for single carbon unit transfer reactions in amino acid interconversions, in purine synthesis and, crucially, in the thymidylate synthetase reaction. Humans cannot synthesise folates de novo. Vegetables and fruits are especially rich in folates as polyglutamate conjugates, but most foods contain some folate.

Absorption occurs in the proximal jejunum. Dietary polyglutamates are, however, very sensitive to heat, and cooking can markedly deplete foods of their available folate. Body stores of folate, mainly in the liver, are modest, amounting to some 10 mg. As up to 200 .tg is required daily, a deficiency state can develop within weeks, in contrast to deficiency of vitamin B_{12}.

Furthermore, folate requirements are markedly increased in pregnancy and in some diseases associated with increased cell turnover, such as chronic haemolysis.

Mechanisms of folic acid deficiency

Causes of folate deficiency are:

- malnutrition (e.g. poor diet, overcooking of food, alcoholism)

- malabsorption (e.g. coeliac disease, tropical sprue, Crohn's disease)
- increased requirements (e.g. pregnancy and lactation, haemolytic anaemias, myelofibrosis, malignancy, extensive psoriasis or dermatitis)
- drugs (e.g. anti-convulsants).

Whereas malnutrition is an unusual cause of deficiency of vitamin B12, it is the most common mechanism of folate deficiency. It is most prevalent in the elderly. Overcooking of food and lack of fresh foods contribute.

During pregnancy, folate and iron deficiency may occur if no supplements are given. In contrast, vitamin B_{12} deficiency is almost unknown, as fertility is impaired in vitamin B_{12} deficiency and the commonest cause, pernicious anaemia, is a disease of late middle age and after.

In some disorders the folate deficiency is likely to be multifactorial, as in malignant disease, where lack of appetite with resultant malnutrition may aggravate folate deficiency secondary to increased utilisation of folate by the malignant tissues.

Phenytoin and phenobarbital used long-term as anticonvulsants probably impair folate absorption and may interfere with folate metabolism.

Some anti-cancer drugs act as folic acid antagonists. Methotrexate inhibits the enzyme dihydrofolate reductase, thus depleting tetrahydrofolate. The antimalarial pyrimethamine acts similarly. Trimethoprim acts as a folate inhibitor in bacteria but is ineffective as an inhibitor in humans.

Blood and bone marrow

In folic acid deficiency, blood and bone marrow changes are indistinguishable from those in vitamin B_{12} deficiency. The concentration of folic acid in serum and erythrocytes (red cell folate) is reduced.

Oral folic acid supplements result in a complete reversal of the pathological features. Even in malabsorption states, sufficient folate can be absorbed from pharmacological doses. The time course of the response is identical to that in vitamin B_{12} deficiency. Contrasting features of vitamin B_{12} and folate deficiency are listed in Table elsewhere in this chapter.

Megaloblastic anaemia is the result of deficiency of vitamin B_{12} or folate in the vast majority of instances. However, other causes include drugs and congenital defects. Prolonged anaesthesia with N_2O causes inactivation of vitamin B_{12} by oxidising the cobalt moiety and has resulted in pancytopenia with megaloblastic erythropoiesis.

Cases of congenital deficiency of enzymes involved in cobalamin or folate metabolism or purine or pyrimidine synthesis are extremely rare. However, several anti-neoplastic drugs act by inhibition of synthesis of purine or pyrimidine (hydroxyurea, cytosine arabinoside) and can cause a reversible marrow pathology similar to megaloblastic haemopoiesis.

Anaemia of Chronic Disorders

Anaemia of chronic disorders is one of the most common anaemias. It is found in association with a range of chronic inflammatory diseases, especially connective tissue disorders, chronic infections such as osteomyelitis or tuberculosis, and malignancies such as carcinoma and lymphoma.

Anaemia is not severe; the haemoglobin concentration is 8 g/dl or greater and the red cells are normocytic and normochromic. A degree of microcytosis and hypochromia may be present, but never to the degree seen in iron deficiency. Bone marrow iron is plentiful. If the underlying chronic disorder remits, the anaemia resolves.

It may also respond to pharmacological doses of erythropoietin. The disorder may represent a cytokine-induced failure of transfer of iron from reticulo-endothelial cells to normoblasts. It has been shown that some cytokines, such as tumour necrosis factor (TNF) can induce apoptosis of erythroblasts. Indeed, treatment of rheumatoid disease with anti-TNF leads to improvement in anaemia.

This type of anaemia occurs in disorders frequently associated with other types of anaemia, resulting in a complicated picture. For example, in rheumatoid arthritis iron deficiency often accompanies anaemia of chronic disorders due to the gastric irritation and bleeding caused by anti-inflammatory medications. There may be folate deficiency due to poor diet, and hypersplenism and immune haemolytic anaemia may also be present.

Dyserythropoietic Anaemias

The term dyserythropoietic anaemias is used to describe some incompletely understood disorders where anaemia is at least in part due to production failure, but haematinic deficiency is not present and marrow cellularity is normal or increased.

There are prominent morphological abnormalities of bone marrow cells, often affecting erythroid, myeloid and megakaryocytic cell lines.

Table 6.5: Comparison of features of vitamin B_{12} and folic acid deficiency states.

Feature	*Cobalamin (vitamin B_{12}) deficiency*	*Folate deficiency*
Nutritional deficiency	Uncommon	Common
Onset	Slow (years)	More rapid (weeks)
Revealed by increased demands	Never	Frequently
Absorption	In terminal ileum as a complex with intrinsic factor. Gastric and terminal ileal (e.g. autoimmune gastritis, Crohn's disease) may cause deficiency	In jejunum. Jejunal disease (e.g. coeliac disease) may cause deficiency disease
Drug-related	Never	May be due to anti-convulsant therapy. Anti-metabolites induce a similar deficiency
Spinal cord and peripheral nerve degeneration	Frequent	None

Most of these conditions are described in the section on Myelodysplastic Syndromes.

Sideroblastic Anaemias

The term sideroblastic anaemias describes a rather diverse and uncommon group of anaemias in which a defect of haem synthesis is present and a characteristic cell is seen in the bone marrow-the *ring sideroblast.*

This cell is a nucleated red cell precursor which has granules of haemosiderin within mitochondria surrounding the nucleus, visible on staining with Perls' reagent. Causes include:

- refractory anaemia with ring sideroblasts (RARS) in the middle-aged or elderly due to somatic mutation/clonal abnormality of erythroid cells
- secondary in patients with a bone marrow malignancy (e.g. myeloma, myeloid leukaemia, etc.)
- those due to drugs and toxins (e.g. vitamin B_6 antagonism by isoniazid; lead poisoning which inhibits synthesis of haem; alcoholism)
- hereditary due to enzyme defect in haem synthesis.

Although deficiency of vitamin B_6 (pyridoxine) causes a similar anaemia in animals, it is never the cause in humans. However, vitamin B_6 antagonism can result from antituberculous therapy, and other sideroblastic anaemias occassionally respond partially to pharmacological doses of vitamin B_{12}.

RARS is a primary acquired sideroblastic anaemia which is classified among the myelodysplastic syndromes. These are neoplastic disorders of bone marrow in which dyserythropoiesis is prominent. They are described anywhere else in this chapter.

Hypoplastic Anaemia

Hypoplastic (aplastic) anaemia is pancytopenia (anaemia, neutropenia and thrombocytopenia) resulting from bone marrow hypoplasia of variable severity. Hypoplastic anaemia probably results from failure or suppression of pluripotent stem cells.

Very occasionally, the defect appears to affect cells committed to the erythroid series only, when 'pure red cell aplasia' results. The cause is often unknown; however, it is occasionally congenital or due to poisoning or to iatrogenic causes. Thus, hypoplastic anaemia may be:

- idiopathic
- due to chemical agents (e.g. benzene, cytotoxic drugs, chlor-amphenicol)

- due to ionising radiation
- due to infection such as hepatitis virus and parvovirus
- congenital (Fanconi anaemia).

Most cases caused by anti-neoplastic drugs are reversible. Aplasia is also often a feature of the rare disorder paroxysmal nocturnal haemoglobinuria, a clonal disorder of bone marrow.

In idiopathic forms of hypoplastic anaemia there is evidence that T-lymphocytes are involved in the suppression of stem cell development. Immunosuppressive therapy is occasionally successful. The reason for an idiosyncratic response to some drugs is unknown.

Chloramphenicol, an antibiotic, and gold, used in treatment of rheumatoid arthritis, are especially likely to produce marrow aplasia, often irreversible. Infection with parvovirus causes a transient suppression of erythropoiesis; this suppression is brief and clinically insignificant in otherwise healthy subjects.

However, where red cell survival is markedly shortened, as in sickle cell disease, such infection may cause a catastrophic fall in haemoglobin. Aplastic anaemia is a rare late complication of viral hepatitis.

There is anaemia (normocytic or slightly macrocytic), leukopenia (including lymphopenia in severe cases) and thrombocytopenia. There is reduced polychromasia, especially in relation to the degree of anaemia, and the reticulocyte count is very low. Morphologically abnormal cells are not a feature.

Marrow aspiration often fails. Trephine biopsy reveals increased fat spaces and little residual marrow activity, although a few small clusters of haemopoietic cells occasionally remain.

Clinically, anaemia, infections and bleeding due to thrombocytopenia occur. Splenomegaly and lymphadenopathy are absent. Without successful treatment of the aplasia, severe forms are fatal within months. Spontaneous remission occasionally occurs. Bone marrow transplantation can be curative.

Anaemia due to Bone Marrow Infiltration

Not infrequently, carcinoma and lymphoma involve the bones and bone marrow. A leukoerythroblastic blood picture may result. In carcinomatosis, numerous other factors are likely to be contributory to the anaemia, such as bleeding from carcinoma of the gastrointestinal tract, folate deficiency and chemotherapy.

In myelofibrosis the marrow is replaced by reticulin and collagen.

Fibrosis of the marrow is also a feature of other myeloproliferative disorders and some other malignant marrow infiltrates.

Other causes of marrow infiltration are very uncommon, e.g. Gaucher's disease, a metabolic defect where glucocerebroside accumulates in the reticulo-endothelial cells of many organs.

ANAEMIAS DUE TO INCREASED CELL LOSS, LYSIS OR POOLING

The haemolytic states are the main members of the group of anaemias due to increased cell loss, lysis or pooling. However, anaemia due to acute blood loss and the pancytopenia of hypersplenism are also conveniently included.

A fall in haemoglobin of much greater than 1 g/dl per week must indicate the presence of haemorrhage or haemolysis, as complete cessation of erythropoiesis would result in a rate of fall of no more than 1 g/dl per week. An exception is the rapid fall in haematocrit due to infusion of cell-free fluids in a dehydrated subject.

Acute Blood Loss Anaemia

Chronic haemorrhage, usually gastrointestinal, causes anaemia by depletion of iron stores. Acute blood loss may result initially in a state of cardiovascular collapse, as described in an earlier section. Following adjustment to the plasma volume over a period up to 48 hours, anaemia will be apparent.

The blood picture is normocytic and normochromic, and an increased number of polychromatic erythrocytes and reticulocytes in the days following a brisk haemorrhage reflects increased haemopoiesis. Transient leukocytosis and thrombocytosis commonly occur.

Haemolytic Anaemias

The haemolytic anaemias are those in which a major feature is a reduction in red cell life-span. In severe *haemolysis* red cell survival may be reduced from the normal 120 days to less than 10 days. Although *erythropoiesis* will increase, anaemia is inevitable under such circumstances.

Even in the presence of normal marrow function and adequate supplies of haematinics, the maximum potential increase in red cell production is some six times the normal rate. In the presence of a defect of red cell production, as in folate deficiency or thalassaemia major, the severity of the anaemia is increased in relation to the degree of shortening of red cell survival.

Classification and Incidence

Haemolytic anaemias can be divided usefully into those due to a defect of the red cell itself and those due to an abnormality outside the red cell. Almost all the former are hereditary; an exception is the uncommon acquired disease paroxysmal nocturnal haemoglobinuria (PNH). Those due to mechanisms 'outside' the red cell are acquired disorders.

The relative incidence of haemolytic anaemias is highly variable geographically. In the United Kingdom the acquired haemolytic states, especially autoimmune haemolytic anaemias, are relatively common disorders. Worldwide, however, thalassaemia, sickle cell disease and malaria are of major importance.

Consequences of Haemolysis

In addition to the particular pathological and clinical features of the various haemolytic diseases, certain consequences of the haemolytic process and the response to it are common to all types of haemolytic disorder. These consequences are:

- raised serum bilirubin (unconjugated) resulting in the formation of pigment gallstones
- raised urine urobilinogen
- raised faecal stercobilinogen
- absent serum haptoglobin, which binds haemoglobin; the complex is removed by the liver
- splenomegaly
- reticulocytosis in peripheral blood
- erythroid hyperplasia in bone marrow, causing bone deformity in children in extreme cases, especially thalassaemia.

Red cell destruction occurs predominantly in the *reticuloendothelial* tissues of the spleen and liver. Splenomegaly is therefore common in chronic *haemolytic anaemia*, and *hepatomegaly* may also be present. Within the spleen there is congestion within the cords and deposition of *haemosiderin*.

Less commonly, the red cells are destroyed within the circulation. Examples are haemolytic red cell antibody in major blood group mismatch, that due to the presence of a foreign surface such as a (malfunctioning) *artificial heart valve*, *malaria* and glucose-6-phosphate dehydrogenase deficiency. Particular features of intravascular haemolysis are the presence of free haemoglobin in plasma and urine (haemoglobinaemia, haemoglobinuria), of *methaemalbumin* in plasma (oxidised haem bound to albumin) and of haemosiderin in urine (in shed renal tubular cells which have reabsorbed haemoglobin from the tubular contents; the haem is incorporated into haemosiderin).

Haemolytic Anaemia due to Red Cell Defects

The major components of the erythrocyte are haemoglobin, enzymes involved in protection of haemoglobin from oxidant stress, and the plasma membrane. Abnormalities of each of these components can be a cause of chronic haemolytic anaemia.

Defects of the red cell membrane

Hereditary spherocytosis and *hereditary elliptocytosis* include several disorders in which diminished red cell survival is due to a defect in one of the structural proteins of the erythrocyte membrane such as *spectrin*. Inheritance is dominant. Spherocytosis is the most common cause of hereditary haemolytic anaemia among Caucasians in the UK. Spherocytes are not confined to hereditary spherocytosis however.

They are also present in the blood film in immune haemolytic anaemia. In hereditary spherocytosis, biconcave erythrocytes are released from the marrow but they rapidly lose membrane and therefore assume a spherical shape. Spherocytes are of reduced deformability, which impedes their traverse through the splenic microcirculation. The cells are retained for long periods in the splenic cords. They become metabolically stressed by glucose lack and acidosis, and are eventually prematurely phagocytosed.

The abnormal red cells in these disorders are more sensitive than normal to lysis under osmotic stress. This increased osmotic fragility is of diagnostic value. Anaemia is usual but varies in severity between affected kindreds. The blood film has many spherocytes; they appear smaller than normocytes and more dense, with loss of the central pallor. Polychromatic cells are increased.

General features of chronic haemolysis are also present. Haemolysis tends to be less severe in elliptocytosis. The clinical features are variable and are those of chronic extravascular haemolysis. Pigment gallstones commonly develop.

The disorder can be subclinical. Occasionally, transient red cell aplasia secondary to parvovirus infection can develop, when several family members may be affected by aplasia simultaneously. Removal of the spleen results in resolution of the anaemia, confirming the role of the spleen in the haemolytic process. Splenectomy is reserved for cases in which symptoms of anaemia are intolerable.

Defects of red cell enzymes

Defects of red cell enzymes render the erythrocyte susceptible to damage by oxidant compounds. The generation of reduced glutathione by the metabolic activity of the red cell normally inactivates oxidants. Reduced glutathione is generated by the hexose monophosphate shunt of the Embden-Meyerhof glycolytic pathway, which is the source of: energy, as ATP, necessary for maintenance of red cell shape, volume and flexibility; NADH for reduction of oxidised haemoglobin; and 2,3-diphosphoglycerate (2,3-DPG) for the regulation of the oxygen affinity of haemoglobin.

Deficiency of several of the enzymes involved in these reactions has been identified. Only two are of pathological and major clinical significance: glucose-6-phosphate dehydrogenase deficiency and pyruvate kinase deficiency.

Glucose-6-phosphate dehydrogenase deficiency

Deficiency or defect of G6PD results in impaired reduction of glutathione. Reduced glutathione protects haemoglobin and red cell membrane from oxidative damage. Inherited G6PD deficiency is an uncommon cause of anaemia in the UK but is among the most common genetic disorders worldwide.

It is a sex-linked disorder: female heterozygotes are usually asymptomatic and may have some protection from falciparum malaria; this probably explains the high prevalence of the disorder in many parts of the world. The common iso-enzymes are traditionally designated 'type B', the most common, 'type A and 'type A-minus', found among American blacks (30% and 11 % respectively).

Type A differs from type B by a single amino acid substitution and is functionally normal. Type A-minus has an additional amino acid substitution resulting in decreased red cell enzyme activity and disease. Typically there is a tendency to the development of an acute haemolytic episode associated with the ingestion of an oxidant drug (for example some anti-malarials and antibiotics) and with other stresses such as surgery or infection.

Clinically, a self-limiting episode of anaemia and jaundice develops. Treatment centres around avoidance of exposure to known oxidant drugs. A further variant is found in Mediterranean populations and is associated with the acute haemolytic tendency known as *favism,* where ingestion of the fava (broad) bean results in acute haemolysis.

The responsible oxidant compound has not yet been identified. Again, oxidant drugs, surgical stress and infections may also lead to haemolysis. Many other less common genetic variants have been recognised. Some result in a more chronic haemolytic state or neonatal jaundice due to haemolysis. The blood picture during haemolytic crisis includes increased poikilocytosis with contracted red cells, 'bite' cells and 'blister' cells (poikilocytes with bite-shaped defects or surface blebs).

Oxidised, denatured haemoglobin is seen as red-cell inclusions (Heinz bodies) attached to the cell membrane, when blood is stained supravitally as in the reticulocyte preparation. Haemolysis is generally selflimiting because of the rapid outpouring of new red cells, with higher G6PD content, from the marrow in response to the falling haemoglobin. The blood picture is normal between haemolytic episodes. Treatment consists essentially of avoidance of known precipitating factors for haemolysis. Health is generally good between haemolytic episodes.

Pyruvate kinase deficiency

Pyruvate kinase (PK) deficiency is an autosomal recessive disorder which results in congenital chronic haemolytic anaemia. The blood film has increased poikilocytosis. The chronic anaemia is associated with increased erythrocyte 2,3-DPG because of the site of the metabolic block. This situation results in reduced oxygen affinity of haemoglobin and increased oxygen delivery to the tissues; the anaemia is thus less symptomatic than would be expected from its severity. No specific treatment is available.

Haemoglobinopathies (Abnormal Haemoglobins)

Abnormal haemoglobins are caused by a single point mutation in the genetic code resulting in an amino acid substitution in the α or β globin chain of haemoglobin A. Variant haemoglobins can be readily identified by their electrophoretic mobility. Several hundred variant haemoglobins have been identified but few are clinically significant and almost all of those involve β chain substitutions. Depending on the site of the substitution, four main types of functional defect result:

- a haemoglobin which becomes crystalline at low oxygen tension, e.g. HbS, causing haemolysis and microvascular occlusion
- an unstable haemoglobin causing chronic haemolysis with Heinz bodies (red-cell inclusions composed of denatured haemoglobin)
- a haemoglobin of increased oxygen affinity causing polycythaemia
- a haemoglobin which tends to the oxidised state (methaemoglobin) causing cyanosis.

The first defect is the most common. HbS is very common worldwide, as are three related haemoglobins: C, D and E.

Sickle cell disease

- Due to homozygous inheritance of a gene coding for a haemoglobin variant which becomes crystalline at low oxygen tensions
- Characterised, by episodes of tissue *infarction* and *chronic haemolysis*
- The heterozygous state (sickle cell trait) is associated with normal full blood count and no *symptoms*

Substitution of valine for glutamic acid in position 6 in the β chain of globin results in a haemoglobin (HbS) which undergoes aggregation and polymerisation at low oxygen tensions. In the *homozygote* for sickle cell disease, where the majority of the haemoglobin content of the erythrocytes is HbS, this results in distortion of the red cells, which acquire a sickle shape.

The consequence of this distortion and the predominant features of sickle cell disease are a chronic haemolytic anaemia and microvascular occlusion, causing ischaemic tissue damage. The results of the latter dominate the clinical picture. The gene for HbS is common in the West and Central African populations, the Mediterranean, Middle East and some parts of the Indian subcontinent. Carriage of the gene may confer some protection against falciparum malaria.

The gene is carried by 8% of black Americans and 30% of black Africans. The heterozygous state, or *sickle cell trait*, results in less than 40% HbS, the remainder being mostly normal HbA. Two major bands are therefore present on electrophoresis of haemoglobin: one corresponding to HbS and one to HbA. The carrier is clinically and *haematologically* essentially normal, sickling occurring only very uncommonly and only under conditions of severe hypoxia.

Haematuria is an occasional feature, due to renal *papillary* necrosis from focal sickling in the renal medulla. Hypoxic sickling in heterozygotes is an avoidable risk of general anaesthesia. In the homozygote the haemoglobin concentration is low (7-9 g/dl). Sickle cells and target cells are present on the blood film, as are features of hyposplenism in the adult. (Splenomegaly due to chronic haemolysis is present during childhood but the spleen shrinks progressively due to *microvascular* occlusion and infarction.)

The bone marrow is *hyperplastic* with erythroid *hyperplasia*. Extramedullary erythropoiesis in the liver and, occasionally, other sites is a minor feature. Pathological changes in other organs result from the effects of local ischaemia. Haemoglobin electrophoresis reveals a characteristic single band of HbS.

Clinical features

These are predictable from the above. There is anaemia and jaundice from infancy. Sickle 'crises' of various clinical types occur from an early age. Vascular occlusion with resultant ischaemia causes severe pain, often in the long bones, abdomen or chest. Ischaemic stroke is common. Acute sequestration of sickle cells in the liver or (in children) spleen may cause pain and acute exacerbation of anaemia. Between episodes of crisis, health may be good. Cholecystitis, due to the presence

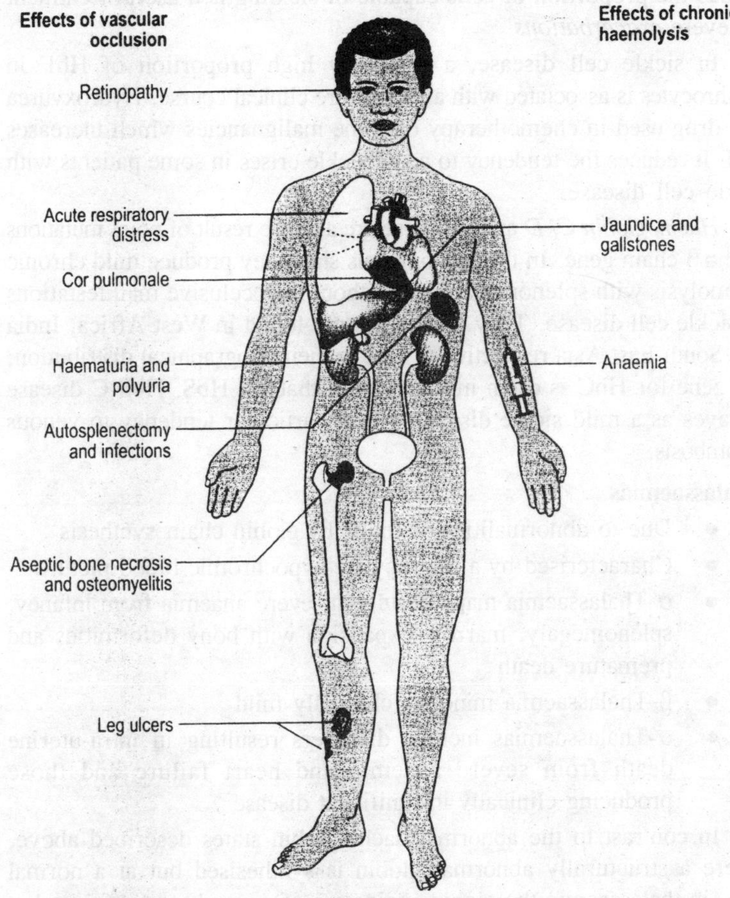

Figure 6.6: The pathogenesis and clinical consequences of sickle cell disease.

of pigment stones, is a frequent occurrence. As in pyruvate kinase deficiency, oxygen affinity of the haemoglobin is low and symptoms of anaemia mild, due to the relatively enhanced O_2 delivery to tissues. Premature death, often from respiratory complic-ations, may occur in early middle age, but longer survival is a feature in some populations.

Treatment

This is essentially conservative, with avoidance of factors known to precipitate crises, especially hypoxia, and provision of warmth and rehydration during crises. *Pregnancy* may be complicated by an increased tendency to acute sickle crises. Exchange transfusion of red cells to reduce the proportion of cells capable of sickling is a useful treatment in severe *exacerbations*.

In sickle cell disease, a relatively high proportion of HbF in erythrocytes is associated with a less severe clinical course. Hydroxyurea is a drug used in chemotherapy of some malignancies which increases HbE It reduces the tendency to acute sickle crises in some patients with sickle cell disease.

Haemoglobin C, D and E. These are also the result of point mutations in the β chain gene. In the homozygous state they produce mild chronic haemolysis with splenomegaly but without the occlusive manifestations of sickle cell disease. They are commonly found in West Africa, India and South-East Asia respectively. Due to their geographical distribution, the gene for HbC is often inherited with that for HbS. HbS-C disease behaves as a mild sickle disease with a particular tendency to venous thrombosis.

Thalassaemias

- Due to abnormalities of (α or β) globin chain synthesis
- Characterised by a microcytie, hypochromic blood picture
- α-Thalassaemia major results in severe anaemia from infancy, splenomegaly, marrow expansion with bony deformities and premature death
- β-Thalassaemia minor is clinically mild
- α-Thalassaemias include disorders resulting in intra-uterine death from severe anaemia and heart failure and those producing clinically insignificant disease

In contrast to the abnormal haemoglobin states described above, where a structurally abnormal globin is synthesised but at a normal rate, in thalassaemia the globin chains are of normal composition, but the rate at which the globin chain (α or β) is synthesised is reduced.

In a-thalassaemia the a globin chain synthesis is so affected; in β-thalassaemia the β chain is affected. Accumulation of an excess of the unaffected globin chains results in damage to the developing and mature erythrocytes.

Again, in contrast to 'variant haemoglobin' conditions (such as sickle cell disease) where point mutations affecting coding regions underlie the disorders, in thalassaemias the genetic lesions are of a regulatory nature, affecting the normal *expression* of the globin structural genes.

Each chromosome 16 has a pair of a globin genes, thus each cell has four genes coding for a globin, all of them functional. The genes for β globin, as well as those for γ and δ are located in close linkage on chromosome 11. In the a-thalassaemia syndromes there is deletion of all four genes or of three of the four. In a-thalassaemia trait, there is deletion of two or only one gene.

More than 100 genetic defects responsible for (3thalassaemia have now been described, predominantly point mutations, in contrast to the deletions which cause much a-thalassaemia. The type of defect tends to vary between racial groups. Some defects result in an absence of chain synthesis (β^0); in others, chain synthesis is severely restricted but present (β^+).

α-Thalassaemia

This is an uncommon cause of anaemia in the UK. Red cells are microcytic. Haemoglobin H disease is seen mainly in Asian populations. HbH is identifiable on electrophoresis in the 3-gene deletion disorder and HbH inclusion bodies are visible in red cells stained supravitally (as in the reticulocyte preparation) in the 3 and 2 gene deletion forms. Electrophoresis is normal in a-thalassaemia trait and the conditions can be confirmed only by direct measurement of rate of synthesis of α and β chains.

β-Thalassaemia major (Mediterranean or Cooley's anaemia). This is a severe disorder due to the inheritance of two genes for β-thalassaemia-β^+/β^+, β^0/β^0 or occasionally. The β-thalassaemia genes are most frequent in Mediterranean countries, the Middle East and parts of Africa and South-East Asia.

The blood picture is that of a severe microcytic, hypochromic anaemia (haemoglobin concentration 3-6 g/dl) developing from 3 to 6 months of age (when β-chain production should have completely taken over from that of the γ chains).

In response to the defective haemoglobin synthesis and haemolysis the red bone marrow is dramatically expanded with gross erythroid hyperplasia. As a result, cortical bone is thinned and new bone deposits on the outer aspect, especially in the skull vault, maxilla and frontal facial bones. Cortical thinning and fractures may develop in the long bones, vertebrae and ribs.

The spleen is grossly enlarged, with expansion of the reticulo-endothelial elements and extramedullary erythropoiesis. The liver is similarly affected. Iron overload is apparent and often gross. Haemoglobin electrophoresis reveals absent or markedly reduced haemoglobin A. Small (normal) amounts of haemoglobin A_2 are present and the remainder of the haemoglobin is E

Predictably, the clinical features are those of severe anaemia, including growth retardation, and haemosiderosis. The latter may result in failure of sexual development due to iron deposition in endocrine organs and gonads, as well as diabetes mellitus, liver and heart failure. Facial deformities result from the bone changes.

Death often occurs, even with transfusion support, in childhood or early adult life. The situation may be improved by iron chelation therapy to reduce tissue iron. At present this can only be efficiently delivered by near continuous subcutaneous infusion of the iron-chelating drug desferrioxamine. Orally administered iron chelators are under investigation. Bone marrow transplantation has been curative.

β-Thalassaemia minor

This is mild and most commonly subclinical. The characteristic pathology is gross microcytic and hypochromic change on the blood film with normal or slightly raised red cell count and normal haemoglobin concentration. Mild anaemia may be present during pregnancy, when the condition is often first diagnosed, as it is often the first occasion when the healthy carrier undergoes a routine blood count.

The blood picture is very similar to that of iron deficiency but the MCV and MCH are disproportionately low for the level of haemoglobin. Iron stores are normal or high. Bone changes and hepatosplenomegaly are absent. Haemoglobin electrophoresis reveals raised haemoglobin A_2 concentration ($>2.5\%$). Diagnosis is important in order that genetic counselling can be offered.

Thalassaemia intermedia

The term thalassaemia intermedia describes disease of intermediate severity, often not requiring transfusion and compatible with prolonged survival. Hepatosplenomegaly and iron overload are present. It is genetically heterogeneous, some cases being severely affected heterozygotes, others homozygotes with an unusually mild β-chain deficiency. Occasional patients are doubly heterozygous for β-thalassaemia and HbS. These patients have a variant of sickle cell disease, often with prominent and persisting splenomegaly.

Paroxysmal Nocturnal Haemoglobinuria

Paroxysmal nocturnal haemoglobinuria is an acquired disorder in which chronic haemolysis is due to a clonal abnormality of erythrocytes which renders them abnormally sensitive to complement lysis. Due to an acquired mutation of PIG-A gene within a stem cell clone, blood cells lack an enzyme required for the synthesis of a phosphatidyl inositol which anchors several proteins to the red cell membrane, including some responsible for complement degradation.

Leukocytes and platelets are also affected. The condition is rare and often chronic. Aplastic anaemia, chronic haemolytic anaemia and venous thrombosis in the portal, hepatic or cerebral veins are major features. Haemoglobinuria occurring at night or in early morning is not a common feature, despite the name (nocturnal) of the disorder.

The presence of haemosiderinuria and tendency of erythrocytes to lyse at low pH, which activates complement (acid lysis or Ham's test) are useful diagnostically. A more specific test which identifies the missing proteins on the red cell surface is now available. Treatment is supportive and death is often ultimately due to sepsis or thrombosis.

Haemolytic Anaemia due to a Defect Outside the Red Cell

Haemolytic anaemias due to a defect outside the red cell are all acquired disorders.

Immune Haemolytic Anaemias

Immune haemolytic anaemias are due to red cell damage by an antibody. The phenomenon may be *autoimmune,* as in idiopathic and drug-induced autoimmune haemolytic anaemias and cold antibody disorders, or *alloimmune* (where the antibody forms to an antigen foreign to that individual), as in haemolysis due to mismatched blood transfusion and that in haemolytic disease of the newborn.

In all cases the presence of antibody or complement on the red cell surface is confirmed by the direct antiglobulin (or Coombs') test which uses antibodies to human immunoglobulin or complement raised in an animal to cause in vitro agglutination of red cells sensitised with antibody or complement in vivo.

In some (the more common) instances of autoimmune haemolysis the auto-antibody is IgG and most reactive at 37°C-'warm antibody' autoimmune disorders. In 'cold antibody' autoimmune disorders an IgM antibody is active at 4°C, becoming less active at higher temperatures, but is still able to bind complement and agglutinate red cells at the temperature (c. 30°C) of the peripheral tissues (hands, feet, nose, ears).

Antibody-coated cells bind to macrophages of the reticuloendothelial system via Fc receptors. Partial phagocytosis results and the erythrocyte loses some membrane. In order to maintain cellular integrity after this reduction of surface area, a sphere is formed. Such spherical red cells

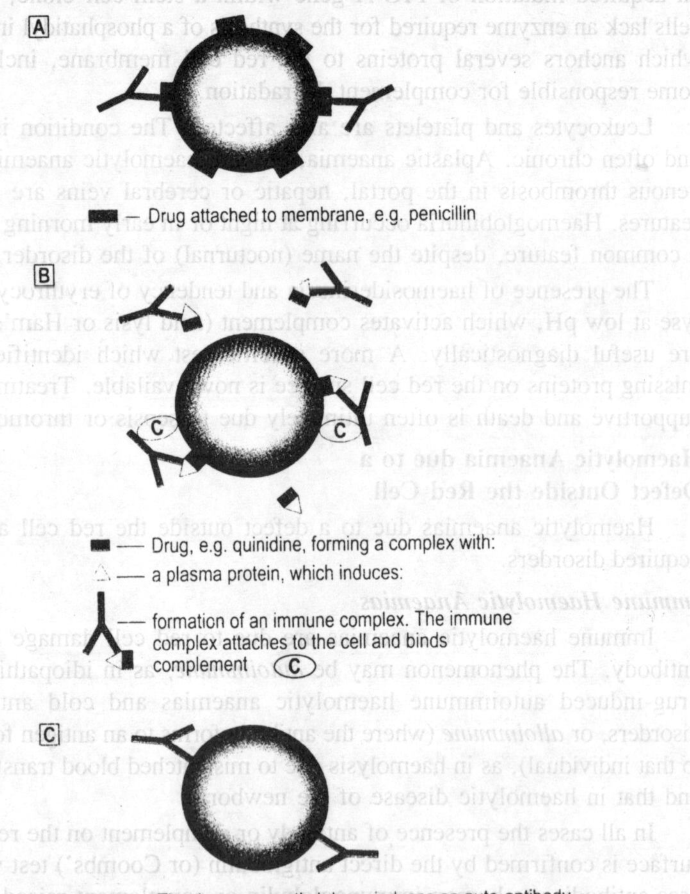

Figure 6.7: Three mechanisms of drug-induced immune haemolysis.

are less deformable than normal; they eventually become trapped in the spleen and are removed by phagocytosis.

'Warm antibody' immune haemolytic anaemia

In 'warm antibody' immune haemolytic anaemia, the autoantibody is usually IgG and may or may not bind complement. Red cell destruction occurs in the cells of the reticulo-endothelial system, especially the spleen. Most cases are idiopathic, occurring at any age. There may be a family history of autoimmune disease.

In about one-third of instances the process is initiated by a drug or it occurs in association with some other disease, particularly a lymphoproliferative disorder, or collagen vascular disease such as systemic lupus erythematosus or rheumatoid arthritis.

Drugs can cause the disorder by one of three mechanisms. Withdrawal of the drug results in resolution of the disorder. The blood picture in warm antibody haemolysis is that of a chronic anaemia with microspherocytes and increased polychromasia (and reticulocytosis). The degree of anaemia is very variable within and between cases but may be extremely severe.

Erythroid hyperplasia is marked in the bone marrow; megaloblastic erythropoiesis may supervene, as in all haemolytic anaemias, due to increased folate requirements. The spleen is moderately enlarged and congested. Features of an underlying disorder, such as lymphoma, may also be present.

Clinical features and treatment

The clinical features are those of haemolytic anaemia-pallor, jaundice and splenomegaly. In those instances where a drug cannot be implicated and withdrawn, treatment by immunosuppression with corticosteroids and other immunomodulatory drugs is employed. In some cases splenectomy is successful in reducing the rate of haemolysis.

'Cold antibody' immune haemolytic anaemias

In 'cold antibody' immune haemolytic anaemias, the IgM antibody attaches to red cells in the peripheral circulation and complement is bound. On re-entering the central circulation the IgM antibody may become detached, but complement activation leads to red cell destruction in the reticulo-endothelial system.

The main consequences of this sequence of events are agglutination of erythrocytes in cooler areas which causes sluggish flow and reduced oxygen saturation, and chronic haemolysis. Severity relates particularly to the thermal amplitude of the antibody, that is its activity at temperatures up to 30°C. The pathological features are those of chronic haemolysis with a tendency to marked agglutination of red cells on the blood film. If the film is prepared at 37°C the agglutination is no longer present. The reticulocyte count is increased.

Clinical features and treatment

The clinical features are of anaemia and of blueness and coldness of the fingers, toes, nose and ears, occasionally progressing to ischaemia and ulceration. Many cases occur spontaneously in older adults. The disorder is chronic and often mild. It occurs as an unusual complication of lymphoma, and also, rarely and transiently, in infectious mononucleosis (glandular fever) and mycoplasma pneumonia.

The degree of haemolysis can be reduced by maintenance of a warm environment. Splenectomy is rarely successful, probably because complement-sensitised cells tend to be destroyed at other sites, especially the liver.

Haemolytic disease of the newborn

Haemolytic disease of the newborn, a previously common disorder, is due to passage across the placenta of maternal IgG antibodies which are reactive against, and cause destruction of, the fetal red cells. This disorder requires the inheritance by the fetus of a red cell antigen from the father which is not present on the maternal red cells, thus provoking antibody development in the mother.

Antibodies against the D antigen of the rhesus blood group system are most commonly implicated, but with improvements in management classical rhesus haemolytic disease is now much less common and an increased proportion of cases are due to antibodies to other antigens in the rhesus system, the A antigen of the ABO system or occasionally other antibodies.

Approximately 15% of the population are negative for the rhesus D antigen and can become sensitised to produce anti-D. Passage of fetal red cells into the maternal circulation occurs normally at delivery or as a result of miscarriage or operative intervention during pregnancy and these D-positive cells sensitise a D-negative mother.

Further stimulation of antibody production occurs in subsequent pregnancies with a D-positive fetus. IgG antibody then crosses the placenta from mother to fetus and causes immune destruction of fetal red cells. Thus, the disorder does not manifest in the first pregnancy. The pathogenesis is similar for other antibodies; however, the fetus may be affected in the first pregnancy in ABO haemolytic disease of the newborn, where IgG antibody to A or B on fetal red cells develops in a group O mother.

Clinicopathological features

The pathological features are those of a haemolytic anaemia of variable severity occurring in utero. In the most severe cases, associated with a high titre of anti-D, the result is death in utero from 'hydrops fetalis': the fetus is extremely pale and oedematous and has gross hepatosplenomegaly, the result of severe anaemia with cardiac and hepatic failure and increased extramedullary erythropoiesis.

In less severe examples the neonate is pale and jaundiced at birth, with hepatosplenomegaly. The blood picture is that of anaemia, polychromasia with increased reticulocytes and often nucleated red cells in the peripheral blood. The direct antiglobulin test on the neonatal red cells is positive, indicating that they are coated with antibody.

When unconjugated bilirubin levels are very high, bile pigment becomes deposited in the central nervous system, especially the basal ganglia, causing severe damage, known as kernicterus. The bilirubin levels rise rapidly after birth due to immaturity of the liver, with further central nervous system damage. Spasticity and mental retardation may be the clinical consequences of this damage.

In some cases of haemolytic disease of the newborn due to anti-D, and most due to anti-A, the disease is mild, with neonatal anaémia and mild jaundice.

Management

The incidence of the disorder has been reduced by the prophylactic removal of fetal cells entering the maternal circulation before sensitisation can occur. This is achieved by injection of anti-D into the D negative mother.

Management of the affected fetus centres around provision of unsensitised red cells by intra-uterine transfusion and removal of bilirubin by exchange blood transfusion postnatally. Mildly affected neonates are treated by phototherapy, in which exposure to light of an appropriate wavelength degrades bilirubin.

Haemolysis due to mismatched blood transfusion

Haèmolytic transfusion reaction constitutes a second type of alloimmune haemolysis. Severe reactions result from transfusion of red cells possessing an antigen, e.g. ABO group antigens to which the recipient possesses complement binding antibody of IgG or IgM class.

Microangiopathic Haemolytic Anaemia

The term microangiopathic haemolytic anaemia describes the dramatic haematological picture which occurs when haemolysis is caused by physical trauma to erythrocytes as they are forced through n or damaged areas in the microvasculature. Characteristic cells are present on the blood film, especially schistocytes.

This type of process is commonly present in disseminated intravascular coagulation; the erythrocytes are damaged on fibrin strands deposited in small blood vessels. It is also a feature of the haemolytic-uraemic syndrome, thrombotic thrombocytopenic purpura, malignant hypertension and of the extensive vasculitis in systemic lupus erythematosus.

In many of these conditions, thrombocytopenia is also present, due to platelet consumption in microthrombi formed on damaged endotheium. Similar erythrocyte damage without microvascular lesions occurs in march haemoglobinuria, originally described in soldiers after prolonged marching; red cell damage presumably occurs in the feet. An analogous situation has been described in marathon runners, bongo drummers and exponents of karate!

In most of these situations the haemolysis is not chronic, and splenomegaly and other features of chronic red cell destruction are absent. The direct antiglobulin test is negative, as antibody is not involved in the pathogenesis. Schistocytes and haemolysis, sometimes catastrophic, are occasionally the result of red cell injury from a malfunctioning mechanical heart valve or other vascular prostheses.

Other Causes of Haemolytic Anaemia

Extensive burns are associated with haemolysis, in part due to direct heat damage of erythrocytes in blood vessels of the burned areas, and in part due to a microangiopathic mechanism. Snake bites, spider bites and chemicals are occasional causes.

Infection with clostridia is a rare cause of haemolysis. Malarial infection is common and results in haemolytic anaemia (Fig. 23.28). Schizonts escape by rupturing the erythrocytes in which they have matured. In chronic malarial infection, extreme splenomegaly is often present.

Histologically, there is marked congestion and expansion of reticulo-endothelial cells: macrophages contain parasites and red cells, and are laden with malarial pigment.

Hypersplenism

Hypersplenism is defined as anaemia (often accompanied by leukopenia and thrombocytopenia) secondary to splenic enlargement. This anaemia is in part due to a haemolytic component, presumed to be due to increased red cell sequestration in the enlarged spleen, with enhanced phagocytosis by macrophages. However, other mechanisms contribute: the plasma volume increases in proportion to the degree of splenic enlargement, for reasons which are not understood.

This results in a dilutional anaemia. Pooling of blood cells also occurs within the spleen. Hypersplenism is associated with splenomegaly from any cause, such as portal hypertension and collagen vascular disease. Hypersplenism in rheumatoid arthritis has the eponym *Felty's syndrome*.

The blood picture in hypersplenism is that of a pancytopenia with no specific features. The haemoglobin concentration would rarely be less than 8 g/dl and the platelet count less than 60 × 10^9/1 due to hypersplenism alone.

NEOPLASTIC DISTORDERS OF THE BONE MARROW

Classification of Bone Marrow Malignancies

Bone marrow malignancies are classified according to their presentation (acute or chronic, and with or without leukaemia) and their histogenesis (e.g. myeloid, lymphoid). Recently the World Health Organization has refined the classification of tumours of the haemopoietic and lymphoid tissues.

The objective of this new WHO classification is to offer pathologists, haematologists, oncologists and geneticists worldwide a system of classification of human haemopoietic neoplasms that is based on their histopathological and genetic features.

This classification takes into account tissue and cell morphology, immunological characteristics of the malignant cells and, where known, specific acquired genetic abberations associated with the malignancies. The advantages of this approach to classification are improved reliability in diagnosis, better prognostic information with the possibility of tailored therapy for a given prognostic group and, finally, more reliable characterisation of patients entered into trials of therapy.

LEUKAEMIAS

Leukaemias are neoplastic proliferations of white blood cell precursors. This proliferation results in the common features of leukaemia:

- diffuse replacement of normal bone marrow by leukaemic cells with variable accumulation of abnormal cells in the peripheral blood
- infiltration of organs such as liver, spleen, lymph nodes, meninges and gonads by leukaemic cells.

Bone marrow failure with anaemia, neutropenia and thrombocytopenia is the most important consequence, particularly in the acute leukaemias.

Aetiology

In the majority of cases the cause is unknown. Leukaemias represent neoplastic monoclonal proliferations of cells within the bone marrow and blood. Whether or not the cell of origin is a pluripotent stem cell or a more committed cell in each type remains contentious. However, current evidence suggests that in most cases of acute myeloblastic leukaemia (AML) a pluripotential stem cell is mutated.

The exception to this is acute promyelocytic leukaemia (APL), which seems to arise from a more committed myeloid progenitor cell. In acute lymphoblastic leukaemia (ALL) the transforming events occur in a very primitive B-cell which has not yet developed the capacity to produce immunoglobulin; most cases of chronic myeloid (or granulocytic) leukaemia (CML), where megakaryocytes and erythroid cells are involved as well as leukocytes, derive from a pluripotent stem cell. Most cases of chronic lymphocytic leukaemia (CLL) are of B-cell origin, but these cells are more differentiated than those in ALL.

In acute leukaemia the typical cells-'blast' cellsaccumulate as a result of a combination of proliferation but failure of maturation. In CML the abnormal myeloid stem cells also accumulate, but maturation still occurs, with increased numbers of mature myeloid cells in blood and bone marrow, as well as blast cells.

It seems likely that several predisposing factors acting together trigger the onset of the disease in most cases. These triggers act by inducing a series of mutations in certain key genes involved in regulating cell proliferation and differentiation. Such genes are known as oncogenes if they promote tumour development, and tumour suppressor genes if their normal, un-mutated form protects against tumour development.

In some leukaemias genetic material is exchanged between two genes (translocation), leading to the development of a novel fusion gene which acts as an oncogene. The best understood examples of these types of mutations in leukaemogenesis include the t(9;22) translocation in CML, in which the fusion gene is a tyrosine kinase, BCR-ABL, and t(15;17) translocation in acute promyelocytic leukaemia.

Such genetic mutations are often first recognised by the identification of gross cytogenetic abnormalities at the chromosome level, for example the Philadelphia chromosome is the small chromosome 22 produced by the exchange of genetic material with chromosome 9. With more sophisticated molecular techniques such as fluorescent in situ hybridisation

(FISH) and gene array technology it is becoming clear that all leukaemias have altered genes. Already such abnormalities are being used to produce new targeted therapies, for example imatinib mesylate (Glivec) in CML, and to identify patients with a good prognosis who do not necessarily need a stem cell transplant, for example AML patients with t(15;17) or t(8;21).

Certain factors known to initiate leukaemic transformation are:

- irradiation (e.g. atomic bomb survivors, spinal irradiation in ankylosing spondylitis, ^{32}P therapy in myeloproliferative disease)
- drugs (e.g. alkylating agents in treatment of lymphomas)
- other chemicals (e.g. benzene exposure)
- viruses (e.g. leukaemia in some animals; HTLV-I in adult T-cell leukaemia/lymphoma)
- genetic factors (e.g. increased incidence in Down syndrome).

Acute Leukaemias

Acute leukaemias arise from mutations in haemopoietic stem cells. The leukaemic clone of cells proliferates but loses the ability to differentiate into mature blood cells. This imbalance between proliferation and differentiation in acute leukaemia leads to the accumulation of blast cells in the bone marrow and the hallmark clinical features of bone marrow failure.

Two broad types of acute leukaemia are recognised: acute lymphoblastic leukaemia (ALL) most common in childhood and acute myeloblastic leukaemia (AML) most common in adults. The incidence of ALL and AML with age is shown in the Figure elsewhere in this chapter.

Acute lymphoblastic leukaemia

ALL is most common between 2 and 4 years of age. It is the commonest cause of cancer death in childhood. Recent data suggest that one of the predisposing genetic mutations for childhood ALL actually occurs in utero and that further genetic mutations in the first years of life lead to the disease.

ALL blasts are described morphologically by the FrenchAmerican-British (FAB) classification according to their size, nuclear:cytoplasmic ratio and whether or not there is marked cytoplasmic vacuolation, as L1, L2 or L3 cells. Routine use of panels of monoclonal antibodies have shown that the majority of cases of ALL derive from B-cell precursors, and the use of these antibodies can classify ALL according to the degree of maturation along the B-cell pathway, i.e. common ALL and pre-B

ALL, which can be of L1 or L2 morphology, or B-ALL which is of L3 morphology and now known as Burkitt's leukaemia because of its biological similarity to Burkitt's lymphoma. A number of acquired genetic abnormalities are recognised in ALL, including the occurrence of a Philadelphia chromosome caused by the t(9;22) translocation in 2% of children but 20-30% of adults with ALL.

Acute myeloblastic leukaemia

The incidence of AML increases steadily with age. In older people AML is more likely to develop from an existing bone marrow disorder such as myelodysplastic syndrome (MDS), whereas the majority of younger patients present with de novo AML. AML has traditionally been classified according to the degree of cell maturation present along the granulocytic, monocytic, erythroid or megakaryocytic lines.

The FAB classification applied to AML therefore includes eight subtypes (M_0 - M_7). In M_0 and M, there is no or minor evidence of maturation. In M_3 there is maturation to promyelocytes; in M_4 and M_5 there is monocytic maturation; in M_6 there is erythroid maturation; and in M_7 there is megakaryocytic maturation.

In all cases there must be at least 20% blast cells in the bone marrow for AML to be diagnosed. Prognosis in AML is very much related to acquired cytogenetic abnormalities. Some of these abnormalities occur in specific subtypes of AML. Patients with balanced translocations t(15;17) in AML M_3, t(8;21) translocation in some cases of AML M_2 and inversion of chromosome 16 in some cases of AML M_4 respond *very* well to treatment and have a long-term cure rate of about 70%.

Much is now known about the genes altered by these chromosome rearrangements. For example in t(15;17) the genes rearranged are PML/ RARA. The retinoic acid receptor a gene (RARA) in its fused form with PML leads both to the development of this leukaemia and its response to pharmacological doses of all-trans-retinoic acid (ATRA), which is now part of standard therapy for this subtype of AML. At the other end of the spectrum are cytogenetic abnormalities which carry a very poor prognosis with cure rates of less than 20°70.

These include loss of a whole chromosome 5 or 7 or complex multiple cytogenetic abnormalities. These cases occur more commonly in elderly people, following on from MDS or in so-called treatment-related AML after exposure to chemotherapy for previous cancers.

Blood and bone marrow changes in acute leukaemia

In peripheral blood the white cell count is usually increased; counts of greater than 100 × 10^9/l are not uncommon. Alternatively, leukopenia is an occasional feature, despite massive marrow infiltration with blast cells.

The majority of nucleated cells are leukaemic blasts. In AML, cells containing diagnostic rod-like granular structures (Auer rods) may be present, as may hypogranular polymorphonuclear variants and pseudo-Pelger cells. Anaemia is present, usually normocytic and normochromic. Thrombocytopenia is marked, particularly in AML.

Bone marrow cellularity is markedly increased. Blast cells constitute at least 20% of nucleated cells present, and often greater than 80%. Extension into areas of previously fatty marrow may occur. Gross bone erosion with fractures is not generally a feature of acute leukaemia. Karyotype analysis reveals abnormalities in the leukaemic blasts, with gains and losses of whole chromosomes as well as translocations.

Changes in Other Organs

Lymph nodes, liver and spleen may be infiltrated with leukaemic blast cells in all types of acute leukaemia. Lymph node enlargement is generally mild and nodes remain discrete, although in some cases of ALL massive involvement of mediastinal lymph nodes is a feature. Splenic enlargement, where present, is also minor in contrast to that in chronic leukaemias.

Histologically, there is effacement of normal node architecture by sheets of leukaemic blasts and focal or diffuse infiltration of the spleen. A diffuse infiltrate of leukaemic cells may also be present in most other organs. Evidence of bacterial, fungal or viral infection may be apparent, as may haemorrhage secondary to thrombocytopenia.

Meningeal infiltration in ALL is an important feature. Leukaemic blasts within the central nervous system are protected from chemotherapeutic agents by the blood-brain barrier. Perivascular aggregates of blast cells later form diffuse lesions and plaques which may result in compression of adjacent nerve tissue.

Infiltration of the gums and skin is a peculiar feature of the monocytic types of AML (M_4 and M_5). Severe, life-threatening coagulation failure occurs in the promyelocytic form of AML (M_3), probably due to coagulation activation and consumption of clotting factors by activators released from the granules of the leukaemic promyelocytes.

Clinical Course

The onset is often very rapid and progression to death from anaemia, haemorrhage or infection occurs within weeks if no treatment is given. The features are those of marrow failure, with anaemia, infection due to neutropenia and mucocutaneous bleeding due to severe thrombocytopenia.

Infections are typically with bacteria and fungi. Septicaemias, pneumonia and skin sepsis are common. Fungal infections can be local, such as in the oral cavity but fungal septicaemia and organ invasion occur. Systemic fungal infection is often fatal.

The situation may be exacerbated, especially in AML, by transient aplasia induced by highly myelotoxic chemotherapeutic agents. The clinical course is, however, often less catastrophic in childhood ALL.

Treatment

Treatment of acute leukaemia is directed by individual prognostic assessment. The aim is to offer curative treatment where possible and minimise the long-term complications in groups of patients who have a high cure rate, while intensifying the treatment or using new modes of treatment in those groups of patients who presently do badly.

Therefore, as an example of this principle, children and young adults with good prognosis ALL or AML will not be routinely offered bone marrow transplantation, while those with poor prognosis disease may be offered bone marrow transplantation as part of initial treatment. Treatment is by chemotherapeutic agents in combination to clear the blood, bone marrow and other sites of leukaemic blasts as far as is possible.

The first one or two courses of treatment are aimed at producing a state of remission, in which the blood counts are normal and there are less than 5% blast cells in the bone marrow as identified by light microscopy. However, light microscopy is not very sensitive and in remission there can still be in the order of 10^9 leukaemic cells in the marrow.

Further courses of chemotherapy are given to consolidate the remission and reduce this leukaemic burden further. In poor prognostic disease it seems chemotherapy alone cannot overcome the leukaemic burden and the additional allogeneic immune attack provided by a bone marrow transplant is required to irradicate the disease.

This attack is called graft versus leukaemia and is mediated by the donor's engrafted Tlymphocytes. New approaches to leukaemia management include more accurate monitoring of minimal residual disease (disease which cannot be detected by conventional microscopy) by PCR or flow cytometry and acting on the results of such tests. New modes of therapy, such as antibodies targeted against the leukaemia cells, and techniques to further enhance the graft versus leukaemia effect are being introduced.

Table 6.6: Acute versus chronic leukaemia.

Acute	*Chronic*
Leukaemic cells do not differentiate	Leukaemic cells retain ability to differentiate
Bone marrow failure	Proliferation without bone marrow failure
Rapidly fatal if untreated	Survival for a few years
Potentially curable	Not presently curable without bone marrow transplant

Intensive support by transfusion of blood products and use of antibacterial and antifungal agents is necessary to support the patient during the treatment while bone marrow function is suppressed.

Survival is months or a few years in adults, with an increasing proportion of long-term survivors with advances in therapy. The outlook is much better in childhood ALL and in adults with good prognosis AML, where significant cure rates are now achieved.

Chronic Leukaemias

The important differences between chronic and acute leukaemia are shown in Table elsewhere in this chapter.

Chronic myeloid (granulocytic) leukaemia

Although a 'chronic' leukaemia, CML is a fatal disorder with a median survival of about 5 years in patients not eligible for allogeneic bone marrow *transplantation*. It occurs in all age groups. Normal bone marrow is replaced by an abnormal clone derived from a *pluripotential* stem cell which, in the majority of cases, is characterised by the presence of a karyotypic *abnormality*, the *Philadelphia* chromosome (*reciprocal* translocation of part of the long arm of chromosome 22 to another chromosome, usually 9).

Erythroid, *megakaryocytic* and *B-lymphocyte* cell lines all carry the defect, as well as the granulocytic series. In most cases the disease eventually enters a more *aggressive* phase due to the emergence and dominance of a clone of myeloid cells which have now lost the ability to differentiate. The disease, called blast crisis, then bears a close resemblance to AML (or less commonly ALL) and is fatal.

Blood and bone marrow changes

Leukocytosis is a uniform feature, with occasional cell counts in excess of $300 \times 10^9/1$. The cell picture in the blood can superficially resemble that in a bone marrow aspirate, with *myelocytes*, *promyelocytes*, myeloblasts and normoblasts present as well as large numbers of band cells and mature polymorphonuclear granulocytes. Basophilia is common. Platelets are increased (sometimes over $1000 \times 10^9/1$), normal or reduced. A normochromic anaemia is often present.

The leukocytes are abnormal, as exemplified by an absence or severe reduction of their content of alkaline phosphatase, a feature unique to CML and of diagnostic value. Serum vitamin B_{12} is elevated due to production of binding protein by the granulocyte series.

The bone marrow is hypercellular with marked reduction of fat spaces; granulocytopoiesis predominates. In the acute, terminal phase increased numbers of blast cells become evident in blood and bone marrow, and anaemia and thrombocytopenia are more marked.

Changes in other organs

The spleen is enlarged, often massively, due to infiltration by CML cells; it may fill the abdominal cavity and extend into the pelvis. Areas of infarction are present due to the rapid enlargement outstripping the available blood supply. Hepatomegaly is also frequently present. Infiltration in other organs is an occasional feature. Infection and bleeding are not common in the chronic phase.

Clinical course

Symptoms may be mild in the chronic phase and are essentially those of anaemia and massive splenomegaly (abdominal fullness and pain from splenic infarction). Rarely, a hyperviscosity state may develop when the white count is greater than $300 \times 10^9/1$. In the acute phase the clinical features are those of acute leukaemia.

Treatment

The treatment of BCR-ABL positive CML has seen a significant change in recent times. The initial proliferative features of the disease are readily controlled by the oral antimetabolite hydroxyurea. Patients who are young enough, fit enough and have a suitable donor can be cured by an allogeneic stem cell transplant. For the majority of patients who do not qualify for a transplant based on the above criteria the standard treatment until recently has been long-term α-interferon.

Such treatment prolongs the chronic phase, and hence survival. However, interferon rarely if ever cures patients with CML. The median survival of CML has increased with interferon from 3 to 5 years. With detailed understanding of the molecular structure of the causitive oncogene BCR-ABL, a drug called imatinib mesylate-trade name Glivec, has recently been developed.

The drug is a small molecule which binds to the ATPbinding site of BCR-ABL and inhibits the function of the protein. In clinical trials this oral drug has had very dramatic positive results with > 90% of patients achieving complete haematological control of their leukaemia and a much higher percentage of patients achieving a complete cytogenetic response than when treated with interferon.

Glivec is also more effective in treating patients in blast crises than conventional chemotherapy. It is too early to know if Glivec will cure patients with CML; however, the introduction of Glivec is a landmark event and marks the proof of principle that a clear understanding of the pathogenesis of a disease at a moleular level can lead to the design of effective targeted treatment.

Chronic Lymphocytic Leukaemia

Aetiology

CLL is a chronic lymphoproliferative disorder with features similar to a low-grade lymphoma but with predominant blood and marrow involvement. During the last few years there has been significant new understanding of the pathology of this disease. The disease process is a relentless accumulation of B-lymphocytes which appear resistant to apoptosis.

In the majority of cases it is a considerably less aggressive disorder than are the other leukaemias. This common form of the disease is a disease of the elderly. It is slowly progressive, usually following a predictable clinical course with a median survival of 25 years and often does not require therapy. In this form of the disease the malignant B-cell has undergone rearrangement of its immunoglobulin genes and the cell has also passed through the germinal centre of the lymph node and been selected for antigen by hypermutation of its rearranged immunoglobulin genes.

Such cells therefore are the Leukaemic equivalent of memory B-cells. In a proportion of patients the disease is much more aggressive in its behaviour with resistance to chemotherapy and a much shortened median survival of 8-9 years. In these cases the leukaemic B-cell has not been selected for antigen by hypermutation of the immunoglobulin genes and is the leukaemic equivalent of a naive B-cell. In both forms of the disease lymphocytes accumulate in blood, marrow, liver and spleen until the total lymphoid mass is expanded up to a hundred-fold.

Blood and bone marrow changes

Leukocytosis is present; up to 99% of nucleated cells are small lymphocytes of B-cell origin in most instances. The lymphocyte count is between $5 \times 10^9/l$ and more than $300 \times 10^9/l$. The CLL cells tend to fragment during preparation of the blood film, producing many 'smear cells'.

Anaemia (normocytic) and thrombocytopenia are late developments. However, in up to 10% of cases a secondary autoimmune haemolytic anaemia develops, with reticulocytosis and microspherocytes and positive direct antiglobulin test. Serum immunoglobulins are low in the later stages of the disease. The bone marrow is hypercellular, with progressive replacement of normal tissue by small lymphocytes, resulting eventually in anaemia and thrombocytopenia.

Advanced stage non-Hodgkin's lymphoma (NHL) may result in blood and marrow involvement superficially resembling CLL. However, extensive involvement usually occurs late in the course of the disease and the lymphoma cells are morphologically distinct from the lymphocytes of CLL.

Immunophenotyping of B-CLL cells shows a distinct pattern of antigen staining with the leukaemic cells staining positively for the B-cell antigen CD19 and also for CD5 and CD23. This pattern of staining is useful for helping to distinguish CLL from other cases of B-NHL appearing in the blood which lack staining for CD5 and/or CD23. Cases of CLL, as with other leukaemias, have acquired cytogenetic abnormalities within the leukaemic cells.

The common ones are deletions of 13q and llq and trisomy 12. As with acute leukaemia, these abnormalities have prognostic significance.

Changes in other organs

The lymph nodes, liver and spleen are characteristically involved. In nodes and spleen the normal architecture becomes completely effaced by the infiltrate of monomorphic small lymphocytes, and similar cells are present in the portal tracts of the liver.

Clinical course and treatment

For the good *prognostic* form of the disease the clinical course is protracted; it is summarised in Figure elsewhere in this chapter. The protracted course means that many cases are diagnosed as a result of routine blood tests or clinical examination for some other reason. Elderly patients with this form of the disease often die from an unrelated cause.

Many of these patients do not require treatment at all or for many years. Treatment is indicated for the development of significant cytopenias, bulky *lymphadenopathy* or *hepatosplenomegaly* or systemic symptoms such as loss of weight or night sweats. Treatment with single agent chlorambucil or fludarabine chemotherapy agents is successful.

For the aggressive form of the disease occurring in younger patients the outlook is much less favourable and treatment regimens involving intensive combinations of chemotherapy, such as fludarabine and cyclophosphamide, stem cell transplantation and monoclonal antibody therapy are being explored.

Other Leukaemias

The *prolymphocytic variant of CLL* is more aggressive and responds poorly to therapy. Splenomegaly is massive. The leukaemic cells in blood and bone marrow are larger and of more primitive appearance than is the case in CLL. *T-PLL* (T-cell prolymphocytic leukaemia) occurs in younger subjects than does the more common B-cell CLL described above. Skin involvement is common. Recently T-PLL has been shown to respond well to the monoclonal antibody MabCampath.

Hairy-cell leukaemia is a rare B-cell leukaemia of the middle-aged and elderly. The characteristic cells in the blood have cytoplasmic projections or 'hairs'. Pancytopenia is typical, as is splenomegaly, which may be gross.

A characteristic feature of the peripheral blood count is a marked monocytopenia. The marrow is diffusely infiltrated by the malignant cells and marrow fibrosis is present. The disorder may run a chronic course and is of particular interest because there are a number of very effective treatments, including interferon, cladribine and deoxycoformycin. Splenectomy is also useful in management and can relieve cytopenias but is used less frequently now with these newer effective therapies.

MYELODYSPLASTIC SYNDROMES

This is a group of neoplastic conditions of bone marrow in which there is dysplastic *haemopoiesis*, resulting in marked morphological abnormalities in blood cells, and a tendency to progress to AML. As such they are *pre-leukaemic* disorders. Their hallmark is the presence of a cellular bone marrow with *cytopenias* in the peripheral blood. The pathogenesis appears to be an abnormal clone arising from a mutated stem cell.

The combination of the high marrow cellularity and blood cytopenias may be explained by development of a mutated clone with predisposition to apoptosis. In some cases the *myelodysplastic* syndrome is secondary to stem cell damage from prior treatment of unrelated *malignancies* with chemotherapy or radiotherapy and is therefore iatrogenic.

Blood and Bone Marrow Changes

There is anaemia, usually macrocytic, with leucopenia and thrombocytopenia. Abnormal cells such as poikilocytes and neutrophils with poorly developed cytoplasmic granules are commonly present. Bone marrow appearances are dysplastic with changes resembling those seen in megaloblastic anaemia.

Typical appearances include binucleate normoblasts, ring sideroblasts, megakaryocytes with a single round nucleus and neutrophils with little granulation and poorly developed nuclear segmentation. Leukaemic blast cells may be present but constitute less than 20% of the marrow cells, unless there has been progression to acute leukaemia.

Abnormalities of marrow chromosomes are commonly present, consistent with the malignant and clonal nature of the disorders. Subclassification is possible depending on the presence of ring sideroblasts and increased leukaemic blasts.

In *refractory anaemia* neither ring sideroblasts nor leukaemic blasts are prominent, whereas in *refractory anaemia with ring sideroblasts* the iron-loaded cells are easily seen. As the number of leukaemic blasts increases the terms *refractory anaemia with excess blasts* is applied. In another variant of myelodysplasia there is a marked excess of monocytes in the blood: *chronic myelomonocytic leukaemia (CMML)*.

Because of the combination of features of myeloproliferative disease and myelodysplasia the term 'crossover syndrome' is sometimes applied to CMML and some other variants of myelodysplasia.

Clinical features

Myelodysplasia occurs in the elderly most commonlymedian age over 65 years. Anaemia is usually the most troublesome problem for the patient. Infections and bleeding also occur. Splenomegaly is rare, except in CMML. Progression to acute leukaemia occurs in around 30%. Treatment is largely supportive with blood transfusions and treatment of infections.

In some cases the anaemia responds to treatment with recombinant erythropoietin. Chemotherapy is used to treat high white cell counts and some patients with excess blasts. In younger patients treatment using allogeneic bone marrow transplantation offers a hope of cure. Overall, survival varies with the subtype; for example it is often less than 1 year in those with excess blasts and in CMML.

MYELOPROLIFERATIVE DISORDERS

- Malignant proliferations of myeloid cells with differentiation to mature forms

- In polycythaemia rubra vera, a pancytosis is accompanied by splenomegaly and hyperviscosity
- In essential thrombocythaemia, thrombocytosis is accompanied by splenomegaly or hyposplenism and by bleeding or thrombosis
- In myelofibrosis, anaemia and marrow fibrosis are accompanied by massive hepatosplenomegaly due to extramedullary haemopoiesis

The myeloproliferative disorders are listed in Table elsewhere in this chapter. This list is something of an oversimplification as intermediate forms exist. More importantly, progression in an individual from one such disorder to another within the group is common.

Myeloproliferative disorders most often represent a neoplastic proliferation of a marrow myeloid stem cell with differentiation to the mature form(s) (in contrast to the acute myeloid leukaemias, where maturation is very limited).

The normal control mechanisms governing the cell line(s) involved are no longer active, allowing accumulation of erythrocytes, platelets or leukocytes. Proliferation of megakaryocytes produces growth factors causing a secondary overgrowth of fibroblasts (myelofibrosis).

Chronic myeloid leukaemia behaves as a myeloproliferative disorder and can be usefully regarded as such, along with the non-leukaemic myeloproliferative disorders polycythaemia rubra vera (PRV), essential thrombocythaemia and myelofibrosis. The main features of these conditions are summarised in Table elsewhere in this chapter and described below. Non-myeloproliferative causes of polycythaemia are also considered here.

Polycythaemia Rubra Vera

Polycythaemia is an increase in the concentration of red cells above normal, usually with a corresponding increase in haemoglobin concentration and haematocrit. In PRV it is an idiopathic, primary condition.

The body red cell mass and plasma volume can be accurately assessed by isotopic labelling techniques. Normal ranges are 25-35 ml/kg for red cell mass (22-32 ml/kg in females) and 35-45 ml/kg for plasma volume.

Blood and Bone Marrow Changes

The haemoglobin concentration is raised, often to 20 g/dl or more, with haematocrit values of up to 75%. Red cell mass may be as high as 80 ml/kg. However, iron deficiency is not uncommon, partly due to

Table 6.6: The myeloproliferative diseases

Disorder	*Morphology of bone marrow*	*Clinical features*
Myelofibrosis	Increased reticulin/collagen	Leukoerythroblastic blood picture Anaemia with tear-drop poikilocytes Gross hepatosplenomegaly due to myeloid metaplasia
Chronic myeloid leukaemia	increased cellularity, particularly of the myeloid series Philadelphia chromosome Splenomegaly, often gross	Leukoerythroblastic blood picture Anaemia, neutrophilia with immature forms Basophilia
Polycythaemia rubra vera	Increased cellularity, particularly of the erythroid series	Erythrocytosis, often neutrophilia and thrombocytosis Plethora Pruritus Thrombosis or haemorrhage Splenomegaly
Essential thrombocythaemia	Increased megakaryocytes	Thrombocytosis Thrombosis or haemorrhage Sometimes splenomegaly

increased requirements and partly to a bleeding tendency with chronic gastrointestinal blood loss due to production of functionally abnormal platelets. In such circumstances of iron-deficient polycythaemia, haemoglobin and haematocrit may be normal or even low, but the red cell count is still high.

Thrombocytosis and neutrophil leukocytosis are present in up to 50% of cases. The serum vitamin B_{12} and uric acid are increased, the former due to production of binding protein by myeloid cells, the latter due to increased cell turnover. The bone marrow is hypercellular. Erythroid hyperplasia is present. Megakaryocytes may be prominent and increased reticulin deposition is common.

Changes in other organs

The spleen is enlarged in 75% of cases, usually to a moderate extent. Splenic sinuses are engorged. Extramedullary haemopoiesis may be present: normoblasts and cells of the developing myeloid series are present in the spleen and often the liver. Infarction of heart, brain and spleen is common due to the high blood viscosity and poor flow.

Haemorrhagic lesions may be a feature, especially in the gastrointestinal tract. Peptic ulceration is common in PRV, for unknown reasons.

Clinical features

Clinical features correspond to the pathological changes described above. The skin is plethoric and cyanosis is common. Itching is typical and usually exacerbated by changes in temperature, as after bathing. The conjunctival vessels appear congested, as are retinal vessels. Hyperviscosity results in headache and lethargy.

The spleen is palpable. Acute gout may be a presenting feature. Evidence of mucosal bleeding or of thrombosis (particularly arterial) may be present.

Treatment is by venesection or myelosuppression by alkylating agents, hydroxyurea or use of radiophosphorus (32p). Survival is for many years. Progression to a myelofibrotic state is common and transformation to acute myeloid leukaemia may occur, especially following 32p treatment. Myeloproliferative polycythaemia (rubra vera) must be distinguished from other causes of polycythaemia, in which splenomegaly and pancytosis are not features.

Secondary and Relative Polycythaemias

Most cases of polycythaemia are not due to PRV, but are due to:

- high altitude

- cyanotic heart disease
- respiratory disease
- smoking
- haemoglobinopathy.

Any disorder resulting in chronic hypoxia results in stimulation of erythropoietin production and secondary polycythaemia, as in severe chronic bronchitis, emphysema or alveolar hypoventilation for any reason. Congenital heart disease in which a right-to-left shunt is present is a potent cause; haemoglobin concentrations of 20 g/dl are not uncommon.

Cigarette smokers have a higher haematocrit than non-smokers, due in part to the carbon monoxide in tobacco smoke. In these situations the polycythaemia is frequently not symptomatic and the blood and bone marrow are otherwise normal. Treatment is rarely necessary.

The following renal disorders and tumours are (very uncommonly) associated with inappropriate erythropoietin production and polycythaemia:

- renal carcinoma or cysts
- renal artery stenosis
- massive uterine fibroids
- hepatocellular carcinoma
- cerebellar haemangioblastoma.

Polycythaemia may also result from a contraction of the plasma volume with normal red cell mass. This situation occurs chronically in so-called *stress polycythaemia,* also known as Gaisbock's syndrome, where the plasma volume may be 30 ml/kg or less.

It is a common disorder, especially in middle-aged, overweight male heavy smokers. It is associated with increased risk of arterial occlusion causing myocardial infarction and stroke. The pathogenesis is obscure.

Myelofibrosis

Also known as myelosclerosis, myelofibrosis is characterised by the predominant features of gross marrow fibrosis with massive extramedullary haemopoiesis in liver and spleen. The fibrosis is reactive (a polyclonal proliferation of fibroblasts is present). Factors released from pathological megakaryocytes which proliferate in the bone marrow are thought to be the stimulus to the fibroblastic response. It is a chronic disorder of late middle age and beyond.

Blood and bone marrow changes

Anaemia is usually present; platelets and leukocytes are often increased, but become subnormal eventually. The blood film is typically leukoerythroblastic. Characteristic poikilocytes with a tear-drop shape are a consistent finding.

Bone marrow cannot be aspirated. Trephine biopsy reveals variable cellularity with increased reticulin, progressing to massive deposition of collagen. Megakaryocytes are often increased. Bony trabeculae may be expanded.

Changes in other organs

The spleen is invariably enlarged, often to a massive degree. Lymphoid follicles are preserved but the red pulp is expanded with diffuse areas of extramedullary haemopoiesis.

The liver is often enlarged, with obvious foci of haemopoiesis present. Occasionally, lymph nodes are also involved. The liver involvement may result in portal hypertension, causing oesophageal varices and ascites.

Clinical features

Symptoms are caused by the anaemia and massive splenomegaly. Symptoms of hypermetabolism may also be present, especially weight loss and night sweats. Sclerosis of bones may be apparent on X-ray examination. Many patients have a history of polycythaemia rubra vera or essential thrombocythaemia; in others, the onset is insidious.

With supportive therapy (blood transfusion), survival is often a few years. If the enlarged spleen is troublesome, splenectomy can be safely performed, surprisingly without exacerbation of the anaemia.

Essential Thrombocythaemia

Essential thrombocythaemia, a myeloproliferative disorder, is an important cause of thrombocytosis. The diagnosis is being made more frequently as an incidental finding now that automated cell counters are routinely used.

Blood and bone marrow changes

The platelet count is raised, often to 1000×10^9/l and even to 3000×10^9/l. Neutrophil leukocytosis may also be a feature. 'Giant' platelets and megakaryocyte fragments may be present. Anaemia, when present, is due to iron deficiency from chronic blood loss.

Howell Jolly bodies and other features of hyposplenism may be apparent due to splenic infarction. Bone marrow cellularity is normal or increased, megakaryocytes predominate and some increase in marrow reticulin is common.

Changes in other organs

The spleen may be enlarged but is usually normal or reduced in size due to infarction. Ischaemic changes in the area supplied by digital arteries may be present, as may evidence of infarction in other organs. Paradoxically, haemorrhagic lesions also occur, often in the gastrointestinal tract.

Clinical features

The disorder may be asymptomatic for many years. Painful ischaemic lesions of the digits are an occasional feature. Paradoxical haemorrhage, which may be serious, occurs particularly in association with platelet counts over $1000 \times 10^9/1$. Treatment with alkylating agents or hydroxyurea is effective and survival prolonged. Progression to myelofibrosis may occur.

PLASMA CELL NEOPLASMS

Plasma cells are the immunoglobulin-producing cells and are normally identifiable in the bone marrow. Diffuse neoplastic, monoclonal proliferation of plasma cells throughout the red marrow is characteristic of the disorder multiple *myeloma.* When the proliferation is more localised an apparently discrete plasma cell tumour develops, usually in bone-solitary *plasmacytoma.*

Monoclonal proliferation of IgM-producing plasma cells and lymphoplasmacytoid cells in the reticulo-endothelial organs, bone marrow, liver and spleen is present in a third type of plasma cell neoplasmWaldenstrom's macroglobulinaemia.

Multiple Myelorna

- Malignant proliferation of plasma cells in bone marrow
- Occurs in older age groups
- Usually associated with the accumulation of a monoclonal immunoglobulin or light chains (Bence Jones protein) in plasma
- Often causes renal failure
- Results in bone destruction in the axial skeleton, with pain and fractures

Multiple myeloma is a common neoplastic disease affecting especially the elderly: almost all cases occur after the age of 40 years. Multifocal plasma cell tumours erode the bones of the axial skeleton; the plasma cells synthesise a monoclonal immunoglobulin or light chain, referred to as the *M-component* or paraprotein in plasma.

The M-component is present in over 99% of cases of multiple myeloma; it is most commonly IgG (60% of cases) but may be IgA or immunoglobulin light chains only (kappa or lambda). IgD and IgE M-components are unusual and IgM types are much more commonly a feature of Waldenstrom's macroglobulinaemia.

In two-thirds of cases of IgG and IgA myeloma, a large excess of free light chains is produced in addition to the complete immunoglobulin molecule, presumably due to a functional defect in the malignant plasma cells. While immunoglobulins cannot pass the glomerular filter, free light chains are small enough to enter the urine, where they are called *Bence Jones protein.*

The plasma concentration of the unaffected immunoglobulins is often markedly suppressed ('immune paresis'). Paraprotein formation is not unique to multiple myeloma; a monoclonal immunoglobulin is present occasionally in CLL and lymphomas and, rarely, in carcinomatous disease. Furthermore, a proportion of elderly subjects are found to have a stable paraprotein without immune paresis and without the other features of multiple myeloma or lymphoproliferative disease-so-called 'monoclonal gammopathy of uncertain significance' (MGUS).

The pathology of the bone disease in myeloma is becoming better understood and leading to improved treatments for this catastrophic manifestation of the disease. The osteolytic destruction of the axial skeleton (sites of haemopoiesis in adults) results from malignant plasma cells stimulating osteoclasts to erode bone. This leads to lytic lesions and pathological fractures and generalised osteoporosis.

For some time it has been recognised that chemical messengers (cytokines) produced from the interaction of malignant plasma cells with their microenvironment stimulate the osteoclast activity. Such cytokines were known as osteoclast activating factors (OAFs) and are now known to include interleukins 1 and 6. Very recently another system of messengers has been shown to be important in the development of the bone disease in myeloma.

A protein called RANKL is expressed by osteoblasts and it binds to its ligand RANK on the osteoclast surface and stimulates the osteoclast to erode bone. A second protein called osteoprotegerin (OPG) normally blocks this interaction. However in myeloma it is suggested that the levels of OPG are reduced and this RANKL stimulation of bone erosion goes unchecked.

This understanding has produced successful treatments to limit the bone disease. A group of drugs called bisphosphonates (e.g clodronate and pamidronate) directly inhibit osteoclasts and are used routinely in myeloma. Recombinant OPG is being used in trials.

Blood and bone marrow changes

Anaemia is common. The blood film often has rouleaux formation: a tendency for the erythrocytes to adhere to each other and form columns one cell across in the blood film, due to the presence of a high concentration of immunoglobulin. The anaemia is normocytic, but automated cell counters may suggest a high MCV, probably due to rouleaux formation.

In advanced disease, pancytopenia is present. Abnormal plasma cells are only occasionally seen in the peripheral blood. The marrow is hypercellular; 10-90% of the cells are morphologically abnormal plasma cells, including multinucleate forms. Increased numbers of osteoclasts actively resorbing bone may be seen on trephine biopsy.

The plasma cell infiltrate and discrete tumours are present in those bones normally containing red marrow, especially the skull, ribs, vertebrae and pelvis. The distal long bones and those of the extremities are rarely involved. Generalised osteoporosis is common.

Changes in other organs

Renal involvement is present in over half of the cases. The most common abnormality is the presence of protein casts in the distal convoluted and collecting tubules with surrounding giant cells and atrophy of tubular cells-'Bence Jones or myeloma kidney'.

Metastatic calcification, changes of pyelonephritis and primary amyloid may also be present in the kidneys. Systemic amyloidosis is present in 10% of cases, particularly in the tongue, heart and peripheral nerves, as well as the kidneys.

Clinical features

The clinical features in multiple myeloma are outlined in Figure elsewhere in this chapter. Not all are present in every case. Bone pain is present in the majority and is often severe. Renal failure is common and prognostically sinister. Hyperviscosity is especially associated with IgA paraproteins because of the physical characteristics of IgA. Treatment involves management of acute problems, including hypercalcaemia, cord compression and renal failure and the routine use of bisphosphonates to limit bone disease.

The disease is not curable but responds to single agent chemotherapy (melphalan) or combination chemotherapy. Radiotherapy provides effective control of localised bone pain. Recent randomised data have shown a

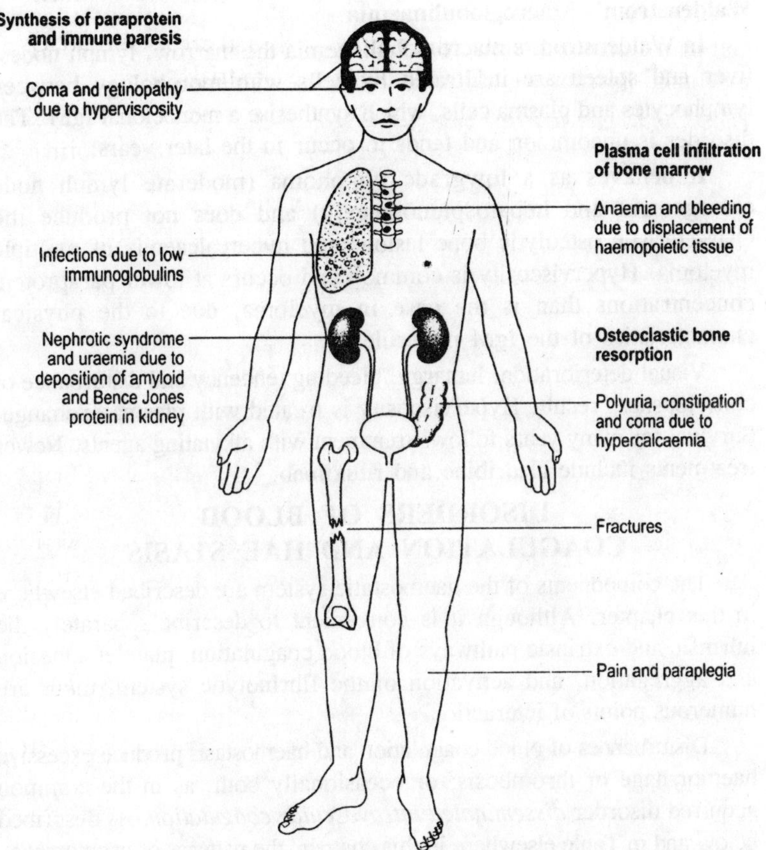

Figure 6.8: Pathological mechanisms and clinical features in multiple myeloma.

survival advantage for high dose therapy and autologous stem cell transplantation which is now offered routinely to younger patients. Survival is 2-3 years in most cases but longer in those treated with high dose therapy. The drug thalidomide is also showing promise in the treatment of end-stage disease, with 20-30% of patients having a useful response.

Solitary Plasmacytoma

Solitary tumours composed of malignant plasma cells identical in morphology to those in multiple myeloma occasionally arise in bone or extra-osseous sites. A paraprotein may be synthesised by the cells of the tumour. Solitary plasmacytoma of the bone may progress to multiple myeloma.

Waldenstrom's Macroglobulinaemia

In Waldenstrom's macroglobulinaemia the marrow, lymph nodes, liver and spleen are infiltrated by cells with morphology between lymphocytes and plasma cells, which synthesise a monoclonal IgM. The disorder is uncommon and tends to occur in the later years.

It behaves as a lowgrade lymphoma (moderate lymph node enlargement and hepatosplenomegaly) and does not produce the characteristic osteolytic bone lesions and hypercalcaemia of multiple myeloma. Hyperviscosity is common and occurs at lower paraprotein concentrations than is the case in myeloma, due to the physical characteristics of the IgM molecule.

Visual deterioration; lethargy, bleeding tendency and disturbance of consciousness result. Hyperviscosity is treated with plasma exchange. Survival for many years follows treatment with alkylating agents. Newer treatments include cladribine and rituximab.

DISORDERS OF BLOOD COAGULATION AND HAE STASIS

The components of the haemostatic system are described elsewhere in this chapter. Although it is convenient to describe separately the intrinsic and extrinsic pathways of blood coagulation, platelet adhesion and aggregation, and activation of the fibrinolytic system, there are numerous points of interaction.

Disturbances of blood coagulation and haemostasis produce excessive haemorrhage or thrombosis, or occasionally both, as in the common acquired disorder *disseminated intravascular coagulation. As* described below and in Table elsewhere in this chatper, the patterns of haemorrhage differ somewhat between disorders of primary haemostasis (platelet disorders) and defects of blood coagulation.

Also, as a general rule, disorders which allow the unchecked generation and deposition of fibrin tend to be associated with thrombosis in the venous circulation (red thrombus), whereas excessive platelet activation tends to result in vascular occlusion in arteries and arterioles (white thrombus), although this is by no means a rigid distinction.

DISORDERS OF PRIMARY HAEMOSTASIS

Theoretically, primary haemostasis could be defective as a result of platelet abnormalities or defects of the small blood vessels. In fact, vascular disease is rarely the cause of clinically important haemorrhage. Bleeding due to primary haemostatic defects is most commonly secondary

Table 6.7: Features that may distinguish bleeding in coagulation defects from that in platelet disorders.

Feature	*Platelet defect*	*Severe coagulation defect*
Purpura	Very common	Absent
Mucosal bleeding	Common from mouth and gut	Relatively uncommon except from urinary tract
Joint bleeding	Absent	Very common in severe congenital factor deficiencies
Muscle haematomas	In response to trauma	Spontaneous
Bleeding after surgery	Immediate	often delayed several hours

to acquired platelet disorders such as thrombocytopenia or disturbance of platelet function.

In bleeding due to disorders of primary haemostasis the skin and mucous membranes are especially involved.

Thrombocytopenias

- Cause spontaneous bleeding when the blood platelet count falls below 20 × 10^9/1
- Due to failure of platelet production or increased destruction/sequestration
- When due to production failure, thrombocytopenia is usually accompanied by other evidence of marrow dysfunction: anaemia, leukopenia or leukocytosis
- When due to increased destruction, immune mechanisms and disseminated intravascular coagulation are common causes

Although a bleeding tendency results from thrombocytopenia, there must be a substantial reduction in platelet numbers before this occurs. No clinical defect of primary haemostasis occurs with platelet counts greater than 80 × 10^9/1 if they function normally.

Increased bleeding after trauma is present with counts of 40-50 × 10^9/1, but spontaneous skin and mucosal haemorrhage occur only when platelet counts fall to 20 × 10^9/1. The time to cessation of bleeding from skin incisions increases progressively as the platelet count falls below 80 × 10^9/l and, when performed in a standardised manner in the bleeding time test, is a good guide to the efficiency of primary haemostasis.

The bleeding time is not usually affected by deficiencies of clotting factors because it relies on adequate platelet numbers and function rather than fibrin formation.

Classification

Thrombocytopenia can be conveniently classified according to pathogenesis:

- failure of platelet production
  - — megaloblastic anaemia
  - — haematological malignancy, including leukaemias, myelodysplasia, myelofibrosis, myeloma and marrow involvement in lymphoma
  - — other marrow infiltration, e.g. carcinoma - hypoplastic anaemia
  - — chemotherapeutic agents and occasionally other drugs, e.g. thiazides
  - — alcohol
  - — some viral infections
  - — congenital absence of megakaryocytes
- increased platelet destruction
  - — acute and chronic autoimmune thrombocytopenic purpura
  - — drug-induced immune thrombocytopenia
  - — neonatal and post-transfusion purpura (alloimmune)
  - — massive blood loss and transfusion
  - — disseminated intravascular coagulation
  - — thrombotic thrombocytopenia/haemolytic-uraemic syndrome
- platelet sequestration
  - — hypersplenism.

Where thrombocytopenia is an isolated finding, with normal haemoglobin and white cells, increased platelet destruction is most likely. Failure of platelet production due to a bone marrow abnormality is most commonly associated with a pancytopenia, or a leukocytosis, in the leukaemias.

Of the causes of thrombocytopenia due to platelet production failure, those due to thiazides, viral infection and congenital megakaryocyte abnormalities are very uncommon. The other disorders resulting in marrow failure have been described earlier.

Autoimmune thrombocytopenic purpura and disseminated intravascular coagulation are the most common disorders in which thrombocytopenia is due to increased destruction/ utilisation of platelets.

Autoimmune thrombocytopenic purpura

In autoimmune thrombocytopenic purpura platelets are destroyed in the reticulo-endothelial system, especially the spleen, due to coating with auto-antibody. The disorder is analogous to autoimmune haemolytic anaemia. It occurs in an acute, spontaneously remitting form in children, as a chronic idiopathic state at all ages, and as a drug-induced phenomenon.

The acute childhood variety may follow an infection such as measles. The chronic type is occasionally symptomatic of a disorder such as chronic lymphocytic leukaemia, or lymphoma, or may occur in association with other autoimmune disease such as rheumatoid arthritis.

Drugs associated with idiopathic thrombocytopenic purpura (ITP) include quinine, heparin and sulphonamides; in most cases, an immune complex mechanism is involved, similar to that in some cases of drug-induced immune haemolytic anaemia.

Blood and bone marrow changes

Thrombocytopenia is present; severity is variable. Platelet counts of less than $10 \times 10^9/1$ are not uncommon. Erythrocytes and leukocytes are usually normal. Iron deficiency anaemia may be present due to chronic mucosal bleeding. In the bone marrow there is a non-specific increase in megakaryocyte size and number.

It may be possible to detect the auto-antibody in serum by tests analogous to the antiglobulin test used in the investigation of haemolytic anaemias, but poor sensitivity and specificity of these assays limit their clinical utility.

Changes in other organs

Changes in other organs are those of haemorrhage. Bleeding into the skin in the form of purpura is common. Purpura (petechiae) of thrombocytopenic type is due to apparently spontaneous leakage of red cells from capillaries and arterioles in the skin. It is usually most prominent in the skin of the lower legs and feet, suggesting that hydrostatic pressure may play a role.

Areas of skin trauma may also be affected. Histological evidence of capillary bleeding may also be present in the serosal linings, mucosae of gastrointestinal and urinary tract and the central nervous system. The spleen is usually of normal size or only moderately enlarged, not extending below the costal margin.

The sinusoids are congested and splenic follicles reactive.

Megakaryocytes may be present in the spleen, a response to the increased platelet turnover.

Clinical features

Clinical features are restricted to excessive haemorrhage. Purpuric rash, skin bruising, epistaxis, menorrhagia and gastrointestinal haemorrhage are common. The acute form in childhood is transient and often requires no treatment. Drug-induced ITP responds to withdrawal of the offending medication.

Chronic 'idiopathic' ITP often responds to immunosuppressive therapy, for example with corticosteroids. Intravenous infusion of a concentrate of normal human IgG prepared from plasma is also often effective. It may act through blockade of the reticulo-endothelial Fc receptors responsible for binding of antibody-coated platelets, or possibly through anti-idiotype activity.

Surgical removal of the spleen (splenectomy) may result in longterm remission. Prognosis is good; the main risk is fatal cerebral haemorrhage.

Other Immune Thrombocytopenias

The immune thrombocytopenia which is occasionally associated with exposure to the anticoagulant drug heparin is unusual, as it is often accompanied by thrombosis rather than haemorrhage. It results from the development of an immune complex formed between heparin, platelet factor 4 (a peptide secreted from the cytoplasmic granules of stimulated platelets) and the auto-antibody to heparinplatelet factor 4.

Binding of the complex to platelet Fc receptors causes platelet activation and consumption with thrombocytopenia. Thrombosis occurs, for example deep vein thrombosis, or arterial thrombosis, resulting in myocardial or cerebral infarction. Heparin must be withdrawn.

Thrombocytopenia is a frequent manifestation of AIDS and, in some cases, has an autoimmune pathogenesis. Neonatal thrombocytopenia due to placental transfer of the platelet-reactive IgG auto-antibody can occur in infants of women with chronic ITP Also, a condition analogous to rhesus haemolytic disease, due to transplacental passage of an antibody, is occasionally recognised as a cause of neonatal thrombocytopenia-neonatal alloimmune thrombocytopenia (NAIT).

The pathogenesis is comparable to that of haemolytic disease of the newborn, the fetus possessing a platelet antigen lacking in the mother, usually HPAla.

Post-transfusion purpura is a very uncommon immune thrombocytopenia in women following blood transfusion. It is also due to formation of an allo-antibody to a foreign antigen on transfused platelets, usually HPAIa. Thrombotic thrombocytopenic purpura and haemolytic-uraemic syndrome. In thrombotic thrombocytopenic purpura (TTP) and haemolytic-uraemic syndrome (HUS) the dominant features are thrombocytopenia due to platelet consumption in microvascular occlusive platelet plugs and a microangiopathic haemolytic anaemia.

Characteristic fragmented erythrocytes-schistocytes-are present on the blood film. Glomerular lesions are characteristic, especially in HUS, but vascular lesions in other organs, especially the central nervous system, are a feature in TTP In children, HUS may occur in epidemics, suggesting an infectious origin.

When it is associated with an acute haemorrhagic colitis, production of verocytotoxin by *Escherichia coli,* usually strain 0157, from contaminated food has been shown to be the cause. TTP is usually sporadic, but can be familial or relapsing. It appears to be due to platelet aggregation by very high molecular weight multimers of von Willebrand factor. Such multimers are normally secreted by endothelial cells but are rapidly degraded into smaller multimers, which are less reactive with platelets, by a protease. In sporadic TTP there is development of an auto-antibody which interferes with the protease activity. In familial TTP there may be a deficiency of the enzyme.

Clinically, haemorrhage and organ dysfunction due to the microvascular lesions predominate. Renal failure is present. Neurological abnormalities, which maybe transient or permanent, including stroke, characterise TTP and distinguish it from HUS.

The disease runs a subacute or chronic course. Spontaneous remission is not uncommon in the childhood form, but chronic renal impairment may result. Renal support, including dialysis therapy, may be required in HUS. In TTP, high volume plasma exchange is effective, presumably through removal of auto-antibody and replacement of the cleaving protease in the transfused plasma.

Qualitative Disorders of Platelets

Disorders of platelet function result in excessive bleeding of platelet type and prolonged skin bleeding time, usually in the presence of normal platelet numbers.

Acquired disorders of platelet function

Acquired disorders of platelet function are due to:

- drugs (e.g. aspirin, anti-inflammatory drugs, high dose penicillin)

- metabolic disorders (e.g. uraemia, hepatic failure)
- myeloproliferative disorders (essential thrombocythaemia, polycythaemia rubra vera)
- plasma cell disorders (e.g. multiple myeloma, Waldenstrom's macroglobulinaemia).

Aspirin and anti-inflammatory drugs block the cyclooxygenase enzyme necessary for platelet synthesis of proaggregatory thromboxane. Any bleeding tendency is very mild, but there may be increased skin bruising and bleeding after surgery.

Gastric haemorrhage from acute mucosal erosions may be life-threatening. In uraemia and liver failure, platelet interactions with subendothelium are abnormal and bleeding may be severe. In myeloproliferative disease, the clonal defect gives rise to functionally abnormal platelets, and in myeloma platelets become coated with immunoglobulin, which blocks surface receptors and prevents platelet aggregation.

Congenital disorders of platelet function

Hereditary platelet disorders causing life-threatening haemorrhage, such as those where the platelet glycoprotein receptors for von Willebrand factor (BernardSoulier syndrome) or fibrinogen (Glanzmann's disease) are absent, are extremely rare autosomal recessive diseases. Life-threatening haemorrhage may occur.

Mild defects of platelet function, causing easy bruising and bleeding after trauma, are more common. In some, a familial pattern is apparent. Various metabolic disturbances of platelets may be responsible, such as a deficiency of adenine nucleotides due to an abnormality of a type of platelet storage granule known as dense bodies (platelet storage pool deficiency). Prolongation of skin bleeding time is a common feature of these qualitative platelet disorders.

Bleeding due to Vascular Disorders

Vascular disorders do not usually cause serious bleeding. Skin haemorrhage and occasional mucosal haemorrhage may occur. In some disorders, the collagen which supports vessel walls is abnormal. This mechanism probably accounts for the bruising of Cushing's syndrome and the bruising, mucosal bleeding and perifollicular skin haemorrhages of scurvy.

Hereditary haemorrhagic telangiectasia

Telangiectases (microvascular dilatations) accumulate from childhood on mucous membranes, in liver and lungs and on the skin of hands and face. It is inherited as an autosomal dominant trait. Nosebleeds and gastrointestinal bleeding may be severe, but bleeding occurs only from telangiectases; coagulation and platelet numbers and function are normal.

Henoch-Schonlein purpura

In Henoch-Schonlein purpura no systemic bleeding tendency is present. It is an immune complex hypersensitivity reaction, usually in children. A rash, superficially similar to thrombocytopenic purpura but with localised oedema causing the lesions to be raised above the skin level, is present on buttocks and lower legs.

Arthralgia, abdominal pain and haematuria may occur. It is usually self-limiting. Although the skin rash resembles thrombocytopenic purpura, the platelet count and skin bleeding time are normal.

Platelet Disorders Causing Thrombosis

HUS and TTP have been described; however, the abnormality causing increased platelet reactivity does not lie within the platelet itself in these disorders. Thrombosis is a feature of myeloproliferative disease with thrombocytosis, especially essential thrombocythaemia and polycythaemia rubra vera.

Laboratory evidence for increased platelet reactivity can be found in subjects with coronary thrombosis, cerebral thrombosis, diabetes mellitus and other disorders. Paradoxically, the heparin-induced immune thrombocytopenia which occasionally develops on exposure to this anticoagulant drug may be associated with extensive arterial and venous thrombosis, due to platelet activation by the auto-antibody.

DISORDERS OF BLOOD COAGULATION

- Coagulation or fibrinolytic disorders may cause thrombosis or haemorrhage
- Can be congenital or acquired
- Acquired disorders are common, due to anticoagulant drugs, vitamin K deficiency, liver disease, and disseminated intravascular coagulation
- The most important congenital bleeding disorders are von Willebrand's disease and haemophilia

Diseases of the coagulation/fibrinolytic system causing thrombosis as well as those causing haemorrhage are recognised. In practice, the majority of bleeding disorders are acquired and due to anticoagulant drugs or to liver disease, or to clotting factor consumption in disseminated intravascular coagulation.

The severe congenital haemorrhagic diatheses are uncommon but clinically important disorders due to an inherited defect of production of a coagulation factor.

Congenital Clotting Factor Deficiencies

Deficiencies of most of the coagulation factors have been described, but deficiency of factor VIII (haemophilia A) and factor IX (haemophilia B or Christmas disease), and of von Willebrand factor (von Willebrand's disease) are the clinically most important disorders in the group.

Factor VIII coagulation protein is a co-factor for fibrin generation in the intrinsic coagulation pathway; it is probably synthesised predominantly by hepatocytes. In order to circulate in plasma with a normal half-life of 12 hours it requires a carrier protein-von Willebrand factor (vWF).

vWF is a large multimeric protein synthesised and assembled by vascular endothelial cells and megakaryocytes. It has no role in the coagulation cascade but is an essential co-factor for interaction of platelets with exposed subendothelium in primary haemostasis.

Factor VIII production is controlled by a gene on the X chromosome. vWF synthesis is under autosomal control.

Haemophilia

Haemophilia A and B are identical clinically and pathologically, differing only in the deficient factor. In each case the disorder is due to sex-linked recessively inherited deficiency of the clotting factor, or synthesis of a defective clotting factor. Males are affected. Female carriers have approximately 50% of the normal factor level and may occasionally be mildly clinically affected.

Mild, moderate and severe forms of haemophilia are recognised, depending on the residual clotting factor activity; degree of severity is constant within a kindred. Predictably, from the place of factor VIII in the coagulation mechanism, the APTT is prolonged and the PT is normal. In severe disease, the blood is incoagulable.

The bleeding is of the coagulation deficiency type. Purpura is not a feature. In severe disease, bleeding from wounds persists for days or weeks. Control can be achieved by clotting factor replacement by the intravenous route, but this must be administered at least 12-hourly to maintain adequate factor VIII levels.

Molecular genetics

Molecular genetic studies have recognised a variety of defects in haemophilia, including partial and complete deletions of the factor VIII gene, as well as single base changes, which create either a translational stop signal (socalled nonsense mutations), with the consequent synthesis of a truncated protein which is ineffective functionally and rapidly degraded, or single amino acid substitutions which alter the stability and function of the proteins.

Table 6.8: Classification of haemophilia A.

Category	*Factor VIII %*	*Features of normal*
Severe	0-1	Frequent and spontaneous haemorrhage into joints and soft tissues from birth Degenerative joint disease
Moderate	1-3	Bleeding after trauma, including dental and other surgical trauma Bruising
Mild	>3	Bleeding after trauma only May be subclinical in mildest form

Mutations occurring de novo account for a substantial proportion of affected subjects (around 30%). Comparable defects in the factor IX gene are seen in haemophilia B.

Clinical features and treatment

Apparently spontaneous haemorrhage into a major joint, especially knees, hips, elbows and shoulders, occurring several times each month is typical of the severe disease. Without factor replacement therapy bleeding continues until the intra-articular pressure rises sufficiently to prevent further haemorrhage.

Slow resolution of this exquisitely painful acute haemarthrosis then occurs. Recurrent bleeds within a joint produce massive synovial hypertrophy, erosion of joint cartilage and para-articular bone and changes of a severe osteoarthritis.

Bleeding into muscles, retroperitoneal tissues and the urinary tract also occurs. Pressure necrosis of adjacent structures such as peripheral nerves may result. The clinical picture in severe haemophilia is one of recurrent spontaneous haemarthrosis and soft tissue haemorrhage from birth. External bleeding from the urinary tract and epistaxis are also common.

By self-administration of clotting factor concentrate at the first symptoms of haemorrhage, or use of prophylactic factor replacement, many of the disabling consequences of haemophilia can now be avoided.

Replacement therapy with clotting factor concentrates prepared from pooled human plasma has led to other diseases in subjects receiving such treatment due to virus transmission in these blood products. Liver disease due to hepatitis C is universal in haemophiliacs treated with concentrates prior to the introduction of virucidal preparation using heat and solvents.

This disease may be progressive, with changes of cirrhosis eventually ensuing in a large proportion of patients. Death from liver failure may occur. Many haemophiliac subjects have also contracted hepatitis B. Many UK haemophiliacs were infected with HIV and developed the pathological features of the acquired immune deficiency syndrome (AIDS), including *Pneumocystis carinii* pneumonia, toxoplasmosis and systemic candidiasis.

Modern virucidally-treated factor concentrates appear to be free of hepatitis viruses and HIV and recombinant factor VIII is now available. In some cases of severe haemophilia exposure to therapeutic factor VIII or IX leads to development of antibody to the clotting factor. The presence of such inhibitors makes management of affected individuals very difficult, as infused clotting factor is rendered ineffective by the antibody.

Rarely subjects without a congenital bleeding disorder develop comparable clotting factor inhibitors, usually directed against factor VIII. The factor VIII concentration in plasma is markedly reduced and bleeding is often spontaneous and life-threatening in these cases of acquired haemophilia.

Other Coagulation Factor Deficiencies

Deficiency of factor XII is common. Although the APTT is prolonged, there is no bleeding tendency, as factor XII is not essential for normal coagulation in vivo. Factor XI deficiency is a relatively common disorder in some populations. Again, the APTT is prolonged but the bleeding tendency is variable and often subclinical. Other coagulation factor deficiencies are very uncommon.

von Willebrand's disease

von Willebrand's disease (vWD) is most commonly a moderate to mild bleeding disorder due to synthesis of vWF in reduced amounts or production of functionally abnormal vWF. It is transmitted as an autosomal dominant disorder in most kindred, and epidemiological studies suggest it may be common in mild or subclinical form.

The majority of cases have a quantitative deficiency of vWF (Type

I), but in around 20% a dysfunctional vWF is synthesised and in these the multimeric structure of vWF is abnormal, with a reduction in the large multimers. There is marked genetic heterogeneity.

The homozygous disease is a serious bleeding diathesis but is extremely uncommon. In the more usual heterozygous form the main manifestations are easy bruising, bleeding after trauma and menorrhagia in females. Haemarthrosis and muscle haematomas are not common features of vWD.

The plasma concentration of vWF is reduced, and, because of the requirement for vWF as a carrier protein, VIII activity is reduced in parallel; levels of less than 10-20% of normal are unusual, however. The bleeding time is prolonged due to the defect of platelet interaction with exposed subendothelium which arises from a reduced availability of vWE The APTT is prolonged due to factor VIII deficiency.

vWF-rich concentrate prepared from plasma is used for treatment of severe haemorrhage. In many patients the vWF level can be temporarily increased by stimulating its release from endothelial cells by administration of an analogue of vasopressin-desdiaminovasopressin (DDAVP). This is also effective in mild haemophilia.

Acquired Disorders of Coagulation

Bleeding due to acquired platelet disorders has been described above. A haemorrhagic diathesis due to coagulation factor deficiency is present in liver disease, disseminated intravascular coagulation, and vitamin K deficiency due to immaturity (haemorrhagic disease of the newborn), obstructive jaundice, pancreatic disease or small bowel disease.

Bleeding may also be a feature of therapy with anticoagulant and fibrinolytic drugs.

Vitamin K deficiency

Vitamin K is obtained from green vegetables and by bacterial synthesis in the gut. It is a fat-soluble vitamin and requires bile for its absorption. Vitamin K is essential for the y-carboxylation of clotting factors II, VII, IX and X (and the inhibitors protein C and protein S); in the absence of vitamin K, these factors are released from the liver in an incomplete and inactive form.

The PT is particularly prolonged as a result. A coagulopathy due to vitamin K deficiency occurs when absorption is defective, particularly in obstructive jaundice. In addition, the neonate tends to have vitamin K deficiency due to lack of gut bacteria and low concentrations of the vitamin in breast milk.

This exacerbates the inefficient coagulation due to low levels of clotting factors secondary to liver immaturity and may produce life-threatening haemorrhage during the first week of *life-haemorrhagic disease of the newborn.* Vitamin K supplementation corrects the defect.

The oral anticoagulant drug warfarin is a vitamin K antagonist and acts by inhibition of the complete synthesis of coagulation factors II, VII, IX and X. Its use is therefore associated with an increased risk of haemorrhage.

Liver Disease

Severe hepatocellular disease is commonly associated with coagulation defects due to failure of clotting factor synthesis, including fibrinogen, and production of abnormal fibrinogen-dysfibrinogenaemia. This is often compounded by thrombocytopenia due to hypersplenism and a qualitative platelet disorder. The skin bleeding time may be prolonged, as is the PT, and often the APTT Life-threatening haemorrhage may result, particularly from oesophageal varices.

Disseminated Intravascular Coagulation

Disseminated intravascular coagulation (DIC) is a common state in which a combination of haemorrhage and thrombosis complicates another disorder. Activation of coagulation leads to the formation of microthrombi in numerous organs and to the consumption of clotting factors and platelets in the process of clot formation, in turn leading to a haemorrhagic diathesis. There are several potential triggers to coagulation activation in DIC and a wide range of disorders can be complicated by this phenomenon:

- infection (e.g. septicaemia, malaria)
- neoplasm (e.g. mucin-secreting adenocarcinoma)
- tissue trauma (e.g. burns, major accidental trauma, major surgery, shock, intravascular haemolysis, dissecting aortic aneurysm)
- obstetric complications (e.g. abruptio placentae, retained dead fetus, amniotic fluid embolism, toxaemia)
- liver disease.

Thus, in obstetric disorders, tissue factor release into the maternal circulation from the placenta or fetus, or in amniotic fluid, may trigger coagulation. Many tumours are also rich in procoagulant substances. Septicaemia may also cause coagulation activation by damage to vascular endothelium and induction of tissue factor expression by endothelial cells and monocytes.

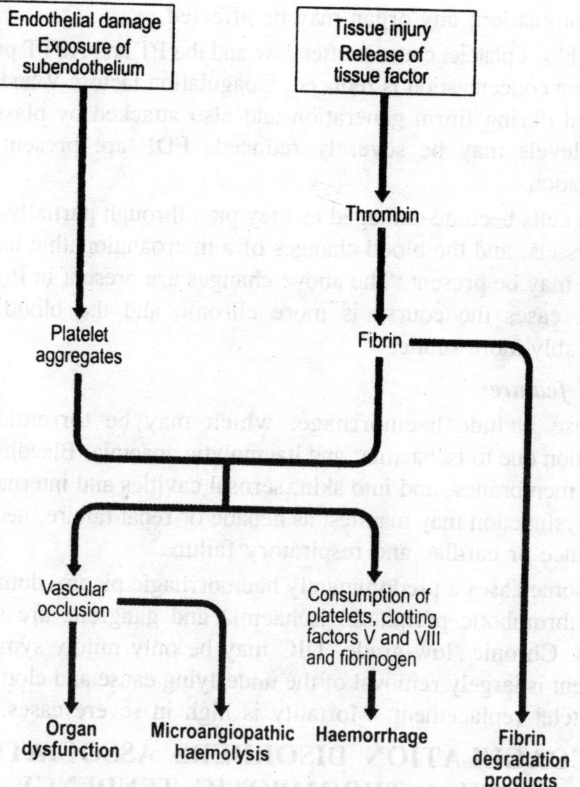

Figure 6.9: The pathogenesis of disseminated intravascular coagulation.

In liver disease there is reduced clearance of activated clotting factors. The fibrinolytic system is activated in DIC and plasmin is generated. This plasmin may attack fibrinogen and coagulation factors V and VIII as well as fibrin.

Digestion of fibrin and fibrinogen generates split products (fibrinogen and fibrin degradation products; FDP) which themselves have an anti-coagulant and anti-platelet effect and contribute to the haemorrhagic diathesis.

Thrombi, composed of platelets and fibrin, may be found in the microvasculature of brain, lungs, kidneys, heart, spleen and liver. Other organs may also be affected. The distribution of affected organs is variable. Micro-infarcts or more major areas of infarction such as renal cortical necrosis or hepatic necrosis may result.

Areas of haemorrhage may also be apparent histologically and on gross examination; any organ may be affected.

The blood platelet count is often low and the PT and APTT prolonged. Fibrinogen concentration is reduced. Coagulation factors V and VIII are consumed during fibrin generation and also attacked by plasmin, and plasma levels may be severely reduced. FDP are present in high concentration.

Red cells become damaged as they pass through partially occluded small vessels, and the blood changes of a microangiopathic haemolytic anaemia may be present. The above changes are present in florid DIC. In some cases the course is more chronic and the blood changes considerably more subtle.

Clinical features

These include haemorrhage, which may be torrential, organ dysfunction due to ischaemia, and haemolytic anaemia. Bleeding is from mucous membranes, and into skin, serosal cavities and internal organs. Organ dysfunction may manifest as hepatic or renal failure, neurological disturbance or cardiac and respiratory failure.

In some cases a predominantly haemorrhagic picture dominates; in others, thrombotic peripheral ischaemia and gangrene are the major features. Chronic 'low-grade' DIC may be only mildly symptomatic. Treatment is largely removal of the underlying cause and clotting factor and platelet replacement. Mortality is high in severe cases.

COAGULATION DISORDERS ASSOCIATED WITH A THROMBOTIC TENDENCY

Familial Thrombophilia

Control mechanisms for the prevention of inappropriate fibrin deposition are an important feature of the coagulation system. These mechanisms include the rapid lysis of fibrin by plasmin generated at the site of a thrombus, neutralisation of thrombin by antithrombin III, and inactivation of factors V and VIII by activated protein C with its co-factor, protein S.

Hereditary defects of these control mechanisms have been described which lead to a life-long tendency to *thrombosis-thrombophilia*. The thrombosis in these familial thrombophilic states is almost always in the venous system: deep venous thrombosis of the limbs and pulmonary embolism. Thrombotic events rarely manifest before adulthood and usually occur when a second risk factor is also present, commonly pregnancy, exposure to female hormones in the combined oral contraceptive or hormone replacement therapy, immobilisation or surgery.

The recognised familial abnormalities associated with such a thrombotic tendency are:

- *antithrombin III deficiency* resulting in failure of thrombin neutralisation
- *protein C and protein S deficiency* resulting in failure of neutralisation of activated V and VIII
- *activated protein C resistance,* the commonest cause of familial thrombophilia, where a point mutation in the factor V gene leads to synthesis of a factor V variant which has normal procoagulant activity but which is not inhibited by activated protein C; this variant, called factor V Leiden, is present in 5% or more of European subjects
- a point mutation in the *prothrombin gene* resulting in an increased plasma concentration of prothrombin
- *dysfibrinogenaemia* resulting in abnormal fibrinogen.

Individuals with antithrombin III deficiency are heterozygous for the defect. Over 30 mutations leading to deficiency of the protein have been discovered, mostly caused by frameshifts or base changes resulting in a protein that is not secreted or is rapidly removed from the circulation.

This type of deficiency is designated 'Type 1'. In Type 2 a dysfunctional protein is produced due to one of several single base changes which alter the amino acid sequence of the synthesised antithrombin III. Subjects deficient in protein C or protein S are also heterozygous, the homozygous condition producing a severe thrombotic disease often manifesting in the neonate.

Type 1 and Type 2 (dysfunctional) defects are also found in protein C deficiency. Several mutations in the genes for protein C and protein S have been identified.

One or more of these genetic thrombophilias, most commonly factor V Leiden, can be found in around 30% of subjects with deep vein thrombosis, and affected family members are also at risk of venous thromboembolism.

Acquired prothrombotic states

Acquired coagulation disorders causing thrombosis are also recognised. In systemic lupus erythematosus (SLE) a predisposition to arterial and venous thrombosis is associated with a paradoxical prolongation of the APTT, apparently due to the development of auto-antibodies which interact with phospholipid-bound proteins involved in coagulation activation ('anti -phospholipid antibodies'). Stroke and deep venous thrombosis are common. These antibodies are also associated with major thrombotic disease in subjects without other evidence of SLE. Women with such antibodies are prone to pregnancy failure due to recurrent miscarriage, possibly secondary to placental thrombosis.

The term *antiphospholipid syndrome* describes these patients with thrombosis or pregnancy failure associated with antiphospholipid antibody. The mechanisms underlying thrombosis in this disorder are not yet known. Long-term therapy with anticoagulant drugs is often indicated, as the risk of recurrent thrombosis is high.

The antibodies can be detected in the laboratory through the ability to prolong clotting times in coagulation tests which involve low concentrations of phospholipid, when the term *lupus anticoagulant* is used, or through binding to negatively charged phospholipid, such as cardiolipin-the *anticardiolipin* antibody.

Thrombosis risk is also increased in a range of other conditions, including myeloproliferative diseases, cancer, nephrotic syndrome, congestive cardiac failure, atrial fibrillation and paroxysmal nocturnal haemoglobinuria. An increased plasma concentration of homocysteine is also associated with a tendency to thrombosis.

The homocysteine level is partly genetically determined, but is also influenced by the dietary content of vitamin B_{12}, folate and pyridoxine. This raises the intriguing possibility of reducing thrombosis risk by dietary manipulation and this approach is currently under investigation.

ANTENATAL DIAGNOSIS OF BLOOD DISORDERS

Several of the more serious haematological disorders can be diagnosed in the fetus. Fetal blood can be obtained from the placenta or umbilical vein with imaging using ultrasound scanning techniques from around the middle of the second trimester.

This material can be used for detection of abnormalities of red cells, white cells or platelets and for diagnosis of clotting factor deficiencies. For example, thalassaemia can be identified by measuring relative rates of globin chain synthesis.

Alternatively amniotic fluid cells can be obtained by aspiration of the amniotic fluid, and techniques have been developed by which fetal material can be safely obtained by biopsy of chorionic villi, this being performed as early as 9-11 weeks gestation.

Fetal DNA can be analysed by restriction endonuclease mapping and RFLP linkage analysis. More recently the application of PCR technology and use of oligonucleotide probes has allowed the very early and rapid diagnosis of haematological disorders. Using these techniques, first trimester prenatal diagnosis of β-thalassaemias and of haemophilia has become possible. Gene probes for the diagnosis of red cell enzyme defects are also becoming available.

BLOOD TRANSFUSION

Donor blood, or fractions of blood, can be safely and beneficially administered intravenously. Transfusion of red cells is valuable in the management of some anaemias and in resuscitation after acute haemorrhage, and is essential for the safe performance of many surgical procedures. Other cellular components of blood, especially platelets, can be usefully transfused, for example to treat bleeding in severely thrombocytopenic subjects.

Blood plasma is fractionated to provide albumin, immunoglobulin and coagulation factors. In red cell transfusion it is essential that compatibility is ensured between antigens on the donor erythrocytes and antibodies present in the recipient's plasma in order to avoid acute haemolysis of the donor cells which may be fatal. The cross-match procedure is used to determine compatibility.

The red cells from the donor unit are incubated with the recipient's serum under a range of conditions that enhance sensitivity to any antibody present. Agglutination or lysis of the red cells indicates the presence of clinically important red cell antibody and that the donor unit is incompatible and cannot be safely administered to the recipient.

Red Cell Antigens and Antibodies

Although there are about 400 red blood cell antigens, most inherited in Mendelian dominant fashion, only a minority are clinically important. An individual lacking a particular antigen may develop an antibody after exposure to red cells carrying the antigen.

Exposure occurs by transfusion of red cells or by passage of fetal red cells into the maternal circulation during pregnancy, the fetal cells carrying paternal antigens foreign to the mother. The important clinical consequences of the development of such an 'immune' antibody are the development of a *haemolytic transfusion reaction* on further exposure to red cells carrying the antigen, and *haemolytic* disease of the *newborn* due to transplacental passage of maternal IgG antibody against fetal red cell antigens.

The most important 'immune' *antibody* is anti-D, an antibody to the major antigen of the rhesus blood group system (Table 23.12). It is a major cause of haemolytic disease of the newborn.

As well as 'immune' antibodies, *'naturally occurring'* antibodies to red cell antigens are also important. In contrast to the IgG immune antibodies, they are predominantly IgM and require no previous red cell antigen exposure. They occur in the ABO blood group system, where naturally occurring anti-A and anti-B are present in subjects whose red cells lack the corresponding antigen.

In addition to the ABO and rhesus blood group systems the major red cell antigen systems of clinical importance are Kell, Duffy and Kidd, as, with ABO and rhesus, their antibodies are responsible for most cases of haemolytic transfusion reaction and haemolytic disease of the newborn.

Table 6.9: The rhesus blood group system.

Allelic genes at closely linked loci code for paired antigens designated C and c, E and e and D. Absence of D is termed d. A set of genes and hence antigens is inherited from each parent and the presence of D determines rhesus 'positivity'.

Genotype	*Rhesus status*	*% Frequency (UK)*
cde\cde	Negative	15
CDe\cde	Positive	32
CDe\CDe	Positive	17
cDe\cde	Positive	13
CDe\cDE	Positive	14
Others	Positive	9

Table 6.10: The ABO blood group system.

There are three allelic genes A, B and O. A and B genes control the synthesis of enzymes which modify the red cell membrane glycolipid. The unmodified molecule is known as H substance and is not modified in the presence of the 0 gene alone, which is an amorph. Thus there are 6 genotypes and 4 phenotypes.

Genotypc	*Phenotype*	*Natural antibodies*	*% Phenotypic frequency (UK)*
OO	O	Anti-A, -B	46
AA or AO	A	Anti-B	42
BB or BO	B	Anti-A	9
AB	AB	None	3

Clinically important platelet antigens are also recognised. Human platelet antigen la (HPA1a) is present on platelets in around 98% of Caucasians. Subjects lacking the antigen are at risk of allo-antibody development from exposure to HPA1a platelets during pregnancy or blood transfusion. Anti-HPAI a is responsible for most cases of post-transfusion purpura and neonatal alloimmune thrombocytopenic purpura.

Haemolytic Transfusion Reactions

Immediate reactions

Massive intravascular haemolysis occurs when complementactivating antibodies, such as anti-A and anti-B, interact with the relevant antigen on transfused red cells. There is typically collapse, with hypotension and pain in the lumbar region. Haemoglobin-stained urine may be passed and oliguric renal failure may ensue. Red cell lysis may trigger disseminated intravascular coagulation.

This clinical scenario can develop after transfusion with only a few millilitres of incompatible red cells. Treatment includes immediate interruption of the transfusion, resuscitation with intravenous fluid, immunosuppression with corticosteroid therapy and management of the renal failure. Fatalities still occur.

The cross-match procedure should prevent exposure to such incompatible blood. However most cases result from clerical error through mislabelling of the cross-match sample or transfusion to the wrong recipient. Because antibodies to the rhesus system are not complement-fixing, cell lysis occurs in the reticuloendothelial system and reactions are generally milder, although they can still be life-threatening.

Delayed reactions

Occasionally a low titre antibody is too weak to be detectable in the cross-match and is unable to cause lysis at the time of transfusion. Transfusion of red cells carrying the relevant antigen leads to a gradual increase in the titre of the antibody, developing over a period of a few days. Delayed, gradual red cell lysis occurs, producing anaemia and jaundice; this is a delayed transfusion reaction.

Other Adverse Effects of Transfusion

Most nucleated cells, including leukocytes, carry antigens of the HLA (human leukocyte antigen) or major histocompatibility complex system. Prior exposure to HLA antigens by transfusion or pregnancy may lead to development of antibody capable of causing fever and rigors on subsequent exposure to the antigens present on leukocytes in transfused blood. This can be avoided by using filters to remove donor leukocytes prior to transfusion. Such *non-haemolytic transfusion reactions* are unpleasant but rarely dangerous. Allergic reactions may also develop in a recipient because of hypersensitivity to a protein present in the donor plasma. Fever, urticaria and oedema may result.

Commonly confused conditions and sntlties relating to the blood and bonew marrow

Commonly confused	*Distinction and explanation*
Pernicious and *megaloblastic anaemia*	*Pernicious anaemia* is a specific example of *megaloblastic anaemia* in which autoimmune gastritis results in loss of intrinsic factor and failure to absorb vitamin B_{12}. Megaloblastic anaemia can also be due to folate deficiency and to other explanations for B_{12} deficiency.
Polycythaemia rubra vera and *secondary polycythaemia*	Both are characterised by an increased concentration of red blood cells. *Polycythaemia rubra vera* is a clonal myeloproliferative condition, whereas *secondary polycythaemia* is usually a physiological response to hypoxia or to inappropriately excessive erythropoietin production.
Myelodysplasia, myelofibrosis and *myeloproliferative diseases*	The *myelodysplastic syndromes* are neoplastic bone marrow disorders at the stem cell level, affecting all myeloid lines, with characteristic morphological changes in the marrow and a tendency to progress to acute leukaemia. *Myelofibrosis is* characterised by marrow fibrosis and the emergence of extramedullary haemopoiesis. *Myelopro-liferative diseases,* a group of disorders with abnormal proliferation of one or more cell lines, include myelofibrosis, chronic myeloid leukaemia, polycythaemia rubra vera and essential thrombocythaemia, and are grouped together because intermediate forms exist and progression from one to another is common.

Virus transmission by blood transfusion remains a significant problem. Transmission of hepatitis B and C, as well as human immunodeficiency viruses, parvovirus and cytomegalovirus, can occur. Careful donor selection and screening of donations have considerably reduced the risk. Some other transmissible infections are syphilis and malaria.

It is not yet known whether the prion responsible for Creutzfeld Jakob disease can be transmitted by transfusion of blood. *Circulatory overload* may result from transfusion of excessive volume. Because bank blood is devoid of functioning platelets, transfusion of large volumes can cause thrombocytopenia and haemorrhage.

Repeated red cell transfusion without blood loss, usually in the management of chronic anaemias such as thalassaemia, inevitably leads to *tissue iron overload.* A unit of blood contains 200 mg of iron, in haemoglobin. Although, initially, deposition occurs in reticulo-endothelial tissues without toxic results, iron later accumulates in skin, liver, myocardium and pancreas.

Pigmentation, liver cirrhosis, heart failure and diabetes mellitus are the consequences. An iron chelating compound, desferrioxamine, is administered by subcutaneous infusion to minimise iron accumulation in tissues.

7

TESTICULAR HISTOLOGY

Diseases of the female genital tract include inflammation, neoplasia, hormonal disturbances and complications of pregnancy. The commonest disorders are discussed here on a topographical basis.

Pathological basis of sign and symptoms in the female genital tract.

Sign or symptom	Pathological basis
Vaginal bleeding	
• In pregnancy	Haemorrhage from placenta (e.g. placenta praevia), placental bed (e.g. miscarriage) or decidua (e.g. ectopic pregnancy)
• Post-coital	Haemorrhage from lesion on cervix (e.g. carcinoma)
• Post-menopausal	Haemorrhage from uterine lesion (e.g. polyp, carcinoma)
Abnormal menstruation	Psychological disturbance
(timing or volume of loss)	Hormonal dysfunction Defects in local haemostasis Fibroids
Pain	Pathological distension or rupture (e.g. tubal ectopic pregnancy)
	Muscular spasm (e.g. uterine contractions)

	Ischaemia or inflammation (e.g. ovarian torsion) Menstrual pain due to adenomyosis
Abdominal distension	Ascites (e.g. peritoneal involvement by ovarian carcinoma) Uterine enlargement (e.g. pregnancy) Ovarian cyst

NORMAL DEVELOPMENT

Female Sexual Development

Female development does not require the presence of a gonad, and the ovary plays no part in primary sexual development. This means that a neuter embryo will always develop along female lines. The testis-determining factor is the SRY gene carried in the sex-determining region of the Y chromosome.

The indifferent gonad develops into an ovary when no Y chromosome is present, although two functional X chromosomes are usually required for normal ovarian differentiation. Disorders of female sexual development are listed in Table elsewhere in this chapter.

Embryological Development

Germ cells arise in the wall of the yolk sac, and migrate to the region of the coelomic germinal epithelium. In the sixth week cords of cells appear within the indifferent gonad, but it is not until after the seventh week that ovarian differentiation is apparent and by 14 weeks these cell cords surround the primordial follicles.

The paired paramesonephric Miillerian ducts arise as an invagination of the coelomic epithelium of the mesonephric ridge lateral to the mesonephric duct. The paramesonephric duct follows the mesonephric duct.

Near the cloaca, the paramesonephric ducts cross from the lateral to the medial side of the mesonephric ducts; together they carry with them some mesoderm from the side walls of the pelvis to create the transverse bar which helps to form the septum dividing the rectum from the urogenital sinus.

At the 30 mm stage (8 weeks), fusion of the paramesonephric ducts creates the utero-vaginal canal, which ultimately forms the uterus and proximal part of the vagina; the unfused parts form the uterine tubes. The trans-pelvic bar, which is a continuation of the mesonephric

Table 7.1: Abnormalities of female sexual development.

Sex chromosomes	Gonads	Possible abnormalities
Normal XX	Bilateral normal ovaries	Congenital adrenal hyperplasia Maternal androgen or progestagen administration in pregnancy Maternal virilising tumour in pregnancy
Normal XX or XY	Abnormal (streak gonads) Ovaries (XY) or testes (XX)	Gonadal dysgenesis Inappropriate gonads for chromosomes
Abnormal		Turner's syndrome Mixed gonadal dysgenesis True hermaphroditism

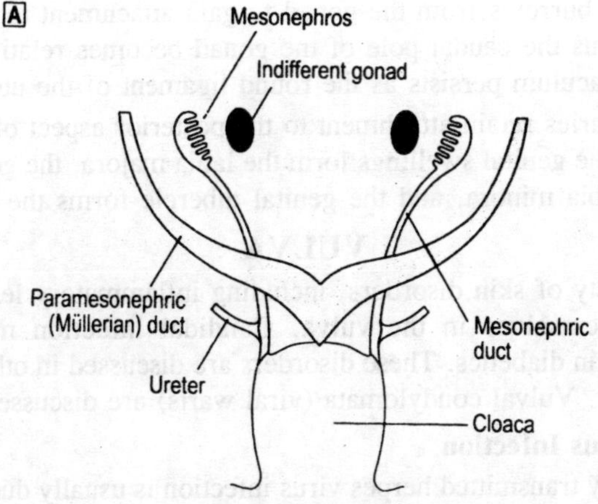

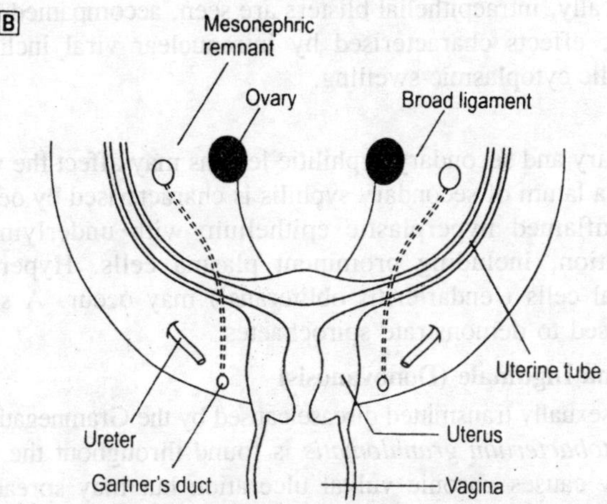

Figure 7.1: Development of the female genital tract.

mesentery, forms the broad ligament; the ovary, projecting medially from the mesonephric ridge in the early stage, comes to lie posterior to the broad ligament. The inferior free end of the fused paramesonephric ducts (utero-vaginal canal) is still solid, and the sino-vaginal bulbs grow out from the posterior wall of the urogenital sinus to fuse with it and, later, give rise to the lower part of the vagina.

The hymen occupies the position where the sino-vaginal bulb and urogenital sinus meet. The gonads are at first elongated and lie in the long axis of the embryo. Later, each gonad assumes a transverse lie. The gubernaculum is formed in the inguinal fold as a fibromuscular band which burrows from the gonad to gain attachment to the genital swelling; thus the caudal pole of the gonad becomes relatively fixed. The gubernaculum persists as the round ligament of the uterus.

The ovaries retain attachment to the posterior aspect of the broad ligament. The genital swellings form the labia majora, the genital folds form the labia minora, and the genital tubercle forms the clitoris.

VULVA

A variety of skin disorders, including inflammatory lesions, may manifest themselves in the vulva. Candidal infection may occur, particularly in diabetics. These disorders are discussed in other chapter of this book. Vulval condylomata (viral warts) are discussed below.

Herpes Virus Infection

Sexually transmitted herpes virus infection is usually due to herpes simplex type 2, and produces painful ulceration of the vulval skin. Histologically, intraepithelial blisters are seen, accompanied by specific cytopathic effects characterised by intranuclear viral inclusions and eosinophilic cytoplasmic swelling.

Syphilis

Primary and secondary syphilitic lesions may affect the vulva. The condyloma latum of secondary syphilis is characterised by oedematous, acutely inflamed hyperplastic epithelium with underlying chronic inflammation, including prominent plasma cells. Hypertrophy of endothelial cells ('endarteritis obliterans') may occur. A silver stain may be used to demonstrate spirochaetes.

Granuloma Inguinale (Donovanosis)

This sexually transmitted disease caused by the Gramnegative bacillus *Calymmatobacterium granulomatis* is found throughout the tropics. It commonly causes chronic vulval ulceration but may spread to other sites in the female genital tract. Characteristically, large macrophages with clear or foamy cytoplasm containing bacilli (Donovan bodies) are seen, demonstrated with the help of Giemsa or silver stains.

Lymphogranuloma Venereum

This sexually transmitted disease is caused by *Chlamydia trachomatis* and is most prevalent in the tropics. The earliest lesion is a vesicle which breaks down to form a punched-out painless ulcer. The primary lesion may become secondarily infected with abundant granulation tissue, fibrosis, fistula formation and lymphatic obstruction characterising the chronic form of the disease. Necrotising granulomas may occur in inguinal lymph nodes.

Candidiasis

Candida may cause chronic irritation and inflammation of the vulva which may be associated with vaginitis. The diagnosis may be made by microscopic examination of skin scrapings or culture. The histological features are nonspecific, although the fungi may be identified within the keratin layer or superficial epithelium with the use of silver stains.

Cysts and tumours

Any benign cyst or tumour of the skin may be seen in the vulva. Two uncommon benign tumours are worthy of comment because of their distinct histological appearance: papillary hidradenoma and granular cell tumour.

Papillary hidradenoma

Papillary hidradenoma is a benign skin adnexal tumour. It presents as a localised lump, and is composed of interlacing papillae lined with epithelium.

Granular cell tumour

Granular cell tumour is uncommon and presents as a well-circumscribed vulval lump. It is composed of uniform large cells with pink granular cytoplasm. This neoplasm is currently thought to be derived from Schwann cells.

Bartholin's Glands

Bartholin's glands are common sites of cysts and of abscesses secondary to infection of a cyst. Bartholin's gland adenoma is uncommon, and adenocarcinoma arising at this site is rare.

NON-NEOPLASTIC EPITHELIAL DISORDERS

The term 'non-neoplastic epithelial disorders' encompasses a group of vulval disorders of uncertain aetiology which affect all age groups, although predominantly peri- and post-menopausal women. In the past, these disorders have been given a confusing variety of clinical labels.

They often appear clinically as 'leukoplakia', a term which refers to the white appearance of the skin and which should never be used in a pathological context. The clinical appearance of 'leukoplakia' is due to hyperkeratosis. In about 5% of cases there is a risk of squamous carcinoma, so that the presence or absence of cytological atypia (vulval intraepithelial neoplasia) in biopsies should always be reported.

There are two basic types of non-neoplastic epithelial disorders of the vulva: squamous hyperplasia and lichen sclerosus; these may sometimes co-exist.

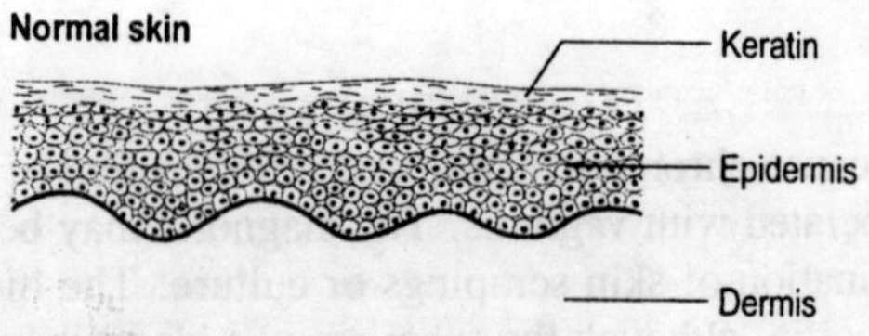

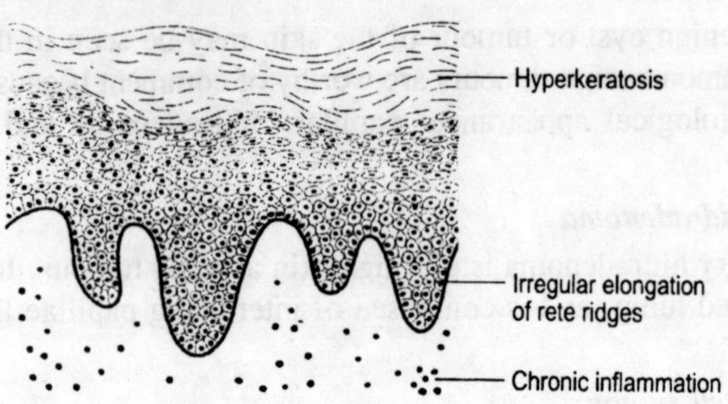

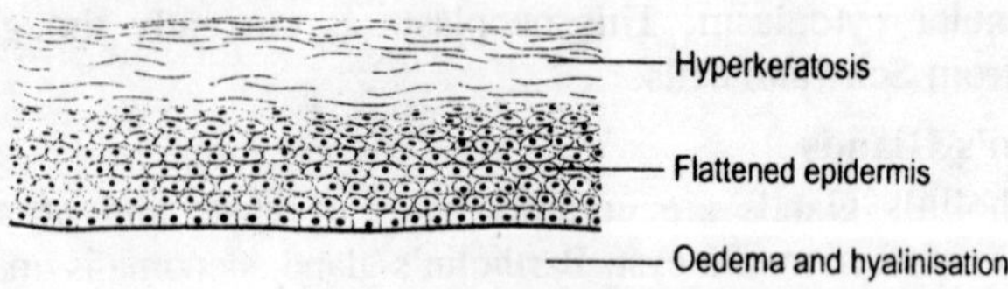

Figure 7.2: Morphological features of vulval non-neoplastic epithelial disorders.

Squamous hyperplasia

Vulval squamous hyperplasia is characterised by hyperkeratosis, irregular thickening of the epidermal rete ridges, and chronic inflammation of the superficial dermis.

Lichen sclerosus

Lichen sclerosus, like hyperplasia, shows hyperkeratosis, but there is thinning of the epidermis with flattening of the rete ridges. The most characteristic feature is a broad band of oedema and hyalinised connective tissue in the superficial dermis. Beneath this, there may be mild chronic inflammation. Lichen sclerosus has a lower neoplastic potential than squamous hyperplasia.

NEOPLASTIC EPITHELIAL DISORDERS

Intraepithelial Neoplasia

The term *intraepithelial neoplasia* refers to the spectrum of pre-invasive neoplastic change affecting the vulva. Its classification is the same as that of similar lesions in the cervix, although it may be incorrect to draw too close an analogy with the cervix as far as natural history is concerned.

It is a condition that predominantly affects young women, and is associated with high-risk human papillomavirus infection (see below). In severe cases, there may be extensive involvement of the perineum, including the peri-anal area. The incidence of malignant change occurring in these lesions is low as compared to the cervix.

There is a tendency for intraepithelial neoplasia to occur multifocally, with synchronous or metachronous involvement of vulva, vagina and cervix.

Squamous Carcinoma

Squamous carcinoma is a tumour predominantly affecting elderly women in whom it is not usually associated with human papillomavirus infection. The recognition of associated intraepithelial neoplasia may be difficult as it may occur in a so-called 'differentiated' form.

The appearances are those of squamous carcinoma in any site; thus the tumour may be well, moderately or poorly differentiated. The prognosis is determined by the size, depth of invasion and degree of histological differentiation of the tumour and the presence and extent of lymph node metastases, which predominantly affect the inguinal lymph nodes.

The pathological criteria for describing early invasive disease are not clearly established in the vulva. In contrast to squamous carcinoma of the cervix, even minimally invasive disease in the vulva is associated with a risk of local lymph node metastasis, although this risk seems to be negligible for carcinoma invading to a depth of less than 1 mm. Tumour thickness of greater than 5 mm and positive lymph nodes are associated with a poor prognosis.

Paget's Disease

The rare occurrence of mucin-containing adenocarcinoma cells within the squamous epithelium of the vulva is analogous to Paget's disease of the breast. Paget's disease of the vulva tends to be chronic, with multiple recurrences.

It may be indicative of an underlying invasive adenocarcinoma (in about 25% of cases), usually of skin adnexal origin, although, unlike the equivalent breast lesion, this is not usual. Adenocarcinomatous differentiation within the squamous epithelium has also been proposed as a possible explanation.

Other Malignant Tumours

Other malignant tumours of the vulva are rare. The most important of these are *basal cell carcinoma,* for which local excision is usually curative, and *malignant melanoma* which, as in other sites, generally has a poor prognosis.

VAGINA AND CERVIX

The commonest diseases affecting the vagina and cervix are infections, many of which are transmitted sexually. Tumours and pre-neoplastic lesions of the cervix, of which squamous cell carcinoma is the most important, are associated with human papillomavirus infection.

Infections

Vaginal infections are common and often sexually transmitted. The organisms of most importance are: *Gardnerella vaginalis, Neisseriagonorrhoeae, Candida albicans* and *Trichomonas vaginalis.*

Vaginal Adenosis

The occurrence of glands within the subepithelial connective tissue of the vagina is uncommon, and is believed to be due to a defect in embryological development. The lining of these glands is usually a mucinous cuboidal epithelium which may undergo squamous metaplasia. Vaginal adenosis particularly affected young females who were exposed to diethylstilbestrol in utero.

This synthetic oestrogenic agent was used in the 1950s in the treatment of threatened miscarriage in the USA and, to a lesser extent, in the UK. Clear cell adenocarcinoma of the vagina may rarely complicate adenosis.

Vaginal Intraepithelial Neoplasia

Vaginal intraepithelial neoplasia is much less common than cervical intraepithelial neoplasia but the same diagnostic criteria are applied. The lesion may co-exist with similar lesions of the vulva and cervix (reflecting the multicentric origin of squamous neoplasia).

Vaginal Squamous Carcinoma

Vaginal squamous carcinoma is an uncommon tumour predominantly occurring in older women. Pathologically, the tumour resembles squamous carcinoma of the cervix but it has a propensity to local invasion and radical surgery may be necessary.

Cervicitis

Non-specific acute and/or chronic inflammation is common in the cervix, particularly in the presence of an intrauterine contraceptive device, ectopy (see below) or prolapse. Chlamydiae are obligate intracellular organisms containing DNA and RNA, and are larger than viruses. *Chlamydia trachomatis* is a common sexually transmitted infection which is often recognised by its persistence following treatment for gonorrhoea in males (post-gonococcal urethritis).

Chlamydiae can be isolated from the cervices of about 50% of asymptomatic female partners of these infected males and from women with chronic cervicitis. Chlamydial infection may produce subepithelial reactive lymphoid follicles, a condition sometimes given the label of 'follicular cervicitis'.

Cervical Polyps

Benign polyps of the cervix are common. They are composed of columnar mucus-secreting epithelium and oedematous stroma. Vessels may be prominent and there may be acute or chronic inflammation of varying severity. These polyps have no malignant potential.

Cervical Microglandular Hyperplasia

Cervical microglandular hyperplasia is a commonly seen complex glandular proliferation that may be confused with carcinoma. Small, tightly packed glands, lined by low columnar or cuboidal epithelium, may form polypoid projections into the endocervical canal.

Accompanying acute inflammation and reserve cell hyperplasia (see below) are often seen. These changes may be seen in pregnancy and in users of the oral contraceptive pill, where they are the result of high levels of progestogen. Microglandular hyperplasia may also rarely be seen in post-menopausal women. It appears to have no malignant potential.

CERVICAL SQUAMOUS NEOPLASIA

- Incidence associated with sexual intercourse (especially number of male partners)
- Human papillomavirus postulated as main causative factor, with cigarette smoking as independent risk factor
- Pre-invasive phase of intraepithelial neoplasia can be detected by cervical cytology
- Cervical intraepithelial neoplasia (CIN) graded from 1 to 3 according to severity of abnormality

Aetiology

Squamous neoplasia of the cervix is associated with sexual activity; early age at first intercourse, frequency of intercourse and number of sexual partners are all risk factors. The sexual behaviour of the male partner is probably also of importance.

There is probably no one single cause of cervical cancer or pre-cancer, but epidemiological evidence points to a sexually transmitted agent or agents. There is now compelling evidence that human papillomaviruses are implicated in the aetiology of cervical squamous neoplasia.

Cigarette smoking is an independent risk factor; some contents of cigarette smoke, which can be detected in cervical mucus, may act as co-carcinogenic agents. The polycyclic aromatic hydrocarbons in cigarette smoke form damaging adducts with DNA; these have been demonstrated in cervical tissue at higher levels in current smokers.

Human papillomaviruses and neoplasia of the lower female genital tract

Genital warts or condylomata have been recognised for centuries. Only comparatively recently, however, has their viral aetiology been established. Electron microscopy showed the presence of viral particles, and immunohistochemistry (using antibodies to viral capsid antigen) and in situ hybridisation (using DNA probes) also confirmed their viral nature. Warts may affect the vulva but may also involve the cervix.

Moreover, it is now appreciated that human papillomaviruses (HPV) may infect the vulva, vagina and cervix in a non-condylomatous manner. Such infections show characteristic morphological features: most important of these is a specific cytoplasmic vacuolation called koilocytosis. The features associated with human papillomavirus infection are:

- koilocytosis
- hyperkeratosis
- parakeratosis
- papillomatosis
- individual cell keratinisation (dyskeratosis)
- multinucleation.

These morphological features are also common accompaniments of vulval, vaginal and cervical intraepithelial neoplasia.

There are now more than 100 subtypes of human papillomavirus recognised and certain of these show a particular predilection for the

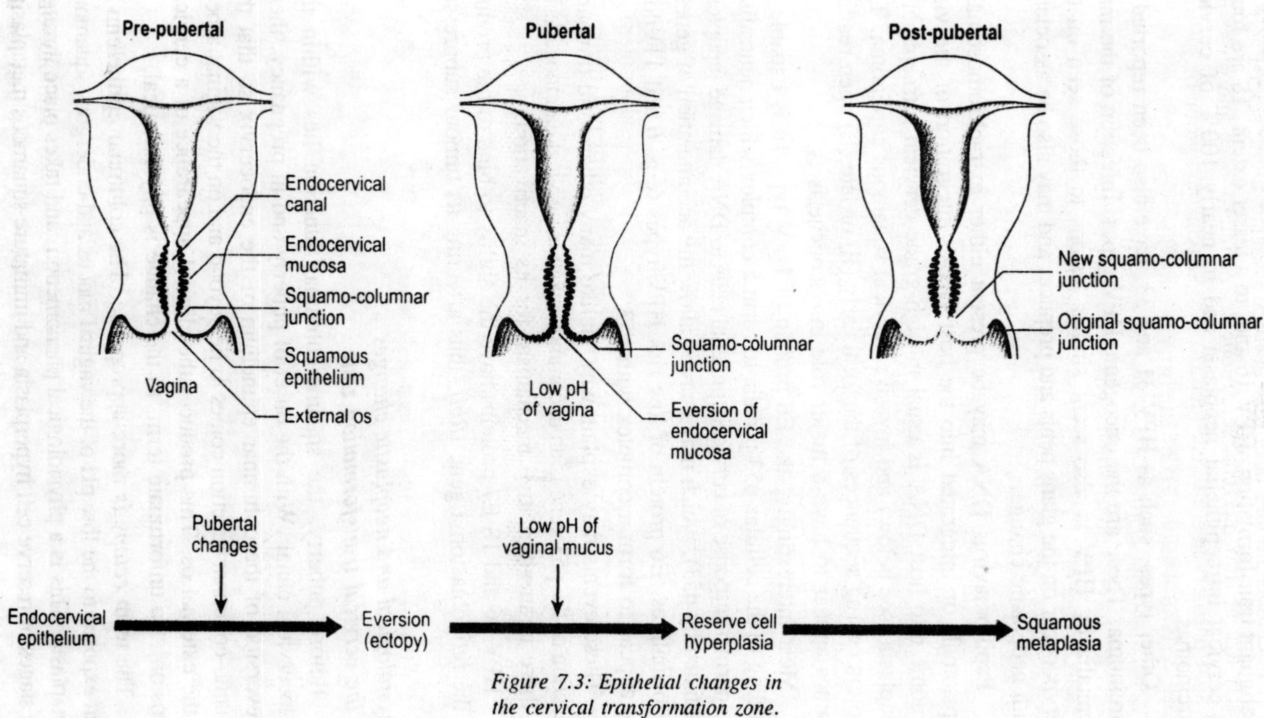

Figure 7.3: Epithelial changes in the cervical transformation zone.

lower female genital tract, notably HPV 6, 11, 16 and 18. HPV 6 and 11 are found in benign condylomata and are only rarely implicated in malignant transformation. HPV 16 and, to a lesser extent, 18 are found in cervical intraepithelial neoplasia and in nearly 100% of cervical carcinomas.

Other types, such as HPV 31 and 33, have also been reported in carcinoma. These are the oncogenic HPV types. Infection of the male genitalia by HPV is also seen; similar lesions to those seen on the cervix occur on the glans penis and prepuce, and may also be associated with neoplastic change.

Papillomavirus DNA may be present either extrachromosomally (episomal) or integrated into the host DNA. Integration of the viral genome into host DNA is usual in high-grade cervical intraepithelial neoplasia (see below) and invasive cervical squamous carcinoma. The protein coding sequences of the viral early (E) or late (L) open reading frames appear to have a major role in oncogenesis.

Most interestingly, the E6 protein of HPV type 16 is capable of binding to the cellular p53 protein to form a complex which neutralises the normal response of cervical epithelial cells to DNA damage (apoptosis mediated by p53), which may thereby allow the accumulation of genetic abnormalities. E6 protein of low risk HPV types (e.g. 6 and 11) does not appear to form a complex with p53.

These events may explain why, unlike many other solid tumours, mutation of the p53 gene is an uncommon event in cervical carcinogenesis, as there is an alternative mechanism for its inactivation.

HPV 16 and 18 E7 proteins have the ability to bind to the product of the retinoblastoma gene *(Rbl),* thus affecting its tumour suppressor role.

Physiological and neoplastic changes in the cervical transformation zone

Before puberty, the squamo-columnar junction lies within the endocervical canal. With the onset of puberty and in pregnancy, there is eversion of the columnar epithelium of the endocervix so that the squamo-columnar junction comes to lie beyond and on the vaginal aspect of the external os. This produces the clinical appearance of a cervical 'erosion', an unfortunate term, as the change is physiological.

The term *ectopy is* more appropriate. The columnar epithelium is then exposed to the low pH of the vaginal mucus and undergoes squamous metaplasia. This is a physiological phenomenon, and takes place through the stages of reserve cell hyperplasia and immature squamous metaplasia.

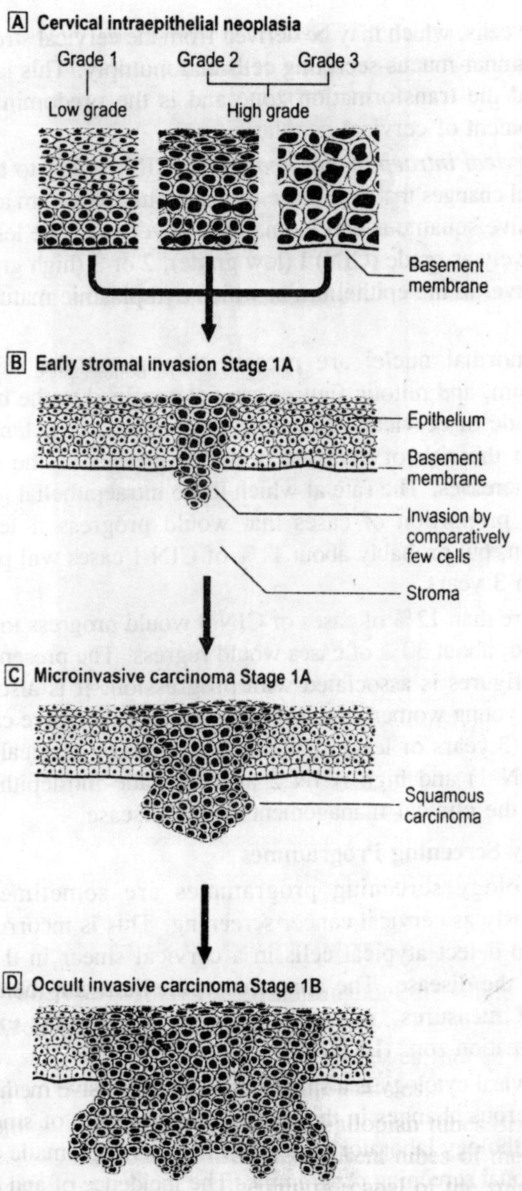

Figure 7.4: Cervical intraepithelial neoplasia (CIN) and invasive squamous carcinoma. A-Cervical intraepithelial neoplasia, B-Early stromal invasion, C-Microinvasive carcinoma, D-Occult invasive carcinoma.

Reserve cells, which may be derived from the cervical stroma, undermine the columnar mucus-secreting cells and multiply. This labile epithelium is called the transformation zone and is the predominant site for the development of cervical neoplasia.

Cervical intraepithelial neoplasia (CIN) refers to the spectrum of epithelial changes that take place in squamous epithelium as the precursors of invasive squamous carcinoma. The severity of the lesion is assessed subjectively as grade (CIN) I (low grade), 2 or 3 (high grade), according to the level in the epithelium at which cytoplasmic maturation is taking place.

Abnormal nuclei are present throughout the thickness of the epithelium, and mitotic figures are not confined to the basal cell layer. Any grade of cervical intraepithelial neoplasia is potentially invasive, although the risk of invasion becomes greater as the severity of the lesion increases. The rate at which these intraepithelial lesions progress and the proportion of cases that would progress if left untreated is uncertain, but probably about 11% of CIN 1 cases will progress to CIN 3 within 3 years.

More than 12% of cases of CIN 3 would progress to invasion if left untreated; about 30% of cases would regress. The presence of abnormal mitotic figures is associated with progression. It is also the case that, in some young women, the lesions progress to invasive carcinoma more quickly (3 years or less). The categorisation of cervical neoplasia into low (CIN 1) and high (CIN 2 and 3) grade intraepithelial neoplasia reflects the clinical management of the disease.

Cytology Screening Programmes

Cytology screening programmes are sometimes referred to erroneously as cervical cancer screening. This is incorrect because the aim is to detect atypical cells in a cervical smear in the pre-invasive stage of the disease. The abnormal epithelium can then be eradicated by local measures, such as diathermy large loop excision of the transformation zone (LLETZ).

Cervical cytology is a simple, safe, non-invasive method of detecting precancerous changes in the cervix. The majority of smears submitted to the pathology laboratory are taken from asymptomatic women as part of a national screening programme. The incidence of and mortality from invasive cervical cancer has fallen in communities where intensive screening has been carried out.

In the United Kingdom the annual mortality from cervical cancer remained static for *many* years at about 2000 women per year, but has now fallen to almost half that figure. The death rate is falling by 7% each year. The rates of cervical cancer would be at least 50% greater if there was no screening programme; attendance for regular screening prevents up to 90% of cervical cancer.

The examination of a cervical smear relies on the identification of abnormal (dyskaryotic) nuclei. The degree of abnormality may be mild, moderate or severe, but does not always correlate with subsequent histological findings in a biopsy specimen. Therefore, even patients with mildly dyskaryotic smears should be referred for colposcopy.

Cytology is not a reliable means of detecting an invasive tumour; the diagnosis of invasive carcinoma of the cervix is largely clinical and is confirmed by biopsy of suspicious areas of the cervix. The morphological abnormalities of the nucleus (dyskaryosis) in cervical smears are:

- disproportionate nuclear enlargement
- irregularity in form and outline
- hyperchromasia
- irregular chromatin condensation
- abnormalities of the number, size, and form of nucleoli
- multinucleation.

In some centres liquid-based cytology, in which cells are received by the laboratory suspended in fluid and prepared as a near monolayer on a slide and stained, is replacing the smearing of cells onto a glass slide from a spatula.

Invasive Squamous Carcinoma

The earliest sign of malignancy is early stromal invasion when small foci (less than 1 mm) are seen to arise from the basal epithelium and to breach the integrity of the basement membrane. The concept of a microinvasive carcinoma is one in which there is a negligible risk of lymph node metastasis so that conservative management is appropriate. The tumour spreads by local and lymphatic invasion.

The two principal factors that determine the prognosis of cervical carcinoma are:

- the size and depth of invasion of the primary tumour
- the presence and (more importantly) the extent of lymph node metastases.

The staging of cervical cancer is based on clinical and pathological assessment. Stage I cervical cancer is strictly confined to the cervix, stage II cancer extends beyond the cervix but has not extended onto the pelvic wall. It involves the vagina but not the lower third. Stage III cancer may extend onto the pelvic wall and involves the lower third of the vagina, and stage IV implies extension outside the reproductive tract. Tumour may then involve the adjacent organs, e.g. the mucosa of the bladder or rectum.

Involvement of para-aortic nodes is associated with a uniformly poor prognosis. The degree of histological differentiation of squamous carcinoma (whether it is well, moderately or poorly differentiated) is also an important factor.

GLANDULAR NEOPLASIA OF THE CERVIX

Glandular neoplasia of the cervix occurs less commonly than squamous neoplasia, but its incidence is increasing. *Cervical glandular intraepithelial neoplasia (CGIN)* is recognised as the precursor of invasive adenocarcinoma and is being recognised more frequently. It occurs at a younger age than malignant glandular neoplasia. The recognition of neoplastic glandular cells in a cervical smear can be difficult.

The use of oral hormonal contraceptive preparations may be implicated in the aetiology of glandular neoplasia. The mode of spread of the malignant tumour is the same as that of squamous carcinoma. It is increasingly recognised that a significant proportion of cervical cancers (perhaps as high as 25%) are mixed adenosquamous carcinomas.

This is understandable if one considers that 'atypical' reserve cells may differentiate along squamous or glandular lines to give pure or mixed tumours.

Other Malignant Tumours

Other malignant tumours of the cervix are rare; they include sarcoma, malignant melanoma and lymphoma. Small cell (neuroendocrine) carcinoma of the cervix is an uncommon, but highly malignant, tumour at this site analogous to small cell carcinoma of the lung.

Uterine Corpus

Diseases affecting the uterine corpus (body of the uterus) may arise primarily within the endometrial lining (e.g. adenocarcinoma) or the myometrial wall (e.g. 'fibroids'). Pathological complications of pregnancy may also affect the uterus, but these conditions are dealt with in a separate section.

CONGENITAL ABNORMALITIES

Atresias and aplasias of the female genital tract are rare, with the exception of imperforate hymen. The majority of congenital abnormalities

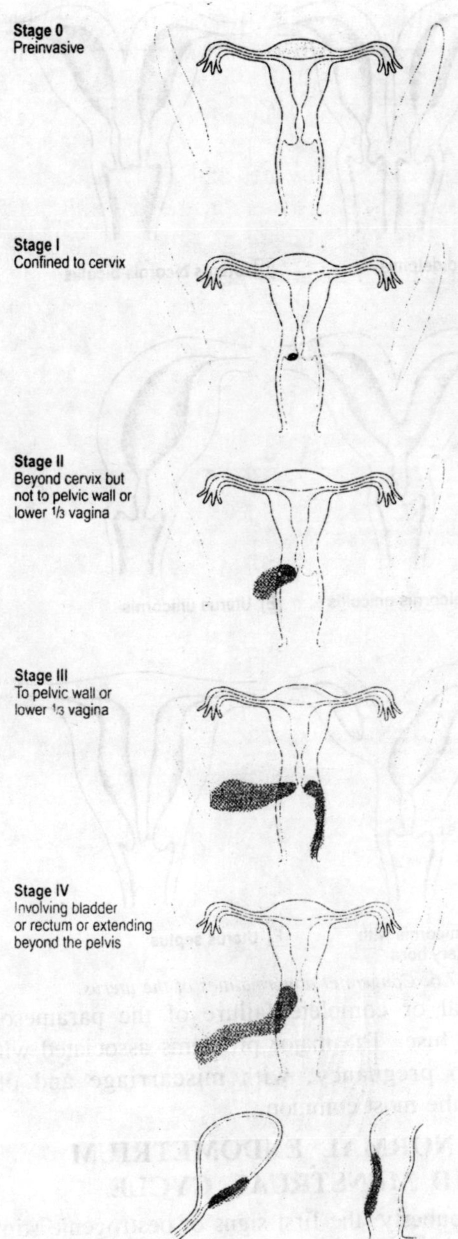

Figure 7.5: Stages of cervical carcinoma.

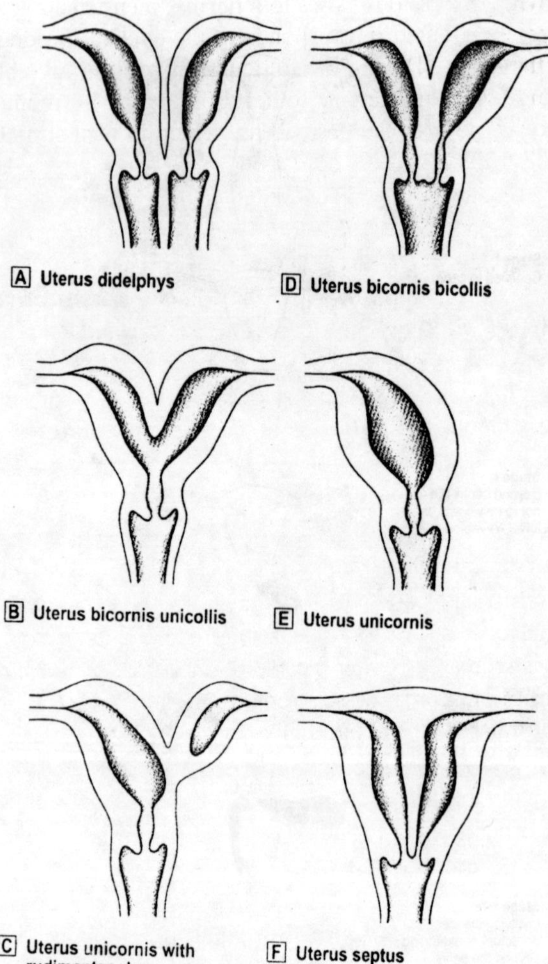

Figure 7.6: Congenital abnormalities of the uterus.

result from a partial or complete failure of the paramesonephric (Mullerian) ducts to fuse. The major problems associated with these anomalies relate to pregnancy, with miscarriage and obstetric complications being the most common.

THE NORMAL ENDOMETRIUM AND MENSTRUAL CYCLE

At the onset of puberty, the first signs of oestrogenic stimulation of the endometrium appear and are soon followed by the first menstrual cycles, most of which are anovulatory.

The following discussion relates to a normal menstrual cycle of 28 days. The normal endometrium responds to the cyclical production of hormones by the ovary. During the follicular or proliferative phase of the cycle, rising levels of pituitary follicle stimulating hormone (FSH) stimulate the ovary to produce oestrogens, which in turn stimulate the endometrium to proliferate.

There is growth of endometrial glands and stroma, both of which show mitotic activity, and vessels become increasingly coiled. Following ovulation at about day 14 of the cycle (mediated by pituitary luteinising hormone and a further output of FSH) the follicle is transformed into a corpus luteum, which continues to secrete oestrogens and also large quantities of progesterone.

This post-ovulatory or luteal phase is associated with secretory changes in the endometrium which can be recognised in three stages:

- *early secretory* (post-ovulatory days 2-5), characterised by prominent subnuclear vacuolation
- *mid-secretory* (post-ovulatory days 5-9), characterised by stromal oedema and luminal secretion
- *late secretory* (post-ovulatory days 10-14), characterised by stromal changes referred to as pre-decidualisation in which there is increased prominence of periarterial stroma, increased tortuosity of stromal vessels (now referred to as spiral arteries) and prominent stromal granulocytes.

These changes prepare the endometrium for implantation of the blastocyst following fertilisation. If this does not occur there is functional decline as the corpus luteum atrophies, with falling levels of oestrogens and progesterone.

This leads to the stromal haemorrhage and crumbling of the menstrual phase endometrium, which is quite variable in duration. Further proliferative activity is initiated with the development of a new follicle.

ABNORMALITIES OF THE ENDOMETRIUM

Disorders of the menstrual cycle leading to abnormal appearances of the endometrium will be discussed, followed by iatrogenic changes, polyps, endometrial hyperplasia and neoplasia. It must be remembered that many cases of abnormal uterine bleeding show a morphologically normal uterus. Defects in local haemostasis and hormonal dysfunction are important causes of bleeding in this context.

Luteal Phase Insufficiency

In some cases of primary or secondary infertility, endometrium examined in the secretory or luteal phase of the cycle shows inadequate secretory maturation for the appropriate estimated post-ovulatory day. Glandular and stromal maturation may also appear to be out of phase (socalled 'irregular ripening'). These changes are usually due to diminished production of progesterone by the corpus luteum.

Irregular Shedding

Irregular shedding presents with abnormal uterine bleeding, and a confusing combination of secretory, menstrual and proliferative changes are seen in endometrial curettings. The changes are the result of a persistent corpus luteum.

Arias-Stella Phenomenon

The Arias-Stella phenomenon is a hypersecretory response of the endometrium to high levels of circulating progesterone. It is characterised by cytoplasmic vacuolation and cytological atypia. The presence of the Arias-Stella phenomenon in the absence of other evidence of intrauterine pregnancy (i.e. trophoblast-see below) suggests the possibility of extra-uterine pregnancy.

Endometritis

It is unusual for the endometrium to be the site of inflammation. The commonest situation in which this occurs is after intra-uterine pregnancy, when the appearances are of non-specific acute or chronic inflammation. This may follow instrumentation or the retention of products of conception. Inflammation may also result from the presence of an intra-uterine contraceptive device (see below).

Two important specific infections of the endometrium are chlamydial infection and tuberculosis.

Chlamydial infection

Chlamydial infection produces a severe acute inflammation or chronic endometritis, with an extensive lymphocytic infiltrate and lymphoid follicle formation.

Tuberculosis

Secondary tuberculous infection of the endometrium may occur. Typical caseating or non-caseating granulomas are best seen in the secretory phase of the menstrual cycle. Definitive diagnosis rests on the demonstration of acidalcohol-fast bacilli by the Ziehl-Neelsen technique. Endometrial infection may be associated with other evidence of pelvic or peritoneal tuberculosis.

Latrogenic Changes in the Endometrium

Changes may be induced in the endometrium as a result of:

- exogenous hormones, including oral contraceptive preparations and hormone replacement therapy
- the use of a mechanical intra-uterine contraceptive device
- tamoxifen administration for patients with breast cancer.

Oral contraceptive preparations

There are two main types of oral contraceptive 'pill':

- combined-both oestrogen and progestogen are taken throughout the cycle; the dose may vary through the cycle and these are then called multiphasic preparations
- *progestogen* only.

The commoner pill now in use is the combined preparation and much smaller doses of oestrogen and progestogen are currently used. The commonest appearance in the endometrium is that of small, tubular, relatively inactive glands in a poorly developed stroma.

Long-term use of the contraceptive pill in women over the age of 35 (particularly smokers) may be associated with hypertension, subarachnoid haemorrhage, thrombo-embolic phenomena and gallstones. For the purpose of contraception, progestogens alone may be administered as a long-term intramuscular injection or as a daily oral preparation.

Glandular atrophy and stromal pseudo-decidualisation are the usual changes produced. Oral progestogen given for the treatment of uterine bleeding secondary to ovarian dysfunction or endometrial hyperplasia produces similar effects.

Hormone replacement therapy

Exogenous oestrogen is used in the treatment of peri- and post-menopausal symptoms. It is of great potential benefit in the prevention of post-menopausal osteoporosis. There is, however, a risk of endometrial hyperplasia (20% after 1 year of treatment) and adenocarcinoma (relative risk 2.3) with unopposed exogenous oestrogen so that postmenopausal hormone replacement therapy in the presence of a uterus should involve a combination of oestrogen and progestogen.

The progestogen opposes the potentially deleterious effects of oestrogen on the endometrium. The two hormones may be taken as 'sequential' or 'continuous combined' preparations. Oestrogens may also be delivered as an impregnated skin patch.

Intra-uterine Devices

The precise mode of action of intra-uterine contraceptive devices is uncertain. They may act by preventing fertilisation or blastocyst implantation, or by inducing very early miscarriage of an implanted pregnancy. The following pathological changes related to the presence of an intra-uterine device may be seen in the endometrium:

- chronic inflammation
- focal acute inflammation
- ulceration
- focal irregular ripening
- papillary metaplasia
- vascular thrombosis
- pseudo-decidual change.

Not all of these changes produce symptoms. Pelvic infection with *Actinomyces-like* organisms may occur with any of these devices.

Some intra-uterine devices contain a progestogen preparation, in which case the endometrial changes associated with exogenous progestogen administration (see above) are also seen.

Tamoxifen

Tamoxifen is an anti-oestrogenic agent used in the treatment of breast cancer. Paradoxically it also has oestrogenic effects and in recent years endometrial abnormalities have been reported following its long-term use; these include endometrial polyps and adenocarcinomas. The risk of developing endometrial cancer in patients treated with tamoxifen is still low (1.2 per 1000 person-years).

Endometrial Polyps

Endometrial polyps are common in peri-menopausal and post-menopausal endometrium, and may be single or multiple. They are the result of the inappropriate reaction of foci of endometrium to oestrogenic stimulation. They are composed of variably sized glands, which are often cystic and are set in a cellular stroma which characteristically contains thick-walled blood vessels.

The epithelium lining the glands may show variable metaplasia, and secondary inflammatory changes may occur. Malignant change is rare.

Endometrial Hyperplasia

The endometrium undergoes hyperplasia in response to unopposed oestrogenic stimulation. The source of oestrogenic stimulation may be endogenous, such as an ovarian tumour, the polycystic ovary syndrome (see below) or exogenous. Obesity is an important cause of a hyperoestrogenic state, as there is increased peripheral conversion of androstenedione to oestrone by the enzyme, aromatase, in fat cells.

The various types of endometrial hyperplasia discussed below are associated with a variable risk of malignant change. The precise factors which determine which type will develop in a particular patient are unknown.

Simple hyperplasia

Simple hyperplasia is a diffuse abnormality affecting the whole of the endometrium. Many of the glands are dilated, and the epithelium shows increased nuclear stratification. The stroma also shows increased mitotic activity but there is no nuclear atypia. This form of hyperplasia is associated with no increased risk of malignancy.

Complex hyperplasia

Complex hyperplasia is usually a focal architectural change in the endometrium. Characteristically, the glands are crowded and irregularly branched. There is a low risk of malignant change (3%).

Atypical hyperplasia

In atypical hyperplasia (endometrial intraepithelial neoplasia) architectural and cytological changes are combined. The nuclei of the epithelial cells may show a variable degree of cytological atypia. There is a close correlation between the risk of malignant change and the severity of the atypia. Thus, for atypical hyperplasia showing a severe degree of cytological atypia, the risk is probably about 25% after 3 years.

Endometrial Adenocarcinoma

- May result from unopposed oestrogenic action or in atrophic post-menopausal endometrium
- Spreads via lymphatic and haematogenous routes

There are two clinicopathological types of endometrial adenocarcinoma.

The first type is endometrioid adenocarcinoma and is usually due to unopposed oestrogenic stimulation and arises from endometrial intraepithelial neoplasia (EIN). This type of tumour characteristically occurs in young women with the polycystic ovary syndrome or in association with obesity.

It also affects perimenopausal women, and may complicate post-menopausal oestrogen replacement therapy. It is generally associated with a good prognosis.

The second type of endometrial adenocarcinoma is nonendometrioid, affects elderly post-menopausal women, is not associated with oestrogenic stimulation, and probably arises on the basis of a pre-existing inactive or atrophic endometrium. High grade serous and clear cell carcinoma are in this category and are associated with a poor prognosis.

A precursor lesion (endometrial intraepithelial carcinoma) of high grade serous carcinoma has now been described. Recently it has been shown that the molecular profiles of these two basic types of endometrial adenocarcinoma (endometrioid and non-endometrioid) are quite different. The lack or presence of p53 mutation is the most important distinguishing molecular feature.

Table 7.2: Molecular profile of endometrial carcinoma.

	Endometrioid	*Serous*
ER/PR	+	–
p53 mutation	–	+
Microsatellite instability	++(20-30%)	+ (11 %)
PTEN mutation	+(34-83%)	–
k-ras mutation	+(10-30%)	–
β-Catenin mutation	+(28-35%)	–

Endometrial adenocarcinoma may be confined to the endometrium. Since the endometrium is composed of glands and stroma, it is possible for a carcinoma to invade its own stroma and still be intra-endometrial. Alternatively, there may be invasion of the myometrium.

The extent of myometrial invasion at the time of diagnosis is the single most important prognostic factor. Involvement of the endocervix also has an adverse effect on prognosis. Thereafter, spread of the tumour occurs via the lymphatic and venous routes to the vagina and pelvic and para-aortic lymph nodes.

Endometrial Stromal Sarcoma

Neoplastic change can occur in the endometrial stroma as well as the endometrial glands, but stromal neoplasms are much less common. Low-grade stromal sarcoma occurs in the uterus of peri- and post-menopausal women and may be diagnosed as an incidental finding in a hysterectomy specimen or following a clinical diagnosis of fibroids. Nodules of bland-looking stroma infiltrate the myometrium, with little or no mitotic activity.

The natural history of these tumours is one of local recurrence, sometimes after many years. Histologically, these recurrences resemble the original tumour. High-grade stromal sarcoma is a highly malignant tumour which may show extensive invasion of the myometrium at the time of diagnosis, with high mitotic activity and focal necrosis.

Mixed Mullerian Neoplasia

Not only do both glandular and stromal components of the endometrium have the propensity to undergo neoplastic change, but they may do so concurrently. This gives rise to the spectrum of mixed Mullerian (mesodermal) neoplasia.

Either component may be benign or malignant. Several variants are recognised, but carcinosarcoma or malignant mixed Mullerian tumour is the most important type and is discussed in more detail below.

Malignant mixed Mullerian tumour

Malignant mixed Mullerian tumour is a highly malignant tumour with a poor prognosis that occurs in elderly women. Clinically, it presents in the same way as endometrial adenocarcinoma, but the tumour is usually advanced with extensive myometrial invasion at the time of diagnosis.

Diagnosis can usually be made on a curettage specimen, where obviously malignant glands and stroma are characterised by cellular pleomorphism, increased mitotic activity and abnormal mitoses. The tumours are usually polypoid and fill the endometrial cavity. If the tumour shows only those components derived from endometrium or myometrium, it is of *homologous type*.

Often, other components foreign to the uterus are seen, including cartilage and bone; it is then of *heterologous type*. Recent molecular genetic evidence suggests a monoclonal origin of these tumours, which should probably be regarded as 'metaplastic carcinomas'.

ABNORMALITES OF THE MYOMETRIUM

Adenomyosis

Adenomyosis is a common finding in hysterectomy specimens and refers to the presence of endometrial glands and stroma deep within the myometrium. It characteristically occurs in peri-menopausal multiparous women and is of uncertain aetiology, although it may be regarded as a form of 'diverticulosis', as there is continuity between adenomyotic foci and the lining endometrium of the uterine cavity.

Neoplastic change may occur within these foci but should not be regarded as evidence of myometrial invasion.

Smooth Muscle Tumours

- Uterine leiomyomas (fibroids) are the commonest benign tumours
- Associated with infertility
- Leiomyosarcomas have varying malignant potential correlated with their mitotic activity

The commonest tumour of the female genital tract is the benign fibroid or *leiomyoma.* These commonly present in later reproductive life and around the time of the menopause. They are associated with low parity, although it is uncertain whether this is a common cause or an effect. The precise aetiology of leiomyomas is unknown. They may present clinically with:

- abdominal mass
- urinary problems due to pressure on the bladder
- abnormal uterine bleeding.

Characteristically, they are multiple, round, well-circumscribed tumours varying in diameter from 5 mm to, in some cases, 200 mm or more. They may show cystic change or focal necrosis. On section, they have a white, whorled appearance.

Histologically, they are composed of complex interlacing bundles of smooth muscle fibres showing little or no mitotic activity. Sometimes, nodules of tumour may be seen within veins (intravenous leiomyomatosis); this is not a sinister feature. Smooth muscle tumours contain steroid hormone receptors, and at least a proportion are oestrogen-dependent.

The crucial factor in the assessment of malignancy in smooth muscle tumours is their mitotic activity. There is a very good correlation between clinical behaviour and the mitotic count but malignancy is always associated with other features, including nuclear pleomorphism, an irregular tumour margin, haemorrhage and necrosis.

The mitotic count is usually expressed in terms of numbers of mitoses per 10 high power fields (hpf) of the microscope (the field area should always be stated). Leiomyomas contain 0-3 mitoses/10 hpf. If there are 10 or more in association with nuclear pleomorphism, then a tumour must be regarded as a leiomyosarcoma and will behave as a malignant tumour, with all the risks of recurrence and metastases.

If there are between 3 and 10 mitoses/10 hpf the behaviour of smooth muscle tumours is unpredictable. They are referred to as 'smooth muscle tumours of uncertain malignant potential', and the patients must be placed under periodical surveillance. Although these criteria may appear arbitrary, their application has proved useful in practice.

OVARY

Ovarian lesions present either with pain due to inflammation or swelling of the organ, or with the remote effects of an endocrine secretion.

OVarian Cysts

Ovarian cysts may be non-neoplastic or neoplastic; many ovarian tumours are partially cystic. The various types of non-neoplastic cysts are:

- mesothelial-lined
- epithelial inclusion
- follicular
- luteinised follicular
- corpus luteum
- corpus albicans
- corpus luteum cyst of pregnancy
- endometriotic.

Inclusion cysts occur in the ovarian cortex probably as a result of surface trauma at the time of ovulation; they may be lined by original peritoneal mesothelium or metaplastic epithelium. This is discussed in more detail below.

The nature and origin of many of the non-neoplastic cysts that occur in the ovary can only be appreciated with knowledge of the normal histology of the ovary, as well as of the development of the follicle and corpus luteum.

Polycystic Ovary Syndrome

The polycystic ovary syndrome is the association of amenorrhoea, hyperoestrogenism and multiple follicular cysts of the ovary. There is usually stromal hyperplasia and little evidence that ovulation has occurred. The syndrome, which is related to defective insulin metabolism, is an important cause of infertility, endometrial hyperplasia and, rarely, endometrial adenocarcinoma in young women.

Ovarian Hyperstimulation Syndrome

This may be induced by gonadotrophins or clomifene used in the treatment of infertility. It is characterised by bilateral ovarian enlargement due to multiple luteinised follicular cysts. The condition may be complicated by ascites and pericardial effusion, hypovolaemic shock and renal failure.

OVARIAN STROMAL HYPERPLASIA AND STROMAL LUTEINISATION

The stroma of the ovary is unlike stromal tissue at other sites because, in addition to a general metabolic and supportive function, the cells may also be directly involved in the endocrine activity of the organ. Ovarian stromal hyperplasia is a proliferative change seen to some extent in the ovaries of many peri- and post-menopausal women.

It is characterised by the non-neoplastic proliferation of stromal cells resulting in varying degrees of bilateral ovarian enlargement. In old age there is a tendency towards atrophy. Atrophic ovaries tend to be small, wrinkled, hard and pearly-white.

Hyperplastic ovarian stroma is associated with increased levels of androgens and oestrogens. Thus there is an association between stromal hyperplasia and endometrial hyperplasia, carcinoma, and polyps. Other steroidogenic cells may be scattered throughout the stroma; such 'luteinised' cells may secrete androgens and may cause virilism. Stromal hyperplasia and luteinisation may also be observed in ovaries containing primary or secondary neoplasms.

ENDOMETRIOSIS

Endometriosis is the presence of endometrial glands and stroma in sites other than the uterine corpus. It is a very important cause of morbidity in women and may be responsible for pelvic inflammation, infertility and pain. The common sites include the pouch of Douglas, the pelvic peritoneum and the ovary.

Endometriosis may also involve the serosal surface of the uterus, cervix, vulva and vagina, and extra-genital sites such as the bladder and the small and large intestines. The occurrence of endometriosis in extra-abdominal sites is very rare. The aetiology of endometriosis is unknown, but retrograde menstruation into the peritoneal cavity along the fallopian tube, or metaplasia of mesothelium to Mulleriantype epithelium are possible explanations.

The glands and stroma are usually subject to the same hormone-induced changes that occur in the endometrium. Thus, haemorrhage in endometriotic foci may cause pain. In the ovary especially, recurrent haemorrhage may produce cysts containing altered blood, so-called 'chocolate cysts'. Uncommonly, hyperplastic or atypical changes may be seen in the epithelial component, with appearances similar to those that affect the endometrium.

At least a proportion of endometrioid tumours of the ovary arise

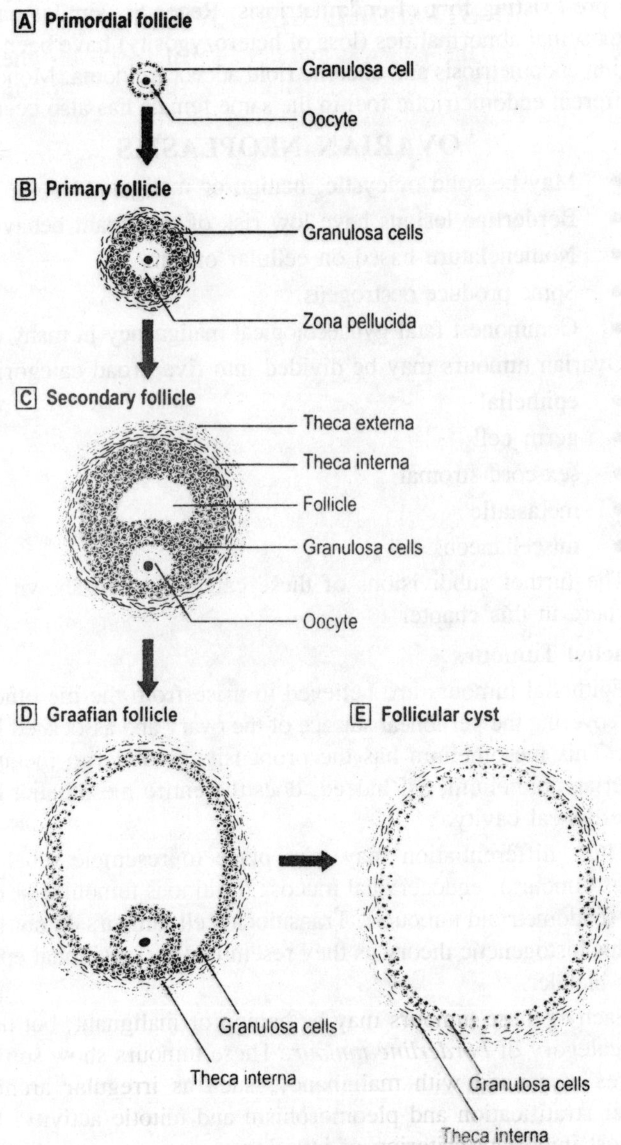

Figure 7.7: Follicle development in the ovary and the origin of a follicular cyst. A: Primordial follicle; B: Primary follicle; C and D: Secondary and Graafian follicles; E: Follicular cysts.

from pre-existing foci of endometriosis. Recently, similar patterns of chromosomal abnormalities (loss of heterozygosity) have been demonstrated in endometriosis and endometrioid adenocarcinoma. Monoclonality of different endometriotic foci in the same female has also been shown.

OVARIAN NEOPLASMS

- May be solid or cystic, benign or malignant
- Borderline lesions have low risk of malignant behaviour
- Nomenclature based on cellular origin
- Some produce oestrogens
- Commonest fatal gynaecological malignancy in many countries

Ovarian tumours may be divided into five broad categories:

- epithelial
- germ cell
- sex-cord stromal
- metastatic
- miscellaneous.

The further subdivisions of these categories are shown in Table elsewhere in this chapter.

Epithelial Tumours

Epithelial tumours are believed to arise from the mesothelial cell layer covering the peritoneal surface of the ovary and associated inclusion cysts. This mesothelium has the propensity to undergo metaplasia to Milllerian epithelium, as, indeed, does the entire mesothelial lining of the peritoneal cavity.

Thus, differentiation may take place to resemble tubal mucosa (serous tumours), endocervical mucosa (mutinous tumours) or endometrium (endometrioid tumours). Transitional cell tumours do not fit neatly into this histogenetic theory as they resemble the transitional epithelium of the bladder.

Each of these tumours may be benign or malignant, but there is a third category of *borderline tumour*. These tumours show some of the features associated with malignancy, such as irregular architecture, nuclear stratification and pleomorphism and mitotic activity, but lack the most important criterion of invasion.

Their biological behaviour is intermediate between that of clearly benign and overtly malignant tumours. Aneuploid tumours are more likely to behave in a malignant manner. A significant proportion of mucinous tumours, particularly in the borderline category, contain

Table 7.3: Classification of ovarian neoplasms.

Origin	Tumour	
	Types	*Subtypes*
Epithelium	Serous	
	Mutinous	Benign, borderline
	Endometrioid	or malignant
	Transitional cell	
Germ cells	Dysgerminoma	
	Teratoma	Mature cystic, immature solid or monodermal (e.g. carcinoid, struma ovarii)
	Extraembryonic	Yolk sac (endodermal sinus tumour), choriocarcinoma
	Malignant mixed germ cell tumours	
Sex-cord stroma	Thecoma	
	Granulosa cell tumour	
	Sertoli-Leydig cell tumour	
	Mixed germ cell stromal tumour (gonadoblastoma)	
	Steroid cell tumour	
Metastatic	Various (most commonly from the gastrointestinal tract)	
Miscellaneous	Haemangioma, lipoma, etc.	

intestinal-type rather than endocervicaltype epithelium. These tumours may be complicated by peritoneal implants producing copious amounts of mucus *(pseudomyxoma peritonei)*. This condition has a poor prognosis and is often complicated by intestinal obstruction.

However, recent evidence suggests that when pseudomyxoma peritonei is associated with appendiceal and ovarian disease, the peritoneal and ovarian lesions are, in fact, metastases from a primary appendiceal

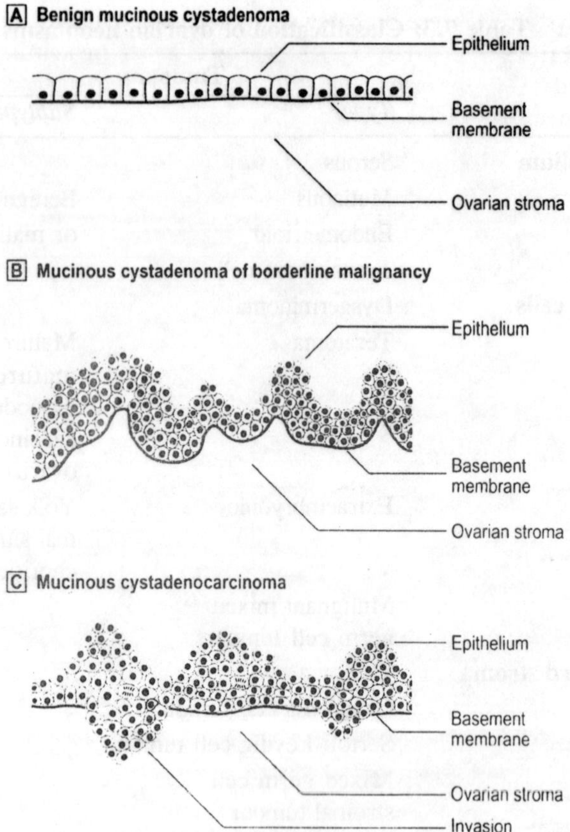

Figure 7.8: Epithelial morphology of ovarian mucinous neoplasms. A: Benign mucinous cystadenoma; B: Mucinous cystadenoma of borderline malignancy; C: Mucinous cystadenocarcinoma.

tumour. The diagnosis of borderline tumour is made on the primary tumour but associated peritoneal implants may be borderline or invasive. The latter are associated with an adverse prognosis.

Benign mucinous and serous tumours are commonly smooth-walled and cystic, while benign transitional cell (Brenner) tumours are solid but may show cystic areas. Endometrioid tumours of the ovary may show the full range of mixed Mullerian neoplasia already referred to in the context of uterine tumours, such as endometrioid adenofibroma and malignant mixed MUllerian turnouts.

The aetiology of epithelial ovarian cancer remains uncertain but certain facts are known. First, ovarian cancer is a disorder of developed societies and shows a higher incidence among women of higher social classes. Second, the oral contraceptive pill and pregnancy offer a protective effect; these probably act by reducing ovulation, although the reduced risk conferred by one pregnancy is much greater than would be expected. Thus repeated ovulatory trauma to the surface epithelium seems to be a crucial factor.

Table 7.4: Number of cases of, and deaths from, various forms of gynaecological cancer in England and Wales.

	Incidence	*Deathst*
Ovary	5388	3962
Cervix uteri	3400	1225
Body of uterus	3912	774
Vulva	776	350
Uterus, part unspecified	425	517
Vagina	210	89
Fallopian tube	44	22
Placenta	9	4

Studies of ovarian cancer in families have shown that sisters and mothers of affected individuals have an approximately five-fold increased risk of ovarian cancer. Among all of the common cancers this is the largest excess risk to relatives and implies genetic susceptibility.

Family studies also show that first-degree relatives are at an increased risk of breast cancer. Mutations of a rare dominant gene, BRCA1, localised on chromosome 17q, increase the risk of cancer at both sites. It must be emphasised, however, that only about 5 10 of cases of ovarian cancer are hereditary; 95% are sporadic.

Ovarian cancers show complex genetic abnormalities with a high incidence of p53 point mutations. Loss of heterozygosity has been demonstrated at a number of other chromosomal sites close to known tumour suppressor genes. Amplification of the erbB-2 (HER-2/neu) oncogene is associated with a poor prognosis.

Ovarian cancer is responsible for more deaths than any other gynaecological malignancy. This is largely because it often presents at an advanced stage, due to its anatomically obscure site. Malignant tumours may be solid and/or cystic and there may be areas of haemorrhage and necrosis, with the tumour projecting into the lumen of a cyst or projecting exophytically into the peritoneal cavity.

Tumour spread occurs predominantly intra-abdominally. The clinical staging of ovarian cancer is shown in Figure elsewhere in this chapter.

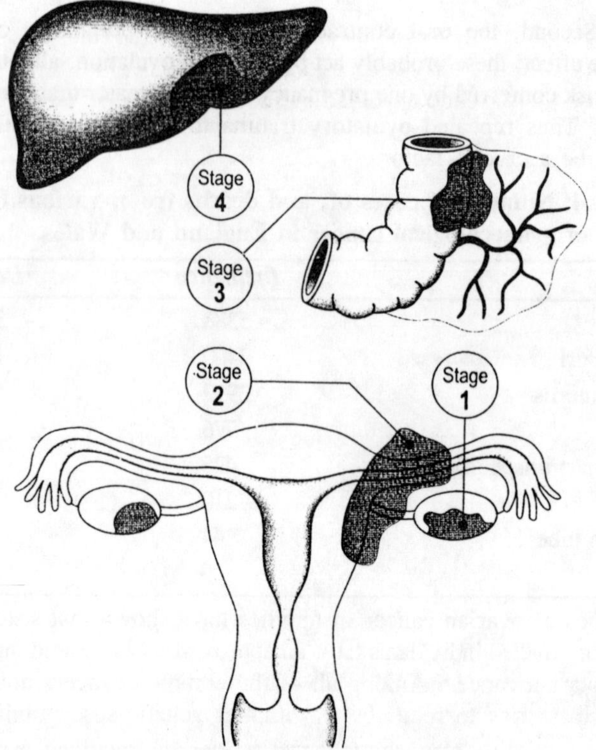

Figure 7.9: Simplified clinical staging of ovarian cancer.

The ovarian cancer related protein CA125 is used routinely as a serum tumour marker, particularly to aid in the recognition of early relapse.

Germ Cell Tumours

A potentially confusing range of tumours may arise from germ cells in the ovary. These may be benign or malignant.

Dysgerminoma

The fundamental or undifferentiated female ovarian germ cell tumour is the dysgerminoma, which is the exact counterpart of the seminoma arising in the male testis. It is a rare malignant tumour arising predominantly in young females; it is usually confined to one ovary and has a fleshy cut surface.

Histologically, it shows a uniform appearance of germ cells admixed with lymphocytes. Occasional giant cells containing human chorionic gonadotrophin may be present, but these do not imply a poorer prognosis. These tumours are highly radiosensitive.

Teratomas

When germ cells differentiate along embryonic lines they give rise to teratomas, that is, a tumour that contains elements of all three germ cell layers-ectoderm, endoderm and mesoderm.

Mature cystic teratoma

The commonest germ cell tumour and, indeed, the commonest ovarian tumour, is the benign or mature cystic teratoma (dermoid cyst). The majority of ovarian mature cystic teratomas arise from an oocyte that has completed the first meiotic division, in a manner analogous to parthenogenesis. It may present at any age, although usually in younger patients, as a smooth-walled, unilateral ovarian cyst.

These tumours characteristically contain hair, sebaceous material and teeth. Histologically, they show a wide range of tissues which, although haphazardly arranged, are indistinguishable from those seen in the normal adult. Squamous epithelium, bronchial epithelium, cartilage and intestinal epithelium may all be seen. These tumours are benign, although in elderly women malignancy (usually squamous carcinoma) may develop very rarely.

Immature teratoma

In contrast to the mature cystic type, teratomas may also be predominantly solid and composed of immature tissues similar to those seen in the developing embryo. These tumours are potentially malignant, and the predominant components are immature neural tissue and immature mesenchyme.

They occur in young patients, and the prognosis is related to the amount of immature neural tissue present. Such tumours may metastasise to the peritoneum, where the assessment of tissue maturity is crucial. Immature neural tissue within the peritoneum may mature, or mature glial tissue may be present from the outset (gliomatosis peritonei).

Monodermal teratoma

Germ cell tumours may be composed entirely, or almost entirely, of tissue derived from one germ cell layer; these are monodermal teratomas. The best examples are struma *ovarii,* composed of thyroid tissue which may be benign or malignant and rarely cause thyrotoxicosis, and *carcinoid* tumours, which are similar to carcinoid tumours arising in the gut.

The carcinoid syndrome may occur even with benign tumours, as metabolic products are released directly into the systemic circulation and are therefore not denatured by hepatic enzymes.

Extraembryonic Germ Cell Tumours

Differentiation of germ cells may take place along extraembryonic (as opposed to embryonic) lines to form the neoplastic counterparts of the non-fetal parts of the conceptus (the primitive yolk sac and the trophoblast of the placenta).

These elements may give rise to yolk sac tumours (also known as endodermal sinus tumours because of their resemblance to the endodermal sinuses of Duval in the developing rat placenta) and choriocarcinoma. These are highly malignant tumours which may be associated with other germ cell elements.

Yolk sac tumours

Yolk sac tumours usually affect young females below the age of 30 years. The tumours are cystic and solid and often haemorrhagic. Histologically, characteristic structures (Duval-Schiller bodies), composed of central vessels with a rosette of tumour cells, may be seen.

Alpha-fetoprotein may be demonstrated immunohistologically and is used as a serum marker. Intra-abdominal metastasis occurs, and the prognosis for untreated patients is poor. Modern combination chemotherapy, however, has considerably improved the outlook for patients with this tumour, and subsequent pregnancy following conservative surgery and chemotherapy is now possible.

Choriocarcinoma

Pure choriocarcinoma of the ovary is extremely rare and is associated with beta human chorionic gonadotrophin (βhCG) production. Theoretically, it could occur either as a germ cell tumour or as a primary or secondary gestational neoplasm (see below), in which case the tumour would contain the paternal haplotype on chromosomal analysis. When choriocarcinoma is seen, it is more usually one component of a malignant mixed germ cell tumour.

Sex-Cord Stromall Tumours

During the fourth month of fetal life and onwards cell cords grow down from the surface epithelium of the ovary to surround the primordial follicles. Sex-cord stromal tumours comprise a range of ovarian neoplasms which frequently produce steroid hormones and are considered to arise from the cells which are the adult derivatives of these primitive sex cords in the fetal ovary. The detailed classification of these tumours is complex, but there are five broad groups.

Thecoma

Thecoma is the commonest sex-cord stromal tumour. It presents in the reproductive years as an abdominal mass, and is a benign tumour of the ovarian stroma. It is usually unilateral and well-circumscribed with a pale, fleshy cut surface.

Histologically, it is a cellular, spindle-celled tumour containing abundant lipid. Its particular importance clinically is that it may be associated with the production of oestrogens, and may therefore give rise to abnormal uterine bleeding, endometrial hyperplasia or rarely endometrial adenocarcinoma.

Granulosa cell tumour

Granulosa cell tumours can occur at any age and all cases are potentially malignant, although there is a close correlation between large size at presentation and malignant behaviour. It is particularly associated with oestrogenic manifestations. (It should, however, be remembered that granulosa cells do not synthesise oestrogens, but merely convert hormonal precursors to oestrogens.)

They present as unilateral multicystic tumours that may be focally haemorrhagic or necrotic. Histologically, they are composed of nests and cords of granulosa cells with characteristically grooved nuclei. Often, cells surround a central space containing eosinophilic hyaline material; this structure is called the Call-Exner body.

Patients often have concomitant endometrial pathology, either hyperplasia or adenocarcinoma. Granulosa cell tumours are characterised by their propensity for late recurrence, in some cases many years after removal of the original tumour. Granulosa cells produce *inhibin* and this may now be used as a serum or immunohistochemical marker for the tumour.

Sertoli-Leydig cell tumours

Sertoli-Leydig cell tumours are rare tumours composed of a variable mixture of cell types normally seen in the testis. Pure Sertoli and Leydig cell tumours may also occur. The tumours may be well, moderately or poorly differentiated and may present with androgenic signs and symptoms. Leydig cells may be identified by the presence of Reinke's crystals within their cytoplasm.

Gonadoblastoma

Gonadoblastoma is a rare lesion, which may not be a true neoplasm, in which primitive germ cells and sex-cord stromal derivatives are present. The latter usually resemble immature Sertoli cells and granulosa cells.

These lesions typically develop in the dysgenetic streak gonads of phenotypic females carrying a Y chromosome. The germ cell component may undergo malignant change, usually to form a dysgerminoma.

Steroid cell tumours

Steroid cell tumours are uncommon and are usually benign and unilateral. In many cases the patient presents with virilisation due to androgen production. Microscopically, the tumour is well circumscribed and composed of cells that resemble adrenal cortical cells and contain abundant intracellular lipid. The precise origin of these tumours is still debated. Although other sex-cord stromal tumours may secrete steroids, the term 'steroid cell tumour' is conventionally reserved for this particular variant.

Metastatic tumours

Tumour metastatic to the ovary may be genital or extragenital. Endometrial adenocarcinoma may spread to the ovary, but it should be remembered that primary endometrial adenocarcinoma may co-exist with primary endometrioid adenocarcinoma of the ovary and be associated with a favourable prognosis.

Large intestine, stomach and breast adenocarcinomas are the most important extragenital tumours. Metastatic colonic adenocarcinoma may be confused with primary mucinous cystadenocarcinoma or endometrioid adenocarcinoma. The term 'Krukenberg tumour' refers to bilateral ovarian neoplasms composed of malignant, mucin-containing, signet ring cells, usually of gastric origin.

Breast carcinoma frequently metastasises to the ovary, but usually these metastases do not manifest themselves clinically. Metastatic malignant melanoma may first present as an ovarian tumour.

FALLOPIAN TUBES

The fallopian tubes may be the site of inflammation, pregnancy, cysts or neoplasia. Inflammatory lesions and tubal ectopic pregnancies commonly present clinically with acute lower abdominal pain, mimicking, for example, acute appendicitis. Loss of tubal patency is an important cause of female infertility.

Inflammation (salpingitis)

Inflammation of the fallopian tube (salpingitis) is usually secondary to endometrial infection or the presence of an intra-uterine device; it may be acute or chronic. Chlamydial infection is now an important cause of chronic inflammation and subsequent secondary infertility due to loss of tubal patency.

Anaerobic organisms, such as *Bacteroides*, are also important as causes of salpingitis, whereas gonococcal infection is uncommon. Infection may be complicated by the accumulation of pus within the lumen of the tube *(pyosalpinx)*. Longstanding chronic inflammation may lead to distension of the tube, loss of mucosa and the accumulation of serous fluid within the lumen *(hydrosalpinx)*.

Cysts and Tumours

Benign fimbrial cysts and *paratubal cysts* are common. They are usually lined by tubal-type epithelium. Rarely, *benign papillary serous neoplasms* may arise in paratubal or paraovarian cysts. Tumours of the fallopian tube are rare. Of most clinical importance is *primary adenocarcinoma of the fallopian tube epithelium.*

This tumour has a similar appearance to that of papillary serous adenocarcinoma of the ovary, for which it may be mistaken. The mode of spread is via lymphatics and the peritoneum. The tumour usually has a poor prognosis.

PATHOLOGY OF PREGNANCY

There is a high rate of fetal loss in early pregnancy, and many early miscarriages are subclinical. Clinical miscarriage is usually the result of chromosomal abnormalities. The chorionic villi of the immature placenta may be oedematous *(hydropic change)*, or the stroma may be fibrotic, which is an involutional change following fetal death.

Hydatidiform Mole

- Characterised by swollen chorionic villi and trophoblastic hyperplasia
- Associated with high hCG levels
- Partial mole: triploid karyotype; fetus may be present
- Complete mole: 46XX karyotype; no fetus
- May be complicated by choriocarcinoma

Hydatidiform mole is a disorder of pregnancy affecting approximately 1 in 1000 pregnancies in the Western world and is much commoner in the Far East. It is characterised by swollen, oedematous chorionic villi, trophoblastic hyperplasia and the irregular distribution of villous trophoblast.

Macroscopically, the placenta appears to be composed of multiple cystic, 'grape-like' structures. A hydatidiform mole usually grows faster than a normal pregnancy, and the patient may present either with a 'large for dates' pregnant uterus, or with bleeding in early pregnancy. If an ultrasound scan is performed, the abnormal cysts can be clearly seen and uterine evacuation is indicated. There are two types of hydatidiform mole-complete mole and partial mole—which are genetically quite different.

Partial Mole

The partial mole is triploid, and may not be diagnosed clinically but only identified histologically in miscarriage material. Most contain one maternal and two paternal haploid sets of chromosomes, with all three sex chromosome patterns possible (XXY, XXX and XYY). It must be remembered, however, that not all triploids are partial moles. A fetus may be present and only a proportion of the villi abnormal; the rest may be fibrotic or may simply be hydropic without trophoblastic hyperplasia. Stromal vessels are present.

***p57*^{kip2}**

p57^{kip2} is a maternally expressed imprinted gene. Its protein product is expressed by the villous cytotrophoblast of partial moles but not androgenetic complete moles.

Complete Mole

The chromosomal constitution of the complete mole is androgenetic (i.e. of paternal origin), characteristically 46XX, and is probably due to the fertilisation of an 'empty' ovum by a spermatozoon carrying an X chromosome which is then reduplicated. Grossly, the placenta is obviously abnormal with swollen villi.

Histologically, the oedema is confirmed; there is an absence of stromal vessels and circumferential trophoblastic hyperplasia affecting all villi. The constituent trophoblast may show varying degrees of cytological atypia.

Complications

The importance of correctly diagnosing hydatidiform mole is that, in a small number of cases, the disorder may be complicated by *persistent trophoblastic disease*. This term encompasses two main pathological entities with similar clinical manifestations, diagnosed by persistently elevated or rising urinary hCG levels following evacuation of molar tissue.

- *Invasive mole;* chorionic villi are present within the myometrium and myometrial vessels. The main complication is uterine perforation.
- *Choriocarcinoma;* this is a rare, malignant neoplasm of trophoblast with a propensity to systemic metastasis. Although there is usually a preceding history of hydatidiform mole, choriocarcinoma may follow a miscarriage or very rarely an

apparently normal pregnancy. It is more common in the Far East and, without treatment, has a high mortality. A biphasic pattern of invading cyto- and syncytiotrophoblast is the characteristic appearance of this tumour.

Cases of hydatidiform mole are monitored by estimation of the serum and urinary hCG. If the level rises, or does not fall, then the patient will receive chemotherapy irrespective of the precise pathological diagnosis. The role of the pathologist in the management of persistent trophoblastic disease is thus limited.

The neoplastic potential of complete mole is greater than that of partial mole. Therefore, all cases of molar disease are followed up, although this may prove to be unnecessary in many cases. Patients are advised not to become pregnant during follow-up as this would cause a confusing rise in hCG levels.

PATHOLOGY OF THE FULL-TERM PLACENTA

The pathology of the full-term placenta is a large complex topic, the details of which are beyond the scope of this book. Only the commoner and/or clinically significant lesions are mentioned here. These may be considered under the following headings:

- abnormalities of placentation
  - extrachorial (may be circumvallate or circum marginate)
  - accessory lobe
  - placenta accreta
- inflammation (villitis)
- vascular lesions
  - perivillous fibrin deposition
  - fetal artery thrombosis
  - placental infarct
  - haemangioma
- immaturity of villous development.

Fascinatingly, long-term follow-up of individuals whose placental weights were accurately recorded earlier this century has shown a strong correlation between low placental weight and adult (e.g. cardiovascular) disease.

Abnormalities of Placentation

Abnormalities of placental shape are usually of no clinical significance. Placenta accreta is an abnormality of implantation.

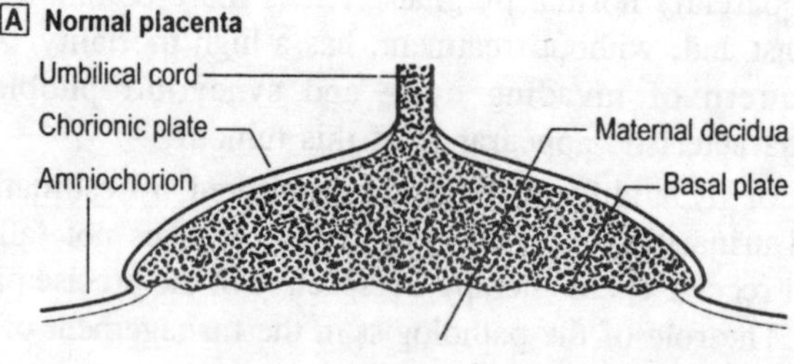

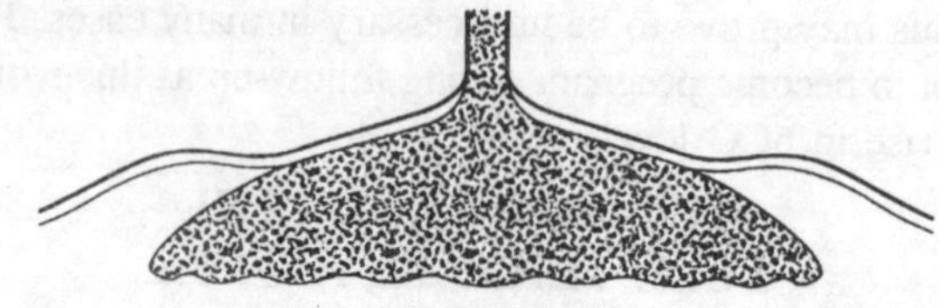

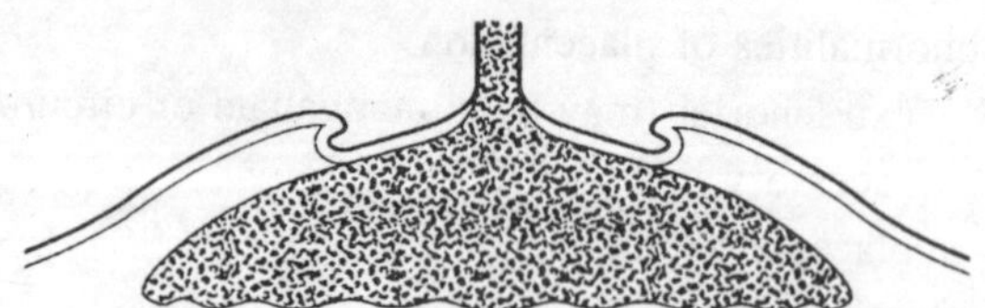

Figure 7.10: Extrachorial placentation.

Extrachorial placentation

Extrachorial placentation is a developmental abnormality in which the fetal surface of the placenta from which the chorionic villi arise (the chorionic plate) is smaller than the maternal surface attached to the uterine decidua (the basal plate).

Thus, the border between the extravillous chorionic membrane and chorionic villi is not at the placental margin but is present circumferentially on the fetal surface of the placenta.

This border may be flat ('circummarginate') or raised ('circumvallate'). Circum-marginate place-ntation is of no clinical significance, but circumvallate placentation is associated with a higher incidence of low birthweight babies, although the causal relationship between the two is still obscure.

Accessory lobe

An accessory lobe to the placenta is usually of no clinical importance, but occasionally the lobe may be retained in utero after delivery of the main placenta.

Placenta accreta

Placenta accreta is a rare disorder in which the chorionic villi are immediately adjacent to, or penetrate, the myometrium to a varying degree. This is associated with a deficiency of decidua, and. may be the result of previous operative intervention, such as curettage or caesarean section, infection or uterine malformation.

The main clinical significance is the risk of ante-partum bleeding. Post-partum bleeding may also occur due to a failure of placental separation resulting from the abnormally adherent chorionic villi.

Inflammation

Inflammation of the placental tissues may involve either the chorionic villi (villitis) or the extraplacental membranes (chorioamnionitis). Inflammation of chorionic villi is usually due to infection through the maternal blood stream. Specific infections, such as listeriosis, toxoplasmosis or cytomegalovirus, are responsible for only a small proportion of cases.

Most examples are of unknown aetiology, and are seen in approximately 5% of all pregnancies as a focal infiltrate of lymphocytes and histiocytes. Villitis is associated with an increased incidence of fetal intra-uterine growth retardation but, again, the pathogenesis is unclear.

Vascular Lesions

Several vascular lesions may occur in the placenta. They are usually of no clinical significance.

Perivillous fibrin deposition

Perivillous fibrin deposition occurs to some extent in all placentae and quite commonly is macroscopically apparent as a firm white plaque. The lesion is of no clinical significance.

Fetal artery thrombosis

Thrombosis of a fetal villous stem artery will produce a well-circumscribed area of avascular chorionic villi, which may be apparent macroscopically as an area of pallor. The inter-villous space appears normal. The aetiology is unknown, although there is an association with maternal diabetes mellitus. Although usually of no clinical significance, extensive thrombosis of fetal villous stem vessels can, rarely, be responsible for fetal death.

Placental infarct

A placental infarct is a localised area of ischaemic villous necrosis due to thrombotic occlusion of a maternal uteroplacental (spiral) artery. (It must be remembered that chorionic villi have a dual blood supply.)

Macroscopically, fresh infarcts are red but progressively undergo fibrosis. When extensive, placental infarction is a manifestation of maternal vascular disease and is thus particularly associated with hypertensive disorders of pregnancy.

Haemangioma

Haemangiomas are uncommon tumours that occur as well-circumscribed, dark nodules. They are of no clinical significance except when large or multiple. They may then be associated with polyhydramnios, premature labour and intra-uterine growth retardation due to diversion of blood through the tumour rather than through normal placental tissue.

Immaturity of villous development

Maturation of the placenta during pregnancy is associated with increased branching of chorionic villi with the production of small terminal villi to maximise the surface area available for materno-fetal transfer.

Syncytiotrophoblast at the tips of villi thins to form vasculosyncytial membranes closely apposed to fetal stromal vessels. These are important sites of oxygen transfer between mother and fetus. Immaturity of chorionic villi and inadequate formation of vasculosyncytial membranes may be associated with intrauterine fetal hypoxia, low birthweight and perinatal death.

PATHOLOGY OF THE UMBILICAL CORD AND MEMBRANES

Umbilical Cord

Mechanical lesions of the umbilical cord include knots, rupture, torsion and stricture, all of which may lead to fetal complications. Abnormal (velamentous) insertion of the cord into the membranes, rather than the chorionic plate, may lead to serious haemorrhage during pregnancy or labour, as unprotected vessels run from the membranes to the surface of the placenta.

A single umbilical artery is often accompanied by congenital fetal malformation. Visible oedema of the cord is associated with a relatively high incidence of fetal respiratory distress, although the reason for this is unclear.

Membranes

Amnion *nodosum* is the occurrence of nodules on the fetal surface of the amnion, particularly around the site of the insertion of the cord. Histologically, these are composed of amorphous material in which cell fragments, and sometimes fetal hair, are embedded. The lesion is usually associated with oligohydramnios.

Chorioamnionitis, or acute inflammation of the membranes, is usually the result of ascending bacterial infection from the vagina and cervix. It may be associated with prolonged rupture of membranes before delivery.

PATHOLOGY OF THE PLACENTAL BED

Within the placental bed there is an intimate admixture of maternal and fetal cells. The former comprise the decidua, residual endometrial glands and a population of macrophages and stromal granulated lymphocytes. The cells of fetal origin are composed of the various populations of nonvillous trophoblast.

These cells develop from the proliferating cytotrophoblast columns of the implanted blastocyst in the early weeks of pregnancy, and invade maternal decidua in a manner reminiscent of a malignant neoplasm. However, this biologically unique and physiologically controlled invasion is essential for the establishment of normal placentation.

The most important types of non-villous trophoblast are the interstitial trophoblast cells, some of which fuse to form giant cells, and the endovascular trophoblast, which invades maternal spiral arteries, destroying their muscular media and replacing it with a fibrinoid matrix.

In this way, these vessels lose their elasticity and become of wide calibre to meet the growing nutritional demands of the developing feto-placental unit. The invasion of non-villous trophoblast occurs in two waves, the first wave occurring in the first weeks of pregnancy and the second between 14 and 16 weeks.

Pre-eclampsia and fetal intra-uterine growth retardation

Pre-eclampsia is a common syndrome of pregnancy characterised by maternal hypertension and proteinuria. It is potentially dangerous for both mother and fetus.

In pre-eclampsia, especially when associated with intrauterine fetal growth retardation, there is a failure of the second wave of endovascular trophoblast migration into the myometrial segments of the spiral arteries. This may also occur in intra-uterine growth retardation uncomplicated by hypertension.

Examination of the placental bed shows that the physiological changes mediated by endovascular trophoblast are confined to the intradecidual segments of the spiral arteries. The pathogenesis of pre-eclampsia is still uncertain; a toxic effect of oxygen free radicals and lipid peroxides on endothelial cells is implicated.

Acute atherosis

Acute atherosis is a necrotising lesion of the uterine spiral arteries characterised by infiltrates of foam cells. It occurs in the hypertensive disorders of pregnancy-pre-eclampsia and eclampsia-either alone or superimposed on other hypertensive disorders, such as renal disease.

Pathological changes in the placental bed or implantation site may be difficult to distinguish from the physiological changes of pregnancy. The decidua away from the implantation site (decidua vera or parietalis) are thus the optimal sites to see this lesion.

Post-partum Haemorrhage

There are three main causes of post-partum haemorrhage:

- retained chorionic villi
- infection
- inadequate involution of placental bed vessels.

Retained chorionic villi are unusual after normal pregnancy, but are more common following miscarriage or termination of pregnancy. Normally, after parturition, the myometrial segments of the uteroplacental spiral arteries are left behind, and rapidly undergo thrombosis to prevent torrential haemorrhage.

Other involutionary changes then take place, and over the course of a few weeks the vessels resume their non-pregnant appearance. However, in a substantial number of cases of post-partum haemorrhage, the vessels are seen to be still distended and only partially thrombosed, so-called *inadequate involution*.

The control mechanisms of normal involution and the causes of its failure are unknown.

ECTOPIC PREGNANACY

- Pregnancy outside uterine cavity
- Fallopian tube is commonest site
- Leads to pain and haemorrhage when it ruptures
- Pregnancy-associated changes in endometrium

Commonly confused conditions and entities relating to female genital pathology

Commonly confused	*Distinction and explanation*
Moles and *hydatidiform* moles	The pathological term *mole* (Latin: moles = mass) is used for the common melanocytic naevus or mole occurring in skin. However, a *hydatidiform mole* is a placental lesion characterised by swollen chorionic villi and trophoblastic hyperplasia.
Dyskaryosis and *dysplasia*	*Dyskaryosis* is a term used for nuclear abnormalities (e.g. enlargement, hyperchromasia) in cervical cytology smears, and can be categorised into mild, moderate or severe according to the degree of abnormality. *Dysplasia is* disordered differentiation and is seen in histological sections of cervical epithelium as loss of stratified structure; dysplasia and carcinoma in situ are merged into 'cervical intraepithelial neoplasia (CIN)'. A cervical smear from a patient with CIN will show dyskaryosis.
Adenomyosis and *endometriosis*	*Adenomyosis* refers to the presence of endometrial glands and stroma in the myometrium, in continuity with the endometrium. In contrast, *endometriosis* is the presence of endometrial glands and stroma outside the body of the uterus, discontinuous with the endometrium.
Benign, borderline and *malignant ovarian tumours*	*Benign* and *malignant* tumours are, by definition, non-invasive and invasive, respectively. In the ovary, a third category of *borderline* tumour is recognised; these lesions exhibit some features commonly seen in malignant tumours (e.g. pleomorphism, mitotic activity) but lack invasion. Their behaviour is intermediate between benign and malignant tumours.

An ectopic pregnancy is the occurrence of pregnancy outside the uterine cavity; its incidence is increasing. The incidence of ectopic pregnancy in the United Kingdom is 10-12 per 1000 pregnancies; 65% of cases occur in the 25-34 year age range.

After one ectopic pregnancy the risk of recurrence is 10-20%. By far the commonest site of ectopic pregnancy is the fallopian tube; the ovary is a much rarer site. Occasionally, there is evidence of a fallopian tube abnormality such as chronic inflammation.

The apparently increasing incidence of ectopic pregnancy may be related to increasing tubal infection. In most cases, however, there is no obvious cause, and a functional defect in tubal transport is assumed. Whether the presence of an intra-uterine device leads to a real increased risk of ectopic pregnancy is controversial.

The presenting symptoms are due to the physical expansion of the developing pregnancy within the limited space of the tube. Thus pain, with or without rupture, and haemoperitoneum are the commonest presenting features.

In most cases, the pregnancy and fetus per se are not abnormal, and the same physiological changes associated with implantation can be seen in the fallopian tube as are seen in the uterus. The finding of pregnancy-associated changes in the endometrium in the absence of trophoblast or a fetus should always alert the pathologist to the possibility of an ectopic pregnancy (Arias-Stella phenomenon).

MATERNAL DEATH

The maternal mortality rate is 10 per 100 000 maternities. The main causes of direct maternal death are:

- thrombosis and thrombo-embolism (including amniotic fluid embolism)
- hypertensive disorders of pregnancy
- haemorrhage.

Early pregnancy deaths are usually due to ectopic pregnancy and abortion, which includes rare cases of legal termination of pregnancy and spontaneous miscarriage. Rare causes of maternal mortality include anaesthetic-related deaths, uterine rupture and genital tract sepsis.

8

OVARIAN HISTOLOGY

PROSTATE GLANDS

Normal Structure and Function

The prostate gland surrounds the bladder neck and proximal urethra. It consists of five lobes, separated by the urethra and ejaculatory ducts. Two lateral lobes and an anterior lobe enclose the urethra. The two lateral lobes are marked by a posterior midline groove, palpable on rectal examination.

The middle lobe lies between the urethra and ejaculatory ducts and the posterior lobe lies behind the ejaculatory ducts. The normal gland weighs about 20 g and is enclosed in a fibrous capsule. Within the prostate there are three main groups of glands arranged concentrically around the urethra: an inner periurethral group, submucosal glands and the external group or main prostatic glands.

From all three groups, ducts converge and open into the prostatic urethra. Individual glandular acini have a convoluted outline, the epithelium varying from cuboidal to a pseudostratified columnar cell type depending upon the degree of activity of the prostate and androgenic stimulation. The epithelial cells produce acid phosphatase and the prostatic secretion that forms a large proportion of the seminal fluid for the transport of sperm.

The normal gland acini often contain rounded concretions of inspissated secretions (corpora amylacea). The acini are surrounded by a stroma of fibrous tissue and smooth muscle. The blood supply to the

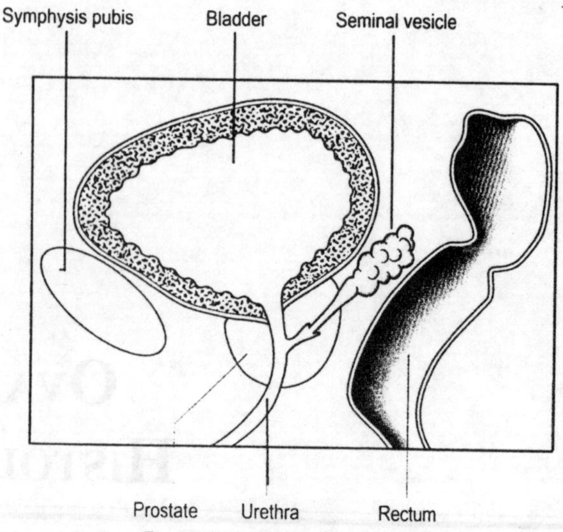

Figure 8.1: Male pelvic organs.

prostate gland is from the internal iliac artery by the inferior vesical and middle rectal branches. The prostatic veins drain to the prostatic plexus around the gland and then to the internal iliac veins.

Pathological basis of distal signs, and symptoms in the male genital tract

Sign or symptom	Pathological basis
Abnormal micturition	
• dysuria (pain)	Inflammation of the urethra, often accompanying a urinary tract infection
• hesitation, poor stream and dribbling ('prostatism')	obstructed urinary outflow, usually due to prostate gland enlargement
• frequency	incomplete bladder emptying due to obstructed urinary outflow
• urinary retention	Severe obstruction to bladder outflow, usually due to prostate gland enlargement
Urethral discharge	Urethritis, possibly due to venereal infections (e.g. gonorrhoea)
Scrotal swelling	
• painful	inflammation or ischaemia of the testis
• painless	Enlargement of scrotal contents due to h[illegible]ia, fluid (e.g. hydrocele), varicocele or tumour

Genital ulceration	Often venereal infection (e.g. syphilis)
Bone pain	if associated with male genital tract disease, possibly due to metastases from prostatic adenocarcinoma
Raised serum acid phosphatase	Secreted by prostatic carcinoma
Raised serum alpha-fetoprotein and/or human chorionic gonadotrophin	Testicular germ cell neoplasia, particularly teratoma
Gynaecomastia	Possible manifestation of interstitial cell tumour of testis
Infertility	impaired spermatogenesis due to endocrine disorders or to testicular lesions, or impaired ejaculation due to obstruction or to neurological disorders

INCIDENCE OF PROSTATIC DISEASE

Diseases of the prostate are common causes of urinary problems in men, the incidence of which increases with age, particularly beyond 60 years. Most prostatic diseases cause enlargement of the organ resulting in compression of the intraprostatic portion of the urethra; this leads to impaired urine flow, an increased risk of urinary infections, and, in some cases, acute retention of urine requiring urgent relief by catheterisation.

The most important and common causes of these signs and symptoms are prostatic hyperplasia and prostatic carcinoma. Inflammation of the prostate gland-prostatitis-is also common, but it less often gives rise to serious clinical problems; indeed, small foci of prostatic inflammation are not uncommon coincidental findings in prostatic tissue removed because of hyperplasia or carcinoma.

The principal clinicopathological features of the common types of prostatic pathology are compared in Table elsewhere in this chapter.

PROSTATITIS

A variable inflammatory infiltrate is commonly seen in the prostatic stroma in glands enlarged by benign nodular hyperplasia. Its significance is sometimes uncertain; it may simply be associated with leakage of material from distended ducts into the stroma. A marked degree of

Table 8.1: Differences between the three most common types of prostatic pathology.

Condition	*Incidence in gland*	*Location*	*Morphology*	*Serum acid phosphatase*	*Metastases*
Benign nodular hyperplasia	75% of men over 70 years	Peri-urethral zone	Nodular hyperplasia of glands and stroma	Normal	None
Clinical (symptomatic) carcinoma	Common tumour; peak 60-85 years	Posterior subcapsular zone	infiltrating adenocarcinoma	Raised in approximately 60% of cases	Bone Lymph node Lung Liver
Latent (incidental) carcinoma	Commoner than clinical carcinoma; 80% of glands over 75 years	Any site	Microscopic focus of adenocarcinoma	Normal	Rare

stromal oedema and periductal inflammation may, however, contribute to urethral obstruction.

Prostatitis implies a more prominent inflammatory lesion of the gland, often associated with a specific infective cause. Prostatitis may be:

- *acute suppurative* prostatitis-caused by coliforms, *Staphylococcus,* or *Neisseria gonorrhoeae* (gonococcus)
- chronic non-specific prostatitis
- *granulomatous* prostatitis-idiopathic, tuberculous, following transurethral resection, or allergic.

Acute Suppurative Prostatitis

Acute prostatitis usually results from spread of infection along the prostatic ducts secondary to urethritis or cystitis. Common causative micro-organisms include coliforms, staphylococci and gonococci. Acute prostatitis may occasionally follow urethral catheterisation or endoscopy; more rarely, the infection is blood-borne.

The lesion is characterised by difficulty in micturition with perineal or rectal pain. There is general malaise and pyrexia and the prostate is palpably enlarged, soft and tender. Histology reveals acute inflammation with acini distended by polymorphs, macrophages and damaged epithelial cells. There may be necrosis with formation of an abscess which may eventually discharge into the urethra.

Chronic non-specific prostatitis

Chronic non-specific prostatitis may develop from recurrent episodes of acute infective prostatitis. The prostate gland shows increased stromal fibrosis with an infiltrate of lymphocytes and plasma cells, associated with acinar atrophy.

Granulomatous prostatitis

Granulomatous prostatitis is a heterogeneous group of lesions, all of which may cause enlargement of the gland and urethral obstruction. The inflammatory component and associated fibrosis produce a firm, indurated gland on rectal examination which may mimic a neoplasm clinically; thus the importance of correctly diagnosing this uncommon group of conditions.

Idiopathic prostatitis may result from leakage of material from distended ducts in a gland enlarged by nodular hyperplasia. There is a periductal inflammatory infiltrate which includes macrophages, multinucleated giant cells, lymphocytes and plasma cells, with associated fibrosis.

The prostate is often involved in cases of genito-urinary *tuberculosis.* This condition is usually secondary to tuberculous cystitis or epididymitis, the infection spreading along the prostatic ducts or vas deferens. The histological features are of caseating granulomas distributed among the prostatic glands and through the stroma.

Some patients may require a second transurethral resection for benign nodular hyperplasia or carcinoma if the first operation fails to relieve the obstructive symptoms. The second biopsy often contains granulomas with necrosis; this lesion may be *ischaemic,* related to damaged blood vessels.

Allergic (eosinophilic) prostatitis is a rare lesion, occurring usually in men with bronchial asthma. There may be a sudden onset of prostatic symptoms. The gland contains granulomas with areas of fibrinoid necrosis and a surrounding zone of histiocytes, giant cells and numerous eosinophils.

BENIGN NODULAR HYPERPLOASIA

- A common non-neoplastie lesion
- Involves peri-urethral zone
- Nodular hyperplasia of glands and stroma
- Not premalignant

Benign nodular hyperplasia is a non-neoplastic enlargement of the prostate gland which occurs commonly after the age of 50 years. About 75% of men aged 70-80 years are affected and develop variable symptoms of urinary tract obstruction. If severe and untreated, benign nodular hyperplasia may lead to recurrent urinary infections and, ultimately, impaired renal function.

Aetiology

Benign nodular hyperplasia is thought to be related to a hormonal imbalance, although the exact mechanism is uncertain. With increasing age, the androgen levels fall, with a relative rise in oestrogens. Oestrogens also increase the prostatic tissue sensitivity to androgens. The central or peri-urethral group of prostatic glands, which are oestrogenresponsive, undergo consequent hyperplasia.

Morphology

The hyperplastic process usually involves both lateral lobes of the gland. In addition, there may be a localised hyperplasia of peri-urethral glands posterior to the urethra and projecting into the bladder adjacent to the internal urethral meatus.

This hyperplasia is described as 'median' lobe enlargement but

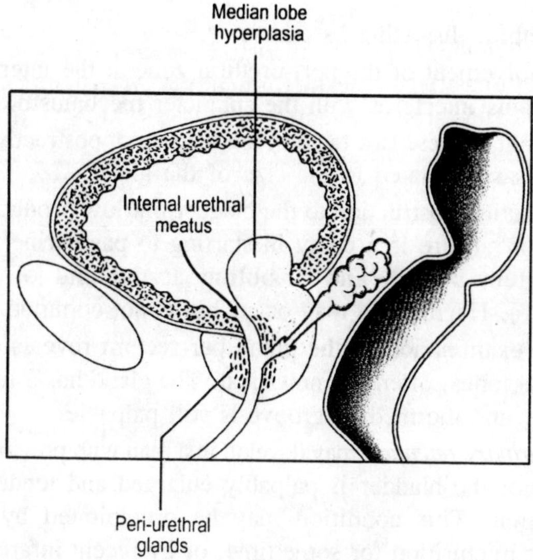

Figure 8.2: Prostatic hyperplasia.

does not correspond to the anatomical middle lobe. The cut surface of the enlarged prostate shows multiple circumscribed solid nodules and cysts.

Histological examination reveals two components: hyperplasia both of glands and of stroma. The acini are larger than normal (some may be cystic) and are lined by columnar epithelium covering papillary infoldings. The acini may contain numerous corpora amylacea.

Phosphates and oxalates may be deposited around these to form prostatic calculi. The stromal hyperplasia includes both smooth muscle and fibrous tissue. Some of the nodules are solid, being composed predominantly of stroma, and others also contain hyperplastic acini. Stromal oedema and periductal inflammation are common and may contribute to the urinary obstruction.

Areas of infarction commonly occur, evident as yellowish necrotic areas with a haemorrhagic margin; these may result from obstruction to the blood supply by the hyperplastic nodules. There is often squamous metaplasia of prostatic ducts and acini at the edges of the infarct. Benign nodular hyperplasia is not a premalignant lesion.

Clinical features

There are two main factors in the development of obstructive symptoms:

- The hyperplastic nodules compress and elongate the prostatic urethra, distorting its course.

- Involvement of the peri-urethral zone at the internal urethral meatus interferes with the sphincter mechanism.

As a result of these two factors, the severity of obstructive symptoms is not necessarily related to the size of the gland.

The resulting obstruction to the bladder outflow produces difficulty in micturition. There is a delay in starting to pass urine with a poor or intermittent stream and dribbling at the end of micturition ('prostatism'). Haematuria may occur but is not common.

Digital examination of the gland per rectum reveals enlargement of the lateral lobes, often asymmetrical. The gland has a firm, rubbery consistency, and the median groove is still palpable.

Acute urinary retention may develop in a man with previous symptoms of prostatism; the bladder is palpably enlarged and tender, requiring catheterisation. This condition may be precipitated by voluntarily withholding micturition for some time, or by recent infarction causing sudden enlargement of a hyperplastic nodule.

Chronic retention of urine is relatively painless. There may be increasing frequency and overflow incontinence, usually at night. The bladder is distended, often palpable up to the umbilicus, but is not tender since the distension is more gradual.

Complications

Continued obstruction of the bladder outflow results in gradual *hypertrophy* of the bladder musculature. *Trabeculation* of the bladder wall develops due to prominent bands of thickened smooth muscle between which *diverticula may* protrude.

This compensatory mechanism eventually fails, with resulting dilatation of the bladder. The ureters gradually dilate *(hydroureter)*, allowing reflux of urine; if untreated, bilateral *hydronephrosis* may develop, with dilatation of renal pelvis and calyces.

As the bladder fails to empty completely after micturition a small volume of urine remains in the bladder. This *residual urine* is liable to *infection,* usually by coliform organisms. The resulting cystitis is characterised by painful micturition with increased frequency and haematuria. An ascending infection in the presence of an obstructed urinary tract may result in *pyelonephritis* and *impaired renal function.* Repeated infections predispose to the development of *calculi,* often containing phosphates, within the bladder. *Septicaemia* may complicate pyelonephritis.

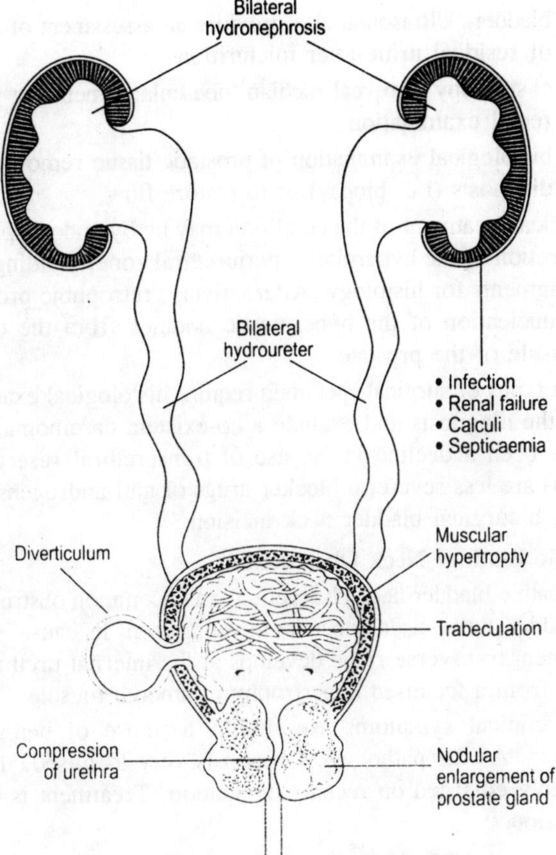

Figure 8.3: Complications of prostatic hyperplasia.

Clinical diagnosis and management

Further investigation of a man with suspected benign prostatic enlargement includes:

- microbiological examination of the urine to detect any infection requiring treatment
- a blood urea or creatinine measurement to monitor renal function; the serum prostatic acid phosphatase activity is not usually raised, although a slight, transient rise may occur following rectal examination or urethral catheterisation
- urinary tract ultrasound to provide an assessment of the upper urinary tract, indicating the severity of obstruction; it may demonstrate an enlarged prostate as a filling defect in the

bladder. Ultrasound also provides an assessment of the quantity of residual urine after micturition

- cystoscopy to reveal median lobe enlargement not palpable on rectal examination
- histological examination of prostatic tissue removed either for diagnosis (i.e. biopsy) or to restore flow.

Surgical treatment of the condition may be by endoscopic transurethral resection of the hyperplastic periurethral zone, yielding numerous tissue fragments for histology. Alternatively, retropubic prostatectomy allows enucleation of the hyperplastic nodules from the compressed false capsule of the prostate.

Both types of surgical specimen require histological examination to confirm the diagnosis and exclude a co-existent carcinoma. Recently, there has been a decline in the use of transurethral resection. If the symptoms are less severe, u-blocker drugs or anti-androgens may be of value, or a surgical bladder neck incision.

Idiopathic Bladder Neck Obstruction

Idiopathic bladder neck obstruction, an uncommon obstructive lesion at the bladder outlet, usually occurs in young men. Its cause is unknown. A prominent transverse ridge develops at the internal urethral meatus, resulting from a localised hypertrophy of smooth muscle.

The clinical symptoms are similar to those of benign nodular hyperplasia. As the pathological lesion is very localised, the gland is not palpably enlarged on rectal examination. Treatment is by bladder neck incision.

PROSTATIC CARCINOMA

- Adenocarcinoma occurring usually >50 years
- Metastasises mainly to bone (osteosclerotic metastases)
- Obstructs bladder outflow
- Many are hormone (androgen)-dependent

Carcinoma of the prostate is one of the commonest forms of malignant disease and is the second leading cause of male deaths from malignancy in Europe and the USA. The incidence has increased during the last two decades, causing approximately 12 000 deaths in 1995 in England and Wales (11% of male cancer deaths). The tumour is rare below 50 years of age; the peak incidence is between 60 and 85 years.

Aetiology

The aetiology of prostatic carcinoma is unknown, although it is probable that the hormonal changes which occur with increasing age are involved. With advancing age there is a decrease in circulating androgen levels. This decrease is associated with involution of the outer zone of the prostate, the area in which most tumours arise.

A family history of the disease is relevant: there is a two- to threefold risk of the tumour developing in men with a first-degree relative in whom prostatic carcinoma was diagnosed under 50 years of age. Benign nodular hyperplasia is not considered a preneoplastic lesion although it is often found coincidentally in the same gland as a carcinoma, as both lesions are common.

Clinicopathological types

Two clinicopathological types of prostatic carcinoma are recognised; they differ in their behaviour:

- clinical (symptomatic) carcinoma
- latent (incidental) carcinoma.

Clinical (symptomatic) carcinoma

- Arises in posterior subcapsular area of gland
- Adenocarcinoma
- Invasion of stroma and perineural spaces
- Asymmetric firm enlargement of prostate may be palpable per rectum
- Metastasises, especially to bone

Clinical carcinoma is the important form of the disease, producing metastases and urinary tract obstruction. Sometimes, the primary tumour in the prostate remains smallan *occult* carcinoma-yet produces widespread symptomatic metastases before the primary is clinically manifest. About two-thirds of patients will have locally advanced disease or metastases at the time of initial presentation.

Most active tumours arise in the posterior lobe of the gland, in the subcapsular area. Figure elsewhere in this chapter compares location of lesions in benign hyperplasia and prostatic carcinoma. A retropubic prostatectomy for benign hyperplasia does not remove the posterior zone; this explains why carcinoma may develop following such a 'prostatectomy'. The tumour appears as an ill-defined, grey or yellow, firm or gritty area.

In the majority of cases the tumour is an *adenocarcinoma,* usually well differentiated, forming acini, tubules or a cribriform pattern. The convoluted outline of the glands is lost and neoplastic acini are formed from a single layer of cells, unlike the glands in benign hyperplasia which have a double-layered epithelium. There is a variable degree of cellular and nuclear pleomorphism, but often the epithelial cells are so well differentiated that it may be difficult to identify -the lesion as a neoplasm.

There is a variable amount of fibrous stroma. Various histological grading systems have been devised for assessing the prognosis of prostatic carcinoma. The most widely used is that devised by Gleason, which grades tumours on a scale of 1-5.

This is based on the degree of glandular differentiation and the architectural pattern of growth. A grade I tumour is composed of circumscribed areas of well-formed, uniform glands. A grade 5 tumour shows an infiltrative growth pattern of sheets of neoplastic cells with only poorly formed glands.

Most tumours are heterogeneous and show a second growth pattern; the combined histological grades are then added to give a Gleason score, which correlates with prognosis. The neoplastic acini invade the stroma of the gland, lymphatics, and perineural spaces. There may be slight mucin secretion within the cells and acini.

Immunohistological techniques to demonstrate *prostate-specific* antigen are helpful to identify metastases as prostatic in origin and thus indicate specific hormonal treatment of an occult primary.

Latent (incidental) carcinoma

- Microscopic focus of tumour found incidentally
- *Common; incidence high in old age*
- Dormant lesions; metastases in 30% after 10 years

Latent carcinomas are microscopic foci of carcinoma found incidentally on histological examination of prostatectomy specimens removed for benign hyperplasia or at autopsy. These minute tumours were formerly thought not to produce clinical manifestations.

Such foci are found in about 30% of prostates over the age of 50 years, the incidence rising to about 80% of glands over the age of 75 years. It is, therefore, much commoner than the clinically active symptomatic form of the disease.

The natural history of these microscopic tumours is uncertain. Recently, the concept of latent carcinoma has been questioned with the recognition that some of them eventually progress and metastasise. Disease progression is related to the length of follow-up and probably occurs in about 30% of these patients after 10 years; it may also be related to the histological grade of tumour.

The majority, however, probably remain as latent or dormant lesions and, in practical terms, the finding of such minute foci of tumour in a prostatectomy specimen is not an indication for immediate hormonal therapy. Latent tumours are adenocarcinomas (like symptomatic lesions) and are usually well differentiated.

Currently, there are no laboratory techniques available to identify which of these microscopic tumours will progress, and most surgeons will follow up the patient without any initial therapy if such tumours are identified in a prostatectomy specimen for benign hyperplasia.

Diagnosis may be attempted at an early stage when the disease is potentially curable; this can be done by screening procedures using rectal examination, serum prostatic antigen and transrectal ultrasound. There are also advocates for radical prostatectomy for the treatment of these small tumours.

Prostatic intra-epithelial neoplasia (PIN)

This is a non-invasive lesion which shows cytological atypia of the prostatic glandular epithelium but with an intact basal cell layer. It is being recognised increasingly in biopsies and resections and is regarded as a precursor lesion, but its behaviour and management is not yet well established.

Mode of spread

Spread of prostatic carcinoma may be:

- direct-stromal invasion, prostatic capsule, urethra, bladder base, seminal vesicle
- *via lymphatics* to sacral, iliac and para-aortic nodes
- *via blood* to bone (pelvis, lumbo-sacral spine, femur), lungs and liver.

Direct spread

Direct spread of the prostatic tumour occurs both within the gland and to extracapsular adjacent structures. There is invasion of the prostatic stroma towards the peri-urethral tissues and the base of the bladder is also commonly involved. Extension through the prostatic capsule is common, involving the seminal vesicles.

The rectal wall is rarely invaded, being protected by the recto-vesical fascia. This extracapsular invasion results in the prostate becoming fixed to adjacent tissues.

Spread via lymphatics

Lymphatics provide an important route of dissemination of prostatic carcinoma, producing metastases in the sacral, iliac and para-aortic nodes. These may result in lymphatic obstruction and oedema of the legs. Less often, the inguinal nodes are involved.

Spread via blood

Vascular invasion by the tumour results in blood-borne metastases, most commonly to bone, lungs and liver. The most frequent sites of bone metastases are the pelvis, lumbo-sacral spine and proximal femur, less frequently the ribs and skull. Tumour emboli may reach the vertebrae by venous spread to the lung, then by passing through the pulmonary capillaries to enter the arterial circulation.

An alternative mechanism is by retrograde venous spread through the vertebral venous plexus, because the blood flow in these veins may reverse due to physiological variation in the intra-abdominal pressure. Bone metastases are usually *osteosclerotic,* with proliferation of osteoblasts and areas of new bone formation occurring in association with the neoplastic cells. The osteoblast proliferation results in a raised serum alkaline phosphatase level.

Clinical features

The clinical presentation and features of prostatic carcinoma include:

- urinary symptoms-difficulty or increased frequency of micturition, urinary retention
- rectal examination revealing hard craggy prostate
- bone metastases-presenting with pain, pathological fracture, anaemia
- lymph node metastases.

Urinary outflow obstructive symptoms caused by prostatic carcinoma usually progress more rapidly than those due to benign hyperplasia. Digital rectal examination is a very important clinical procedure, revealing a hard nodule of tumour in the posterior lobe; the induration is due to the fibrous stromal reaction to the adenocarcinoma cells.

The gland may be enlarged. If capsular invasion has occurred, the capsule is irregular and the median groove is obliterated. Less often, the rectal mucosa is fixed to the prostate. Induration may, however, be due to a non-neoplastic lesion such as prostatic calculi or granulomatous prostatitis.

Bone metastases often present as *localised bone* pain, back pain from vertebral metastases being a common initial manifestation of the tumour. *Pathological fracture* is another clinical presentation. Anaemia may result from extensive neoplastic infiltration of several bones with replacement of haemopoietic tissue. Finally, peripheral *lymphadenopathy* due to metastatic carcinoma is occasionally the initial presentation.

Diagnosis

Useful diagnostic investigations include:

- *diagnostic* imaging-ultrasound, skeletal X-rays, isotope bone scan
- cystoscopy-including transurethral resection
- *chemical pathology-serum* acid and alkaline phosphatase and prostate-specific antigen
- haematology-leukoerythroblastic anaemia
- biopsy-transurethral resection, needle biopsy, fine needle aspiration cytology.

Ultrasound examination is important to assess upper urinary tract dilatation caused by the tumour. Transrectal ultrasound identifies suspicious areas within the prostate and aids selection of sites for needle biopsy. *Skeletal X-rays are* also vital for the detection of bone metastases.

However, Paget's disease of bone is also a common lesion in the lumbo-sacral spine in elderly men and may produce similar radiological appearances to osteosclerotic metastases. An isotopic bone scan is also helpful in the detection of small metastases in the bones.

Serum *prostate-specific antigen* (PSA) is a glycoprotein produced by prostatic epithelium which has a physiological role in the liquefaction of semen. It is also produced by malignant prostatic epithelium and is now most commonly used as the initial biochemical investigation in cases of suspected prostatic carcinoma.

About 60% of patients with a localised carcinoma of the prostate and about 80% of patients with associated bone metastases have a raised level *of serum* acid *phosphatase;* this enzyme is produced by the neoplastic cells. Most of the increase is due to the prostatic iso-enzyme of acid phosphatase.

The *serum alkaline phosphatase* is increased by the presence of osteosclerotic bone metastases as a result of osteoblast proliferation. With widespread carcinomatous infiltration of the bone marrow *a leukoerythroblastic anaemia* develops, evinced by the presence of primitive red and white cell precursors in the peripheral blood. In about 10% of patients with prostatic carcinoma the tumour stimulates *increased fibrinolytic activity* in the serum, which may cause excessive haemorrhage after prostatectomy.

Needle core biopsy of the prostate is now used increasingly in making the diagnosis.

Clinical management

At the time of diagnosis, about 75% of patients already have locally extensive or metastatic disease. It is not yet possible to distinguish histologically between the clinically important cancers and the biologically latent tumours which may not require aggressive treatment.

About 75% of patients with clinical prostatic carcinoma benefit from treatment which reduces androgen levels. This reduces the rate of growth of both the primary tumour and its metastases, and relieves the pain from bone metastases.

Oestrogens suppress the production of pituitary gonadotrophic hormones, thereby inhibiting Leydig cells and reducing androgen production in the testis; this was the first clinical application-of the hormonal treatment of malignancy, instituted by Huggins in Chicago in 1941.

A successful therapeutic effect is indicated by histological changes in the tumour, which include cytoplasmic vacuolation and nuclear pyknosis in tumour cells or actual necrosis of the tumour. Oestrogens also cause squamous metaplasia of normal prostatic duct epithelium and the bladder neck mucosa, often seen in a post-treatment transurethral resection.

The side effects of oestrogen therapy include gynaecomastia and retention of sodium and water. The latter factor may produce oedema and precipitate cardiac failure in elderly men with pre-existing ischaemic heart disease. There is also an increased incidence of both arterial and venous thromboses.

Gonadorelin (gonadotrophin-releasing hormone) analogues are also effective. They act by stimulating luteinising hormone (LH) release from the pituitary which then stimulates testicular testosterone secretion; the high testosterone levels achieved then suppress LH release.

Orchidectomy is also used to reduce androgen levels. More recently, a progestagenic anti-androgen, *cyproterone,* has been used therapeutically. Cyproterone competes with testosterone at prostatic androgen receptors, thereby blocking the effects of testicular androgens.

Radiotherapy is an alternative effective means of palliation for bone metastases.

Radical prostatectomy is a surgical option if the local extent of the tumour and the absence of evidence of metastases are such that it is likely to be curative.

Screening for prostatic cancer

The benefits and limitations of screening for prostatic cancer are debatable. There is no reliable evidence that early detection of the disease improves survival.

A combination of digital rectal examination, together with serum PSA estimation, is effective in the diagnosis with subsequent transrectal ultrasound-guided needle core biopsy. The value of screening asymptomatic men is still debatable; it may, however, detect some localised latent cancers which will not progress and become clinical cancer.

PENIS AND SCROTUM

Diseases affecting the penis, ranked in order of frequency, are:

- venereal infections
- congenital malformations
- tumours.

It is common practice to examine carefully the external genital region of male neonates to detect major malformations; minor abnormalities may remain undetected until the prepuce can be fully retracted. In adolescents and adults, venereal infections (e.g. gonorrhoea) constitute a major public health problem in many countries; the penis is also one route of transmission of other serious infections, notably HIV-the cause of AIDS. The commonest tumours are benign warts, occurring usually in young adults; carcinomas are relatively uncommon.

Congenital Lesions

Congenital lesions of the penis and scrotum include:

- hypospadias
- epispadias.

Hypospadias

Hypospadias is the commonest congenital abnormality of the male urethra, resulting from a failure of fusion of the urethral folds over the urogenital sinus. Normal fusion of these folds starts at the posterior end and extends forward along the penile shaft to the tip.

If fusion is incomplete, the urethra does not reach the tip of the penis, but opens on to its inferior aspect. The commonest site is a meatus on the inferior aspect of the glans. Less often, the meatus is on the penile shaft, and is associated with a downward curvature of the penis (congenital chordee). Rarely, there is a complete hypospadias with the urethral opening on the perineum behind the scrotum.

Epispadias

The congenital abnormality epispadias is much less common than hypospadias. The urethra opens on to the dorsum of the penis, the commonest site being at the base of the shaft near the pubis. This lesion results in urinary incontinence and infections. Epispadias is sometimes associated with exstrophy of the bladder.

INFLAMMATION AND INFECTIONS

Balanoposthitis

Inflammation of the inner surface of the prepuce (posthitis) is usually accompanied by inflammation of the adjacent surface of the glans penis (balanitis). Such a balanoposthitis is often associated with a tight prepuce *(phimosis)*.

Sebaceous material and keratin may accumulate beneath the prepuce, which may become infected by pyogenic bacteria. These bacteria include staphylococci, coliforms or gonococci. In diabetic patients, *Candida* infection is a further risk.

There is redness and swelling of the prepuce and glans with an associated purulent exudate. If treatment is delayed or there are recurrent episodes of infection, fibrous scarring can occur with the formation of preputial adhesions or severe phimosis.

Phimosis

Phimosis, and the closely related condition of paraphimosis, are the commonest medical indications for male circumcision. In phimosis, the prepuce cannot be retracted over the glans penis. In most cases this is an acquired lesion, being the late sequel of an ammoniacal preputial dermatitis in infancy.

Ammonia is formed by the action of some bacteria on the urine, producing blisters over the glans and inner aspect of the prepuce. This blistering results in the formation of numerous minute skin ulcers with associated acute inflammation and eventual fibrosis, narrowing the opening in the prepuce.

Paraphimosis

If a tight prepuce is retracted behind the glans it may obstruct the venous return from the glans and prepuce. The resulting oedematous swelling of the glans and prepuce produces a paraphimosis in which the prepuce cannot be returned easily to its normal position.

Balanitis Xerotica Obliterans

Balanitis xerotica obliterans is an uncommon penile lesion

characterised by thickened white plaques and fissures on the glans and prepuce. The symptoms are of a non-retractile prepuce or preputial discharge, often necessitating circumcision. Similar lesions may develop around the urethral meatus with resulting scarring. The condition most commonly affects men of 30-50 years of age.

The histological features are of hyperkeratosis and atrophy of the epidermis with basal layer degeneration. The papillary dermis shows hyalinisation of the collagen with an underlying infiltrate of lymphoid cells. Similar changes are seen in lichen sclerosus of the vulval skin.

Genital Herpes Aetiology

Herpes is an acute infectious disease caused by herpes simplex virus (HSV). There are two antigenic types of the virus: HSV types 1 and 2. Most genital tract lesions are caused by type 2 as a sexually transmitted disease. HSV type 2 produces a recurrent, acute vesicular eruption on the skin, usually around the mouth or on the genitalia. The incidence of genital herpes is increasing.

The majority of *primary herpes infections* are subclinical, but following this initial infection the virus may remain latent for many years. The virus may remain either locally in the skin or in the nerve ganglion supplying that skin segment, by migrating along the axons to the ganglia. *Recurrent herpes infections* are caused by reactivation of the virus and may be precipitated by a febrile illness, immune suppression, emotional stress or by ultraviolet light.

Clinicopathological features

The primary lesion of herpes genitalis in the male is preceded by itching followed by the appearance of several closely grouped *vesicles* surrounded by erythema on the glans penis or the coronal sulcus. The acute skin lesion is an intra-epidermal vesicle with evidence of cellular damage associated with the virus.

There may be vacuolation of the epidermal cells, some of which are multinucleated and contain viral inclusions. The vesicles soon burst to produce shallow painful *ulcers*. Less often, there is a more diffuse balanitis which may heal with a resulting phimosis, and occasionally vesicles develop on the shaft of the penis or on the scrotum.

Herpetic lesions are less common in circumcised men. In some patients, the infection is asymptomatic with no visible lesions, although these patients may still transmit the disease. The clinical features may be sufficient to enable a diagnosis but laboratory confirmation can be obtained by isolation of the virus from vesicular fluid.

A swab or scrape from this source, collected in a suitable viral transport medium, can be used to demonstrate a cytopathic effect in tissue culture. Viral particles may also be identified by examining vesicle fluid by electron microscopy.

Genital Warts

Genital warts are increasing in prevalence and are now probably the commonest type of lesion seen in patients attending departments of genito-urinary medicine.

Aetiology

Genital warts are caused by the human papillomavirus (HPV), a DNA virus of the papovavirus group. The HPV types causing genital warts (HPV6 and 11) differ from those causing the common skin wart (HPV1, 2 and 4). Other HPV types are incriminated in the aetiology of squamous cervical cancer.

Clinicopathological features

In the male, the characteristic lesion is a hyperplastic, fleshy wart or *condyloma acuminatum*. This wart occurs most commonly on the glans penis and inner lining of the prepuce or in the terminal urethra. Less often, lesions develop on the shaft of the penis, the peri-anal region or the scrotum.

Histologically, the epidermis shows papillomatous hyperplasia. Many of the epidermal cells show cytoplasmic vacuolation, a feature indicating a viral aetiology. There is no epidermal dysplasia and these lesions are not premalignant.

The clinical diagnosis is usually obvious and laboratory diagnosis is rarely required. The clinical management is complicated by a high infectivity and a tendency to multiple recurrences.

SYPHILIS

- Causative organism is a spirochaete: *Treponema pallidum*
- Primary chancre on penis: ulcerated nodule and endarteritis with lymphocytes and plasma cells; associated inguiral lymphadenitis
- Secondary stage: condylomata lata, generalised lymphadenitis
- Tertiary stage: gumma, often in the testis

Aetiology

Syphilis is now a less prevalent sexually transmitted infection in the developed world. It is caused by a spirochaete, *Treponema pallidum*. In the male, the primary lesion develops between 1 and 12 weeks after infection, usually on the penis at the site of inoculation. The organism probably enters the tissues through a mucosal abrasion and, by the time the primary lesion develops, the organism has already disseminated via lymphatics.

Clinicopathological features

The *primary chancre* usually develops on the inner aspect of the prepuce, the glans penis or corona. It forms a painless indurated nodule which soon becomes an ulcer with rounded margins.

There is regional lymphadenopathy. Examination by dark-ground microscopy of the serous exudate in the base of the ulcer reveals numerous spirochaetes.

Initially, the tissue response consists of oedema with necrosis and an associated exudate of fibrin and polymorphs. At a later stage there is an endarteritis with a perivascular infiltrate of lymphocytes and plasma cells. Thrombotic occlusion of these vessels produces necrosis and ulceration of the epidermis.

There is usually an associated unilateral or bilateral inguinal lymphadenitis. Without treatment the primary chancre heals in a few weeks, leaving an atrophic scar.

The secondary and tertiary stages of syphilis develop later as a result of dissemination of the infection and are accompanied by an immunological reaction. Secondary syphilis develops within 2 years of the primary lesion and may include several different cutaneous manifestations.

One of these is the development of *condylomata lata* on the prepuce and scrotum-proliferative epithelial lesions containing numerous spirochaetes. There is a generalised lymphadenitis in many cases. The tertiary stage of syphilis may involve the formation of a *gamma* in the testis, but is also associated with thoracic aortic aneurysms and central nervous system changes.

Clinical diagnosis and management

Syphilis is diagnosed in the primary stage by microscopy of the exudate in the chancre or ulcer; the characteristic spirochaetes can be seen by dark-ground illumination.

In this and later stages, the diagnosis is confirmed serologically by seeking specific antibodies in the patient's blood; the fluorescent treponemal antibody absorption (FTA-Abs) test and the *Treponema pallidum* haemagglutination assay (TPHA) are the most specific.

Treatment is usually with penicillin, but it is essential to trace and possibly treat the patient's sexual partners.

LYMPHOGRANULOMA VENEREUM

- Caused by *Chlamydia trachomatis,* serotypes L1-L3
- Primary genital lesion
- Inguinal lymphadenitis: acute suppurative inflammation with necrosis; chlamydial inclusions

Lymphogranuloma venereum is a sexually transmitted disease seen more commonly in the tropics. Infections seen in the UK, for example, have usually been acquired abroad.

Aetiology

The disease is caused by the bacterium *Chlamydia trachomatis,* serotypes L1-L3 (different from those associated with non-specific urethritis).

Clinicopathological features

Following a short incubation period of 2 to 5 days, about 50% of infected males give a history of a *primary genital lesion.* This lesion is a painless papule on the penis which may ulcerate but usually heals within a few days.

Between 1 and 4 weeks later the patient develops an *inguinal lymphadenitis* and this is the usual manifestation of the disease in the male. There is usually unilateral enlargement of the inguinal lymph nodes.

The nodes are tender and initially discrete, becoming matted together as a result of pericapsular inflammation. The nodes may also become fluctuant. This lymphadenitis is often accompanied by constitutional symptoms with pyrexia and malaise. If untreated, the lymphadenitis may resolve but with some residual local lymphoedema.

The histological features are of an acute inflammation of the node with foci of necrosis surrounded by a margin of polymorphs, histiocytes and plasma cells. This inflammatory infiltrate extends through the capsule of the lymph node into the perinodal adipose tissue and may result in the development of sinuses to the overlying skin.

Clinical diagnosis

Surgical biopsy of the lymph node may be performed if the diagnosis is unsuspected; the histological features are almost pathognomonic.

The diagnosis may also be made by aspirating pus from the lymph node and examining smears by specific immunofluorescence or stained by the Giemsa technique for the presence of chlamydial inclusions.

A serum complement fixation test is also available.

Elephantiasis

In elephantiasis, the skin of the penis, scrotum and legs is greatly thickened by chronic oedema resulting

from lymphatic obstruction. Two main groups can be distinguished:

- non-tropical elephantiasis
- tropical elephantiasis.

The tropical form is relatively common in parts of Africa and other countries with a similar climate in which the causative parasite is prevalent.

Non-tropical elephantiasis

In non-tropical elephantiasis, an earlier inflammatory process such as a recurrent cellulitis results in obliteration of the lymphatics in the skin. Another cause is disruption of lymphatic flow after surgical dissection of the inguinal lymph nodes as treatment for metastatic carcinoma of the penis or scrotum.

Tropical elephantiasis

Tropical elephantiasis is a late sequel of infection by the nematode parasite *Wuchereria bancrofti*. The adult worm lives in the lymphatic spaces, where the female produces microfilariae which re-enter the blood. These are ingested by blood-sucking mosquitoes, developing further in the insects' salivary glands.

They re-infect humans at the time of a further bite, passing back to the lymphatics. In this site the parasite induces a granulomatous inflammation with associated fibrosis, leading to lymphatic obstruction. Mechanical blockage of the lymphatic lumen by numerous parasites contributes to the oedema.

Peyronie's Disease

Peyronie's disease is a rare penile lesion presenting usually in the fifth and sixth decades with painful curvature of the penis on erection and, sometimes, difficulty in micturition. The lesions may gradually progress for a few years, and some later resolve spontaneously.

One or more ill-defined plaques of fibrous tissue develop along the dorsal aspect of the shaft of the penis, initially involving the corpora cavernosa. Histological examination shows fibroblast proliferation, with increasing amounts of collagen as the lesion progresses.

In the early stages of Peyronie's disease, there is also an inflammatory component with an infiltrate composed predominantly of lymphocytes and plasma cells. The nature of the lesion is uncertain. Some cases are associated with palmar fibromatosis (Dupuytren's contracture), although the inflammatory component is unlike most fibromatoses. Peyronie's disease may be related to idiopathic retroperitoneal fibrosis.

Idiopathic gangrene of the scrotum (Fournier's syndrome)

Idiopathic gangrene of the scrotum (Fournier's syndrome) is a rare necrotising subcutaneous infection which involves the scrotum and sometimes extends to involve the penis, perineum and abdominal wall. It usually affects middle-aged to elderly men.

Aetiology

Several predisposing factors may be associated with Fournier's syndrome: local trauma, anal fistula or ischiorectal abscess. There is an increased risk in patients with diabetes mellitus. The common aetiological factor of local tissue trauma allows bacteria to enter the subcutaneous tissue.

The causative organisms are of the faecal flora, including coliforms and anaerobes such as *Bacteroides,* some of which are gas-forming organisms. A mixed infection is common.

Clinicopathological features

The scrotum is red and swollen with crepitus on palpation due to the presence of subcutaneous gas. This initial stage is soon followed by necrosis of the skin and subcutaneous tissue, eventually exposing the testes. Later, the tissue slough separates, sharply demarcated from the adjacent viable skin. Finally, if the patient survives, there is regeneration of the skin.

Thrombosis of blood vessels in the scrotal skin results in necrosis of the subcutaneous tissue and dermal gangrene.

Tumours of the Penis

Tumours of the penis are of two types:

- intra-epidermal carcinoma (Bowen's disease)
- invasive squamous carcinoma.

Intra-epidermal carcinoma

A localised area of intra-epidermal carcinoma may develop on the penis as on other sites on the body surface, presenting as a sharply delineated erythematous patch with a moist keratotic surface. On the glans penis this lesion is sometimes termed *erythroplasia of Queyrat,* with the appearance of a well-defined slightly raised red plaque.

The histological features are of a pre-invasive squamous cell carcinoma. The epidermis is thickened with loss of cellular polarity and stratification. There is cellular and nuclear pleomorphism with hyperchromatic nuclei and an increased number of mitoses.

Many of these abnormal cells keratinise at deeper levels within the epidermis (dyskeratosis). The basal layer of the epidermis remains sharply demarcated from the dermis at this stage, although this lesion carries a significant risk of progression to invasive squamous carcinoma.

Invasive squamous carcinoma

Carcinoma of the penis is rare in the UK although common in parts of Africa and the Far East. It occurs only in uncircumcised men and does not occur in those circumcised at birth. Human papillomavirus infection may be an aetiological factor.

The usual site at which the tumours develop is on the glans penis or inner aspect of the prepuce, forming an indurated nodule or plaque which later ulcerates. It rarely develops on the outer surface of the prepuce or on the shaft of the penis.

The tumour is usually a well-differentiated squamous carcinoma and invades the corpora cavernosa. Infiltration down to the urethra occurs late in the course of the disease. Metastases may develop in the inguinal lymph nodes.

Carcinoma of the Scortum

Carcinoma of the scrotum was the first recognised example of a tumour caused by occupational exposure to carcinogens. In 1775, Percival Pott recognised this association in chimney sweeps. During the sweeps' work, soot containing carcinogens became retained in the rugose skin of the scrotum, later inducing a tumour.

Since that time, other occupational factors have been identified in the development of this type of tumour, such as Lancashire cotton mill workers being exposed to mineral oils used to lubricate the machinery. Workers handling arsenic or tar are also at risk.

Nevertheless, this tumour is now rare in the UK. It develops in elderly men, often many years after possible exposure to industrial carcinogens. It presents as a nodular, often ulcerated mass which may involve an extensive area of the scrotal skin.

The tumour is a squamous carcinoma, usually well differentiated with keratinisation. The inguinal lymph nodes may be enlarged by metastatic carcinoma or as a result of reactive changes resulting from ulceration of the primary tumour.

URETHRA

Urethral Obstruction

The commonest cause of urethral obstruction is extrinsic compression due to prostate gland enlargement. Intrinsic lesions include:

- congenital valves
- rupture
- stricture.

Congenital urethral valves

Congenital urethral valves are a rare cause of urinary tract obstruction in the male neonate. In most cases this presents acutely with urinary obstruction and resulting bladder distension and muscle hypertrophy.

The causative lesion is single or paired mucosal folds in the prostatic part of the urethra. Less often, a milder degree of this abnormality is first diagnosed in early adult life.

Traumatic rupture of the urethra

Traumatic rupture of the urethra is a rare event confined to males, and results from trauma such as a fall astride a hard object or complicating a fractured pelvis. The resulting damage to the wall of the urethra may involve its whole circumference or only part of it and may involve both the mucosa and muscle layers. Any part of the urethra may be involved.

The rupture leads to *extravasation of urine* into the periurethral tissues, which may later become the site of *a secondary infection*. There is *difficulty in passing urine* with *bleeding* from the urethral orifice and *localised pain*. A late complication of this lesion is the development of a *urethral stricture*.

Urethral structure

A urethral stricture is usually an acquired lesion developing secondary to some other pathological condition of the urethra. The commonest cause is *a post-inflammatory stricture* following *a gonococcal urethritis*. This infection usually involves the peri-urethral glands and, if treatment is delayed, this condition may be associated with fibrosis around the glands and a fibrous stricture which encircles the urethra.

Proximal to the stricture, the urethra becomes dilated, with hypertrophy of bladder muscle and urinary obstruction. The patient complains of difficulty in micturition with a poor stream and dribbling of urine. The retention of urine may be complicated further by the development of cystitis.

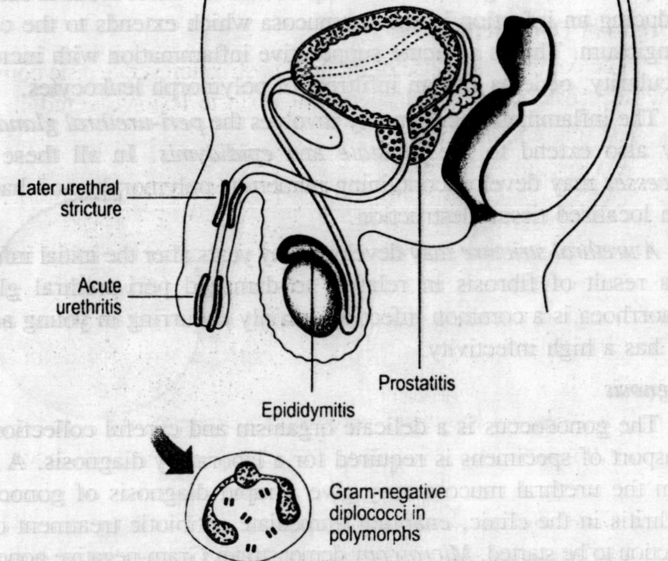

Figure 8.4: Complications of gonococcal urethritis.

Urethral strictures may also be ***post-traumatic,*** complicating a rupture of the urethra, or develop after transurethral instrumentation or resection. A congenital stricture of the urethra occurs more rarely.

Urethritis

Urethritis (inflammation of the urethra) may occur in association with a more proximal infection in the urinary tract or adjacent to a local urethral lesion such as a calculus or an indwelling urinary catheter. The commonest causes, however, are the following specific primary infections of the urethra occurring as a sexually transmitted infection:

- gonococcal urethritis (gonorrhoea)
- non-gonococcal (non-specific) urethritis.

Gonococcal urethritis (gonorrhoea)

In gonococcal urethritis, the bacterial organism *Neisseria gonorrhoeae* (syn. gonococcus) produces an acute inflammation of the urethra. Following a short incubation period of 2-5 days after intercourse, a purulent urethral discharge develops, with pain on passing urine. If the infection spreads to the proximal urethra there may also be increased frequency of micturition.

About 90% of males develop such symptoms as a result of infection, in contrast to females in whom about 70% of gonococcal infections are asymptomatic. The gonococcus can penetrate an intact urethral mucosa, producing an infection in the submucosa which extends to the corpus spongiosum. This is an acute suppurative inflammation with increased vascularity, oedema and an infiltrate of polymorph leukocytes.

The inflammation commonly involves the *peri-urethral glands* and may also extend to the *prostate* and *epididymis*. In all these sites *abscesses* may develop containing numerous polymorphs and bacteria with localised tissue destruction.

A urethral stricture may develop many years after the initial infection as a result of fibrosis in relation to damaged peri-urethral glands. Gonorrhoea is a common infection, mainly occurring in young adults, and has a high infectivity.

Diagnosis

The gonococcus is a delicate organism and careful collection and transport of specimens is required for a laboratory diagnosis. A swab from the urethral mucosa may give a rapid diagnosis of gonococcal urethritis in the clinic, enabling immediate antibiotic treatment of the infection to be started. *Microscopy* demonstrates Gram-negative gonococci within polymorphs.

Microbiological culture of the organism requires urethral swabs to be transferred promptly to the laboratory. Such a culture will provide confirmation of the diagnosis. Laboratory *antibiotic sensitivity tests* may also be required because of the recent emergence of strains of gonococci resistant to penicillin due to penicillinase (β-lactamase) production.

Non-Gonococcal (Non-Specific) Urethritis

Non-gonococcal urethritis (synonymous with non-specific urethritis) is the commonest sexually transmitted disease. In males, a mucopurulent urethral discharge and dysuria develop within a few days to a few weeks of the infecting intercourse. The discharge contains pus cells but gonococci cannot be detected by microscopy or culture.

Aetiology

Evidence from both microbiological culture and serological studies suggests that at least two micro-organisms are a significant cause of non-specific urethritis, although their exact importance as aetiological factors is still uncertain. These organisms are *Chlamydia trachomatis* and *Ureaplasma urealyticum*.

Chlamydia trachomatis is an obligate intracellular organism which structurally resembles a bacterium. Serotypes D-K are associated with genital tract infections. The infectious form of the agent, the elementary body, enters the urethral mucosal cells, enlarging to produce an initial body which is metabolically active.

This body multiplies to form more organisms within a vacuole, seen on microscopy as a basophilic cytoplasmic inclusion. These organisms are released by cell rupture to infect adjacent cells.

Ureaplasma urealyticum is a mycoplasma, a related type of micro-organism.

TUMOURS

Tumours of the urethra include:

- viral condyloma
- transitional cell carcinoma.

Viral Condyloma

Recent studies have shown that minute viral 'warts' may occur in the penile urethra. These 'warts' may be associated with the better-known condyloma of the female ectocervical epithelium, caused by a human papillomavirus. The relationship of this type of lesion to neoplasia and its possible premalignant potential are still uncertain.

Transitional Cell Carcinoma

A papillary transitional cell carcinoma may rarely develop in the urethra, in association with a similar tumour in the bladder. This condition may be a separate, multifocal tumour of the urothelium, or may develop occasionally as a result of tumour implantation in the urethra following instrumentation of the bladder.

TESTIS

Normal Structure and Function

During its development, each testis descends from the posterior abdominal wall to the scrotum, carrying with it a covering layer of peritoneum which forms the *tunica vaginalis,* a closed serous cavity around the testis.

Blood vessels and lymphatics enter and leave the testis on its posterior surface at the hilum, which is not covered by tunica vaginalis. Blood is supplied by the *spermatic artery,* a branch of the aorta, which passes along the spermatic cord. The venous return surrounds the spermatic artery as a network of intercommunicating veins, the *pampiniform plexus.*

This plexus becomes the main testicular vein which, on the right side, drains to the inferior vena cava and, on the left, joins the left

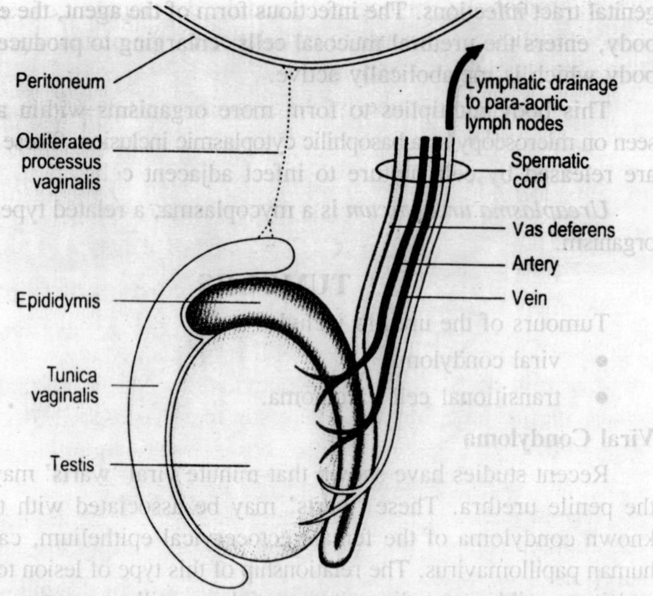

Figure 8.5: Anatomy of testis and vascular connections.

renal vein. Lymphatic drainage of the testis is to the *iliac* and *para-aortic lymph nodes*.

The testis has a fibrous capsule, the *tunica albuginea*. From this capsule, fibrous septa divide the testis into about 250 lobules, each containing up to four convoluted *seminiferous tubules*. These tubules converge on to a network of spaces, the rete testis, at the hilum, from where 10-12 *efferent ductules* lead to the *epididymis*.

The rete testis and the efferent ductules are both lined by a ciliated epithelium. The epididymis lies along the posterior aspect of the testis and is the main storage site for freshly formed sperm. The epididymis is a convoluted tubular structure lined by columnar epithelium.

The seminiferous tubules are each lined by a layer of *germinal epithelium* four or five cells thick; the more immature spermatogonia are situated close to the basement membrane. During spermatogenesis, meiotic division occurs at the spermatocyte stage; maturation of spermatids into sperm occurs near the tubular lumen. *Sertoli cells* lie in contact with the tubular basement membrane and insinuate between the germinal epithelial cells, providing local support and phagocytic function.

In the interstitium between the seminiferous tubules, *Leydig cells* occur in small groups. These cells produce the hormone testosterone, which promotes spermatogenesis and the development of secondary sex characteristics, in response to stimulation by the pituitary gonadotrophic hormone, luteinising hormone.

From birth until puberty, the seminiferous tubules are small, being lined by Sertoli cells and primitive germ cells only. Spermatogenic activity starts at puberty.

INCIDENCE OF TESTICULAR LESIONS

Most testicular lesions are non-neoplastic disorders (e.g. mumps orchitis, torsion), but the possibility of a tumour must be considered fully in each case of testicular swelling or pain. Many testicular lesions present with a hydrocele, an accumulation of fluid around the testis; when this has been drained the testis must be examined carefully by palpation and, if necessary, by ultrasound imaging to exclude the possibility of an underlying testicular tumour.

The incidence of testicular tumours is rising slowly in many countries, but improvements in therapy are having a beneficial impact on patient survival.

DEVELOPMENTAL AND CYSTIC LESIONS

Undescended Testis (Cryptorchidism)

During fetal development, the testis descends from the posterior abdominal wall to the scrotum and in most cases is intrascrotal at birth. In about 5% of boys, one or both testes are undescended at birth, although many descend by the first birthday.

An undescended testis cannot be palpated in the scrotum because the testis is situated in the inguinal canal or in the abdominal cavity. This condition must be distinguished clinically from a retractile testis, in which a normally situated testis is drawn up into the inguinal canal by contraction of the cremaster muscle.

If an undescended testis is not surgically drawn down to the scrotum before puberty, adequate spermatogenic activity does not develop. The seminiferous tubules remain small and are lined by Sertoli cells only. There is associated peritubular fibrosis. A longer-term risk of undescended testis is neoplasia; an undescended testis carries a higher risk of tumour development than a normally situated testis.

Hydrocele

The commonest intrascrotal swelling is a *hydrocele*, an accumulation of serous fluid within the tunica vaginalis of the testis. The smooth, pear-shaped swelling may be tense but is usually fluctuant and can be transilluminated. The contained testis is not palpable as it is surrounded by a layer of fluid.

A congenital hydrocele, appearing in the first few weeks of life, results from persistence of the processus vaginalis, the channel between the peritoneal cavity and the tunica.

A secondary hydrocele may be associated with an underlying lesion of the testis or epididymis. This may be either *inflammatory,* such as mumps orchitis or gonococcal epididymitis, or *neoplastic*. The accompanying inflammation of the mesothelial lining of the tunica vaginalis results in the overproduction of fluid which cannot be drained adequately by the lymphatics in the tunica outer layer.

An *acute inflammatory hydrocele* accumulates rapidly and may produce pain. The straw-coloured fluid contains protein, fibrin, erythrocytes and polymorphs. *A chronic hydrocele,* however, causes only gradual stretching of the tunica and, although it may become large and produce a dragging sensation, it rarely produces pain.

In this instance the fluid may also contain cholesterol crystals. A rough exudate of fibrin lines the hydrocele sac with an associated proliferation of mesothelial cells and the wall of the sac gradually becomes thickened by fibrosis.

Haematocele

A haematocele is haemorrhage into the tunica vaginalis. The usual cause is local trauma to the scrotal contents; this includes trauma to a blood vessel in a hydrocele sac as a result of a therapeutic tap. Another cause is an underlying testicular neoplasm.

In this condition, the tunica is lined by a shaggy layer of organising blood clot. Microscopy of the tunica reveals fibrosis, haemosiderin-containing macrophages and an associated reactive proliferation of mesothelial cells.

ORCHITIS

Orchitis is the name given to any inflammatory condition of the testes.

Mumps Orchitis

Mumps is an acute infectious febrile illness with parotitis, usually occurring in children. In adults, about 25% of cases are complicated by an orchitis, which develops as the parotitis begins to subside. The condition is usually unilateral. The testis is enlarged and very tender due to stretching of the tunica albuginea. There is vascular dilatation and oedema of the interstitium of the testis, with an infiltrate of lymphocytes.

Increasing pressure within the swollen testis produces ischaemia from blood vessel compression and necrosis of seminiferous tubules. If the inflammation is mild, resolution may be complete. In many cases, however, the testis becomes atrophic with increased fibrosis in the interstitium.

Spermatogenesis is then reduced; the tubules are lined by Sertoli cells only. If the involvement is bilateral, this scarring may result in subfertility.

Idiopathic Granulomatous Orchitis

Granulomatous orchitis is an uncommon chronic inflammatory lesion of the testis of unknown aetiology. The peak age incidence is 45-60 years. Granulomatous orchitis produces a firm, unilateral testicular enlargement which may mimic a neoplasm clinically.

The testis is enlarged with a firm or rubbery consistency and a lobulated appearance on its cut surface; there may also be a secondary hydrocele. Histology reveals loss of the germinal epithelium in the seminiferous tubules.

The tubular architecture remains recognisable, but there is a dense granulomatous inflammatory infiltrate centred on the tubules and extending into the interstitium. This infiltrate comprises lymphocytes, plasma cells, macrophages and giant cells.

Although the aetiology is unknown, there is often a history of a *urinary tract infection,* suggesting that reflux of urine along the vas may be an aetiological factor. A reaction to *extravasated sperm* in the interstitium is another possible explanation.

Syphilitic Orchitis

Although the lesion is now rarely seen, the testis was a common site for the development of a *gumma* in the tertiary stage of syphilis. There is unilateral painless enlargement of the testis which may mimic a neoplasm clinically.

There is an irregular area of necrosis on the cut surface of the body of the testis and there may be a hydrocele. Histology shows tissue necrosis, although the architectural outline of the seminiferous tubules remains. At the edge of the necrotic area, there is an infiltrate of lymphocytes and plasma cells with an endarteritis.

TESTICULAR TUMOURS

Tumours of the testis are relatively uncommon, although their incidence has increased in recent years. They account for less than 1%

of all cancer deaths in the UK. Testicular tumours are important, however, as many occur in young men and are the commonest form of malignancy in males under 35 years. Many are highly malignant, although recent advances in chemotherapy have greatly improved the prognosis.

Aetiology

Maldescent of the testis is the only known risk factor for tumour development. An undescended testis is 10 times more likely to develop a tumour than an intrascrotal testis. About 10% of all testicular tumours develop in testes that are, or have been, cryptorchid.

Local trauma is not considered a causative factor, but trauma to a testis containing a tumour may first draw attention to its presence. Environmental factors may be involved, possibly an increase in exogenous oestrogens.

Finally, there is current interest in in situ neoplastic changes within seminiferous tubules adjacent to an established tumour. Patients exhibiting this feature have a significantly increased risk of developing a contralateral tumour.

Clinical features

Testicular tumours may present with:

- painless unilateral enlargement of testis
- secondary hydrocele
- symptoms from metastases
- retroperitoneal mass
- gynaecomastia.

The majority of testicular tumours present as slow, painless enlargement of one testis. On examination, there is a smooth or irregular firm enlargement of the testis. There may be a loss of testicular sensation on palpation.

Less often, the patient notices a more rapidly enlarging scrotal swelling due to a secondary hydrocele around the tumour. Some of the more malignant tumours may produce symptoms from metastases initially, for example haemoptysis from lung deposits, or pain from hepatomegaly.

A retroperitoneal mass may be the presenting feature. This mass may be a para-aortic lymph node metastasis from either a small viable primary tumour in the testis or a regressed testicular primary.

Regressed testicular tumours are rare, but are almost always seminomas as evinced by the histology of their metastases; all that remains in the testis is a small hyaline scar. Gynaecomastia is

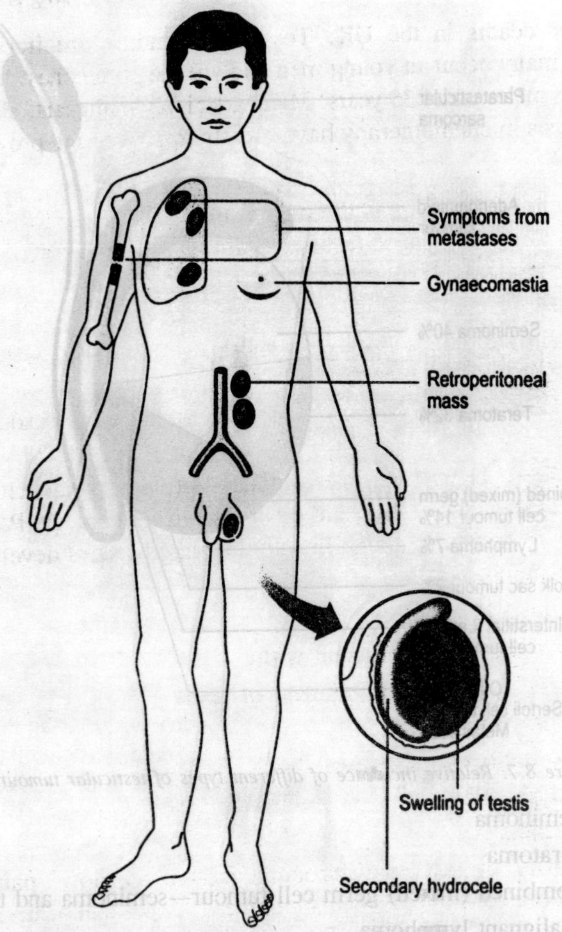

Figure 8.6: Presenting features of testicular tumours.

occasionally the initial feature of sex hormone-secreting interstitial cell turnouts, before a testicular swelling is noted.

Classification

Testicular tumours may be derived from germ cells or nongerm cells; 85-90% are of germ cell origin. Germ cell tumours include seminomas, teratomas and their subtypes. Non-germ cell tumours include those arising from the Sertoli cells of the seminiferous tubules and the interstitial cells.

The most widely used classification of testicular neoplasms in the UK is as follows:

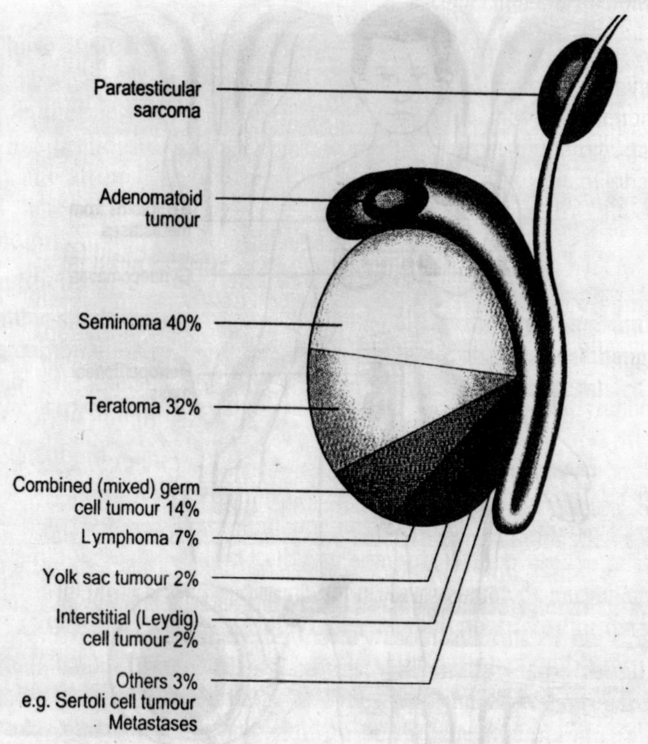

Figure 8.7: Relative incidence of different types of testicular tumour.

- seminoma
- teratoma
- combined (mixed) germ cell tumour—seminoma and teratoma
- malignant lymphoma
- yolk sac tumour
- interstitial (Leydig) cell tumour
- Sertoli cell tumour
- metastatic tumours
- adenomatoid tumour
- paratesticular sarcoma.

Germ Cell Tumours

Seminoma

Seminoma has a germ cell origin, arising in the seminiferous epithelium.

Incidence

Seminoma is the commonest type of testicular tumour, comprising 40% of the total incidence. The peak age incidence is between 30 and 50 years. It is the commonest type of tumour to develop in a maldescended testis.

Morphology and classification

The testis is enlarged by a homogeneous firm white solid tumour. This tumour replaces all or part of the body of the testis. A rim of residual testis may be compressed at one edge of the tumour.

Five histological subtypes of seminoma are recognised:

- classical
- spermatocytic
- anaplastic
- with syncytiotrophoblast giant cells
- combined with other types of germ cell tumour.

Classical seminoma. This is the commonest subtype. It is composed of uniform cells with well-defined cell borders. The cytoplasm is vacuolated and contains glycogen. In most of these tumours the stroma contains a variable lymphocytic infiltrate, a favourable prognostic feature. Some tumours may have a histiocytic granulomatous response in the stroma with fibrosis, which correlates with a better prognosis.

Spermatocytic seminoma. About 3-5% of seminomas are of the spermatocytic type, which occurs in an older age group. The tumour cells resemble spermatocytes and show a marked degree of nuclear pleomorphism with a high mitotic rate.

The tumour cells do not contain cytoplasmic glycogen. There is no lymphocytic or granulomatous response in the stroma. Although the histological features suggest an aggressive tumour, the prognosis of this subtype is excellent.

Anaplastic seminoma. This is a histological subtype with marked cellular pleomorphism and a high mitotic rate. The prognosis is slightly worse than for the classical seminoma.

Seminoma with syncytiotrophoblast giant cells. About 5-10% of seminomas contain multinucleated syncytiotrophoblast giant cells, distributed through the tumour. Immunocytochemistry demonstrates the presence of human chorionic gonadotrophin (hCG) within these cells. The prognostic implication of this finding is uncertain.

Teratoma

- Germ cell origin

- Peak incidence 20-30 years
- More aggressive than seminomas
- Histological subtypes: differentiated; intermediate; undifferentiated; trophoblastic
- OhCG and alpha-fetoprotein are useful tumour markers

Teratomas are composed of several types of tissue representing endoderm, ectoderm and mesoderm. They are now thought to be of germ cell origin, and not from totipotent cells that have escaped the influence of organisers in the embryo.

Teratomas have a peak incidence between 20 and 30 years of age and are more aggressive tumours than seminomas.

Classification

In the classification used in the UK and elsewhere, there are four histological subgroups of teratoma:

- differentiated teratoma
- malignant teratoma intermediate
- malignant teratoma undifferentiated
- malignant teratoma trophoblastic.

A similar classification, based on the World Health Organization system, is used in the USA. The main differences between the UK and USA classifications are with regard to teratoma undifferentiated and teratoma trophoblastic, which approximate respectively to *embryonal carcinoma* and *choriocarcinoma* in the USA (WHO) classification.

Differentiated teratoma

In this type of teratoma all the component tissues are fully differentiated; there are no histological features of malignancy. Such tumours are rare, usually occurring in infancy. The differentiated tumour (TD) is cystic; the cysts are lined by different types of epithelia. The stroma contains mature cartilage, muscle and bone.

Malignant teratoma intermediate

The malignant teratoma intermediate (MTI) group of tumours are partly solid and partly cystic. There are areas of organoid differentiation, with muscle and stromal cells arranged in a circumferential pattern around spaces lined by bronchial or alimentary type epithelium. There are also histologically malignant areas with cellular pleomorphism and necrosis.

Malignant teratoma undifferentiated

Malignant teratoma undifferentiated (MTU) tumours are composed entirely of sheets and trabeculae of undifferentiated cells with marked nuclear pleomorphism and a high mitotic rate. There is usually extensive tumour necrosis. There are no areas of organoid differentiation.

Malignant teratoma trophoblastic

The malignant teratoma trophoblastic (MTT) contains areas of syncytiotrophoblast and cytotrophoblast arranged in a villous pattern. A teratoma should be included in this category even if only a small area of the tumour is composed of trophoblastic tissue. Trophoblastic teratomas are often haemorrhagic.

Vascular invasion by the tumour is a characteristic feature and blood-borne metastases are common. hCG and alpha-fetoprotein (AFP) are valuable markers for this type of teratoma and may be measured in the serum and also demonstrated in the syncytiotrophoblast cells by immunocytochemistry.

The above classification has prognostic value, with differentiated teratomas having an excellent prognosis and trophoblastic teratomas a poor prognosis.

Intra-tubular germ cell neoplasia

The testicular tissue at the edge of most germ cell tumours shows a proliferation of atypical cells within the seminiferous tubules. This is considered as an in situ stage of malignancy and the precursor lesion of germ cell tumours. Immunohistochemical demonstration of placental-like alkaline phosphatase (PLAP) is helpful in the identification of these atypical cells.

Combined germ cell tumours

A mixed pattern occurs in 14% of all testicular tumours. Areas of seminoma and teratoma may be intermingled within the same tumour or occur as separate nodules.

In these combined tumours, immunocytochemistry is of value in identifying small foci of more aggressive tissue components such as trophoblast. The prognosis in mixed tumours is determined by the subtype of teratoma.

Non-Germ Cell Tumours

Malignant lymphoma

Malignant lymphoma comprises about 7% of testicular tumours with a peak incidence between 60 and 80 years. The tumours are often bilateral and, in some cases, may be the first manifestation of a diffuse disease involving lymph nodes, liver and spleen.

The testis is enlarged and replaced by a homogeneous fleshy white tumour. This is *a non-Hodgkin's lymphoma,* usually a poorly differentiated B-cell lymphoma with a diffuse pattern. Typically, the neoplastic cells infiltrate between the seminiferous tubules without destroying the tubular architecture. There is also neoplastic infiltration of the walls of veins within the tumour.

Yolk sac tumour

Yolk sac tumour usually occurs before the age of 3 years and is the commonest type of testicular tumour in the child; its other name is *orchioblastoma*. It may also occur in adults, usually as one component of a mixed germ cell tumour and less often in pure form.

Histology shows an adenopapillary pattern with columnar or flattened cells containing intracytoplasmic eosinophilic globules. There are also characteristic structures termed Schiller-Duval bodies formed by a perivascular layer of tumour cells.

AFP is a valuable marker for this type of tumour and may be detected in the serum and by immunocytochemistry within the neoplastic cells. Occasionally foci of yolk sac differentiation are seen in malignant teratomas.

Interstitial (Leydig) cell tumour

Tumours arising from the interstitial or Leydig cells of the testis are uncommon, comprising only 2% of testicular tumours. The peak age incidence is between 30 and 45 years. This type of tumour may produce androgens and cause precocious sexual development in boys. Paradoxically, gynaecomastia may be the initial manifestation.

An interstitial cell tumour forms a solid yellow-brown nodule within the body of the testis, composed of uniform eosinophilic cells arranged in sheets or columns. The majority of interstitial cell tumours are benign.

Sertoli cell tumour

The Sertoli cell tumour is a type of benign testicular tumour which is rare in man. It more commonly develops in dogs, producing feminising features.

Metastatic tumours

Various tumours may occasionally metastasise to the testis but such metastases are usually found only incidentally at autopsy and very rarely present clinically as testicular enlargement. Carcinoma of the bronchus or prostate and malignant melanoma are among the more frequent primary tumours involved.

Testicular infiltrates of acute lymphoblastic leukaemia cells resist chemotherapy; the testes and central nervous system are 'privileged sites' in this respect. Consequently, irradiation of the testes has been advocated, even though this causes hypogonadism and infertility.

Dissemination

Testicular tumours initially invade the body of the testis and spread locally to the rete testis and epididymis. Invasion of the fibrous tunica albuginea occurs at a late stage.

Invasion of lymphatic spaces leads to spread along the spermatic cord to the internal iliac and para-aortic lymph nodes and then to the mediastinal nodes. Vascular invasion results in visceral metastases, most frequently in the lungs and liver, as well as skeletal deposits. Seminomas tend to spread by lymphatics to para-aortic nodes; teratomas tend to spread haematogenously and, occasionally, to lymph nodes.

The microscopic structure of the metastases usually reflects the histology of the primary tumour but sometimes it may consist of one or more other histological types.

This discrepancy may be explained by further differentiation of the tumour in the metastasis, either spontaneously or as a result of chemotherapy. Alternatively, a small focus of some other tumour type may have been missed in the initial histological examination of a mixed germ cell tumour.

Clinical Diagnosis and Management

If a testicular neoplasm is suspected clinically, a surgical exploration of the testis is required. If the testis is enlarged or nodular, orchidectomy is performed. There is no place for open biopsy, frozen section diagnosis or needle biopsy in the diagnosis of these tumours.

Such techniques carry the risk of tumour implantation and may lead to a sampling error in the diagnosis of a heterogeneous tumour. An inguinal orchidectomy is the treatment of choice; a scrotal incision carries the risk of scrotal recurrence if the tunica albuginea is incised. Histology of the orchidectomy specimen is essential to confirm the clinical diagnosis of a neoplasm and determine its type.

This examination must include adequate sampling of the tumour to detect more aggressive components such as yolk sac tumour or choriocarcinoma. Immunocytochemical staining of the tumour may aid the detection of areas of yolk sac tumour or trophoblastic tissue.

The degree of local spread is assessed by examination of the rete testis and the resection margin of the spermatic cord. The presence of

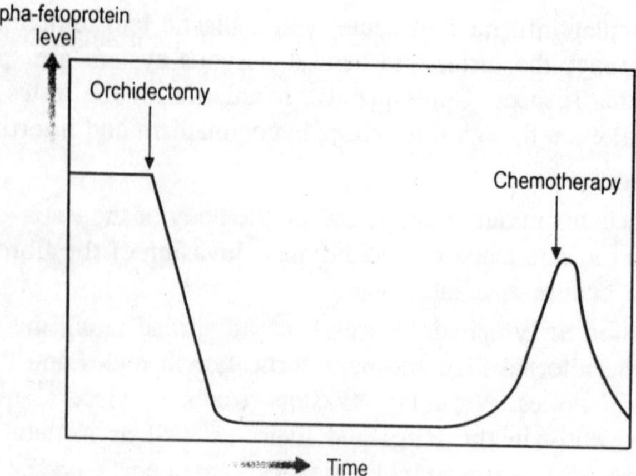

Figuren 8.8: Monitoring tumour growth by serum markers.

vascular invasion by tumour is also an important prognostic factor. A variety of imaging techiques are available for the detection of metastases.

These include conventional radiography using chest X-ray to identify mediastinal lymph node or pulmonary metastases. Intravenous urography will indicate ureteric distortion by para-aortic lymph node metastases.

A more accurate assessment of possible iliac and para-aortic lymph node metastases is available by non-invasive imaging techniques including abdominal ultrasound, magnetic resonance imaging (MRI) and computer assisted tomography (CAT scan) for the detection of small visceral and nodal metastases.

In the investigation of a patient with a testicular neoplasm, these techniques are used after the orchidectomy to assess the presence and extent of metastatic disease before planning therapy. They enable an accurate staging of the disease to be made, as follows:

Stage I — tumour confined to the testis and its coverings
Stage II — tumour involving the testis and para-aortic lymph nodes
IIA — radiological evidence of node metastases
IIB — bulky, palpable retroperitoneal disease
Stage III — involvement of lymph nodes in the mediastinum and/or supraclavicular region
Stage IV — visceral metastases.

Tumour markers

Certain tumour products appear in the serum with some testicular tumours and are of value in monitoring the response to therapy. These tumour products also provide an early indication of tumour recurrence.

This allows a lead time for further courses of treatment, enabling early detection of relapse when the tumour load is minimal and therefore chemotherapy is more effective.

The most useful markers are alpha-fetoprotein (AFP), produced by elements of yolk sac tumour, and the a subunit of human chorionic gonadotrophin (3hCG) produced by trophoblastic components. The placental-like isoenzyme of alkaline phosphatase (PLAP) is proving a useful marker for seminoma.

An ideal protocol for the measurement of serum markers includes a pre-operative sample followed by frequent post-orchidectomy samples. Levels should be measured twice each week during the first two months postoperatively, or until basal levels return, then weekly for 6 months.

If tumour recurrence is detected, more frequent measurements will be required. Tumour markers have biological half-life decay times of 4 days for AFP and one day for βhCG.

Prognosis

There has been a marked improvement in the prognosis for patients with testicular tumours during the last few decades. Seminoma is a very radiosensitive tumour which has an excellent prognosis.

The main improvements, however, have occurred in patients with non-seminomatous germ cell tumours and are due to three main factors: the development of more precise imaging techniques to improve staging; the development of assays for tumour markers; and the use of improved chemotherapeutic agents.

As a result, the cure rate is now similar to that of seminoma. Until recently, the management usually involved orchidectomy followed by prophylactic irradiation of the paraaortic lymph nodes. This regimen resulted in a 90-95% cure rate for seminoma.

A more recent and now accepted management of both seminoma and teratoma is orchidectomy followed by surveillance with imaging techniques and serum markers; recurrences of tumour are then treated with chemotherapy. If the patient survives for 2 years after completion of chemotherapy with no evidence of recurrence then cure is likely.

Male Infertility

Male infertility may be due to:

- endocrine disorders-e.g. gonadotrophin deficiency; oestrogen excess-e.g. hepatic cirrhosis
- testicular lesions-cryptorchidism; Klinefelter's syndrome; maturation arrest of spermatogenesisidiopathic, varicocele,

pyrexial illness; irradiation; defective spermatozoa (e.g. immotile cilia)

- post-testicular lesions-blockage of efferent ducts, congenital or secondary to an inflammatory process; impotence-neurological disorders.

The clinical assessment of infertile men includes thorough investigation to determine the precise nature of the problem. This may include a testicular biopsy to assess the integrity of the seminiferous tubules and the degree of spermatogenesis.

EPIDIDYMIS AND CORD

Congenital Anomalies

In about 10% of men, the epididymis is situated anterior to a normal intrascrotal testis, instead of in its usual posterior position. This abnormality may cause diagnostic problems in palpation of other lesions. *Maldescent* of the testis may be accompanied by an abnormality in the position of the epididymis, which then lies along the course of the spermatic cord.

Rarely, an *extra vas deferens* is present on one side, or one may be *absent*. This latter condition may be associated with absence or hypoplasia of the corresponding epididymis. These abnormalities are of practical importance to the surgeon at vasectomy.

Several vestigial structures adjacent to the epididymis or mesorchium may become enlarged and cystic. These include aberrant ductules and the appendix of the epididymis. They usually remain small but may undergo torsion, with resulting infarction, presenting as an acute painful swelling.

Epididymal Cysts and Spermatoceles

Acquired cysts of the epididymis are more common than the congenital types. An obstruction to the passage of sperm along the narrow lumen of the vas or obstruction of an epididymal tubule results in cystic dilatation of the duct system in the epididymis and efferent ductules of the testis.

The resulting *spermatocele* forms a swelling in the epididymis, above and behind the testis on palpation. It is usually a multilocular cyst with opalescent fluid containing sperms.

Varicocele

A varicocele is varicosity of the pampiniform plexus of veins around the spermatic cord. This may be a *primary varicocele* with no obvious underlying cause, more common on the left side. It may be related to maldevelopment of valves in the pampiniform veins or the testicular vein; on the left side the testicular vein drains into the left renal vein almost at 90°.

A *secondary varicocele* is the result of venous obstruction and occurs with equal frequency on both sides. One cause is a carcinoma of the kidney invading the renal vein and obstructing the testicular vein.

A varicocele may raise the intrascrotal temperature as a result of increased blood flow, reducing spermatogenesis and causing *subfertility*.

Torsion of the Spermatic Cord

Torsion of the spermatic cord involves twisting of the testis and epididymis together on their axis. It is an acute surgical emergency, presenting as a swollen, hard, painful testis. The patient is usually aged 13-16 years.

An earlier peak incidence occurs under the age of 1 year. Torsion of the spermatic cord is often precipitated by exertion, which causes contraction of the cremaster muscle. There is sometimes a history of preceding minor, less painful episodes of testicular pain.

Several anatomical abnormalities, often bilateral, predispose to this lesion. They include maldescent of the testis, an abnormally long spermatic cord, or an abnormally long mesorchium. The torsion usually occurs within the tunica vaginalis, involving only the testis and epididymis. If it occurs above the level of the tunica it involves all structures in that side of the scrotum.

Torsion produces an initial occlusion of the venous return from the testis, although the arterial flow continues for a time. There is congestion of the testis followed by haemorrhagic infarction as the arterial supply becomes impaired with rising pressure within the tunica. If treatment is delayed the infarction progresses, finally resulting in a shrunken, fibrotic testis and epididymis.

Inflammatory Lesions

Acute epididymo-orchitis

An acute inflammation of the body of the testis *(orchitis)* most frequently develops in association with an initial *epididymitis* which later spreads to the testis. The commonest underlying cause is *a urinary tract infection* with coliform organisms; it may also develop after *a prostatectomy*.

A urethritis, either gonococcal or non-specific, may be complicated by an epididymo-orchitis. In all these instances, the infection spreads along the vas deferens or the lymphatics of the spermatic cord to the

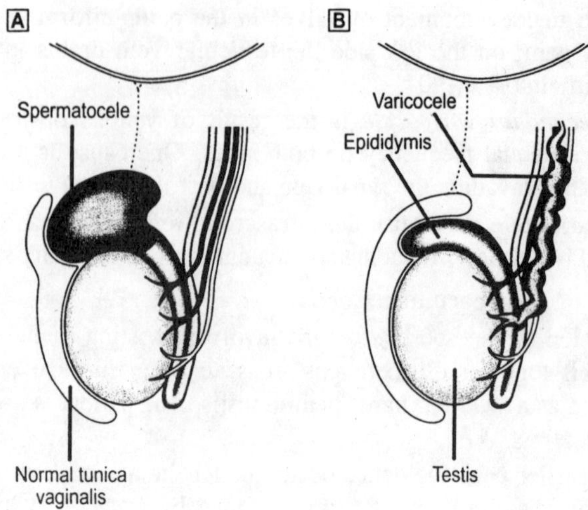

Figure 7.9: Spermatocele and varicocele.

epididymis. The process may be unilateral or bilateral. The epididymis and testis are enlarged, warm and painful.

These signs are accompanied by fever and malaise. Histology shows an acute inflammatory process. There may be a secondary hydrocele. The inflammation is usually mild and resolves either spontaneously or with antibiotic therapy; in severe cases it may, however, progress to suppuration. Less often, an epididymo-orchitis may complicate a septicaemia (e.g. meningococcal).

Tuberculous epididymo-orchitis

Tuberculous infection of the male genital tract is now rare but the epididymis used to be the commonest site of involvement in the male. Infection of the epididymis is secondary to a tuberculous lesion elsewhere in the urinary tract, such as the kidney or bladder, with extension of the infection along the vas deferens.

In about one-third of cases the infection is bilateral, resulting in nodular enlargement of the epididymis. There may be a secondary hydrocele and, in an advanced infection, the inflamed epididymis becomes adherent to the scrotal skin with the formation of sinuses.

The infection may spread directly to the *testis* with the formation of areas of caseation necrosis and the characteristic granulomatous inflammation. There may also be extension to the prostate or seminal vesicles. Microscopy of the urine shows a 'sterile' pyuria with acid-alcohol-fast bacilli.

Commonly confused conditions and entitles relating to male genital pathology

Commonly confused	*Distinction and explanation*
Phimosis and *paraphimosis*	Both are due to chronic inflammation of the prepuce. In *phimosis* the prepuce cannot be retracted over the glans penis, whereas in *paraphimosis* the retracted prepuce cannot be returned to its normal position.
Hydrocele, spermatocele and *varicocele*	*A hydrocele* is formed by serous fluid accumulating in the tunica vaginalis surrounding the testis. A *spermatocele* is an epididymal cyst containing opalescent (due to spermatozoa) fluid. *A varicocele* contains blood because it is due to varicosity of the pampiniform venous plexus.
Prostatism and *prostatitis*	*Prostatism* is a set of symptoms (dribbling, hesitancy, frequency) suggesting urethral obstruction due to prostatic enlargement. In contrast, *prostatitis* is inflammation of the prostateone of several causes of prostatism.
Clinical and *latent prostatic carcinoma*	*Clinical prostatic carcinomas* are those presenting with signs and symptoms and warranting clinical intervention (curative or palliative). *Latent prostatic carcinomas* are often found incidentally in prostate tissue either removed for benign disease or examined at autopsy; many are considered to be only slowly progressive lesions.
Teratoma and *seminoma*	Both are germ cell tumours and may occur together. However, *teratomas* have a greater metastatic potential and are treated more aggressively than *seminomas,* which have an intrinsically better prognosis.

Sperm granuloma

Sperm granuloma is an uncommon chronic inflammatory lesion involving the epididymis and resulting from extravasation of sperm from the tubules into the interstitium. There is an associated inflammatory reaction composed mainly of histiocytes and polymorphs, with secondary fibrosis. The process results in the formation of a firm swelling in the epididymis. The cause is uncertain, although there may be a preceding history of an epididymitis.

A similar cellular sponse to extravasated sperm may sometimes be seen in the spermatic cord at the site of recent vasectomy, forming a localised nodule at the operation site.

Tumours

Tumours of the epididymis and spermatic cord are relatively rare, together forming only 1-2% of the total group of testicular tumours. They include:

- adenomatoid tumour
- paratesticular sarcoma.

Adenomatoid tumour

Adenomatoid tumour is an uncommon, benign neoplasm of the epididymis, which may develop over a wide age range, and presents as a slowly enlarging painless firm nodule in the epididymis. Examination reveals a circumscribed solid nodule 10-20 mm in diameter, composed of irregular clefts and spaces lined by flattened or cuboidal cells.

These cells merge with an intervening stroma of fibrous tissue and smooth muscle. The histogenesis of this lesion is debatable, but current opinion favours a mesothelial origin. A similar neoplasm may occur in the female over the uterine serosa or in the fallopian tube.

This localisation to the genital tract has led to the alternative view that these tumours arise from Miillerian remnants.

Paratesticular sarcoma

Paratesticular sarcomas of the spermatic cord are rare neoplasms which present as an inguinal or scrotal swelling, the tumour forming a mass separate from the body of the testis and epididymis. The types of tumour which occur vary with age: in children and adolescents, the majority are rhabdomyosarcomas; in adults, the lesion may be a leiomyosarcoma, liposarcoma or fibrosarcoma. These tumours have a poor prognosis and metastasise by lymphatics and veins.

INDEX

D

E

I

J

K

L

S

T

U

V

W

X